SCIENCE COMICS

CARS

Engines That Move You

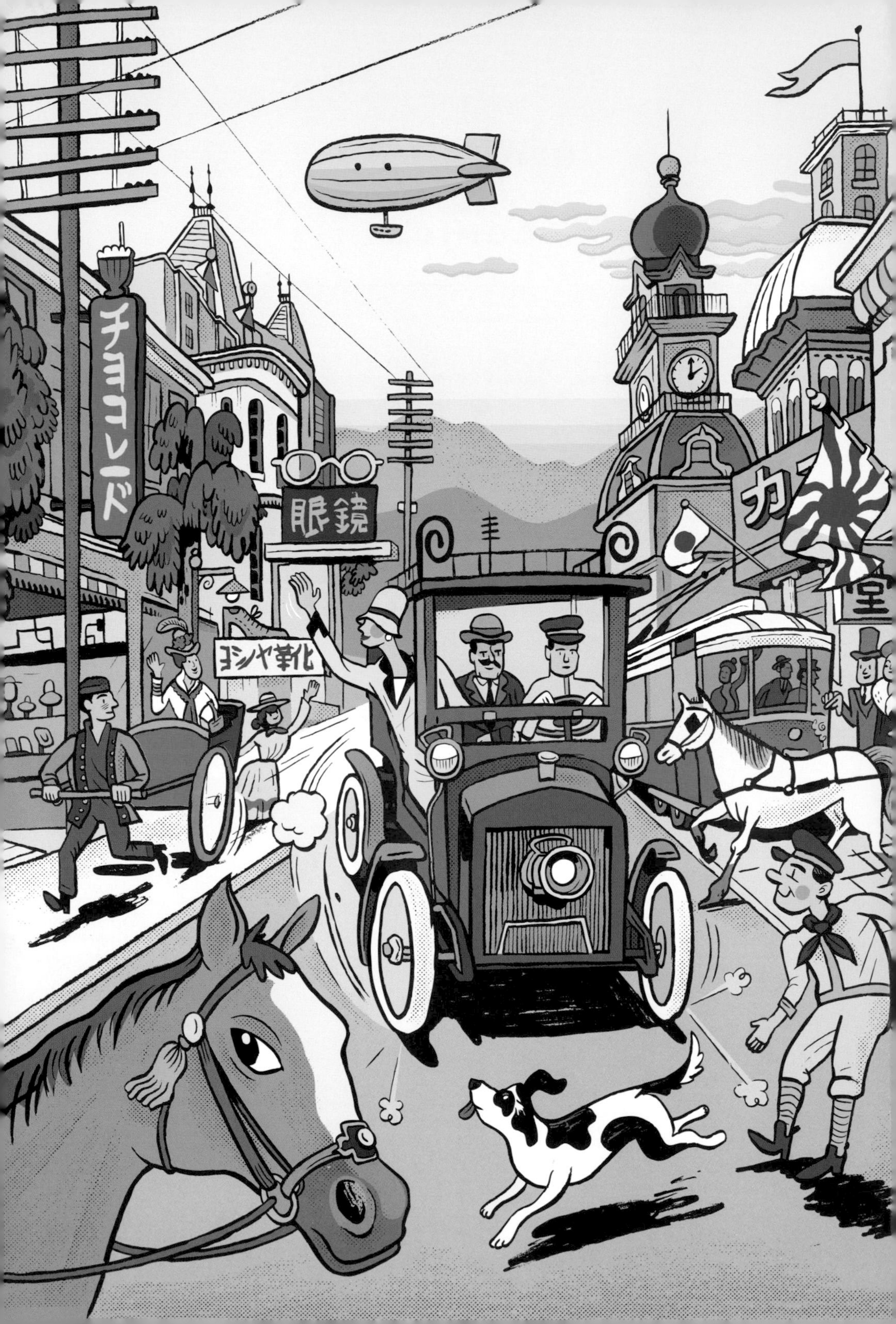
チヨコレード
眼鏡
ヨシノヤ革化

CARS

Engines That Move You

Dan Zettwoch

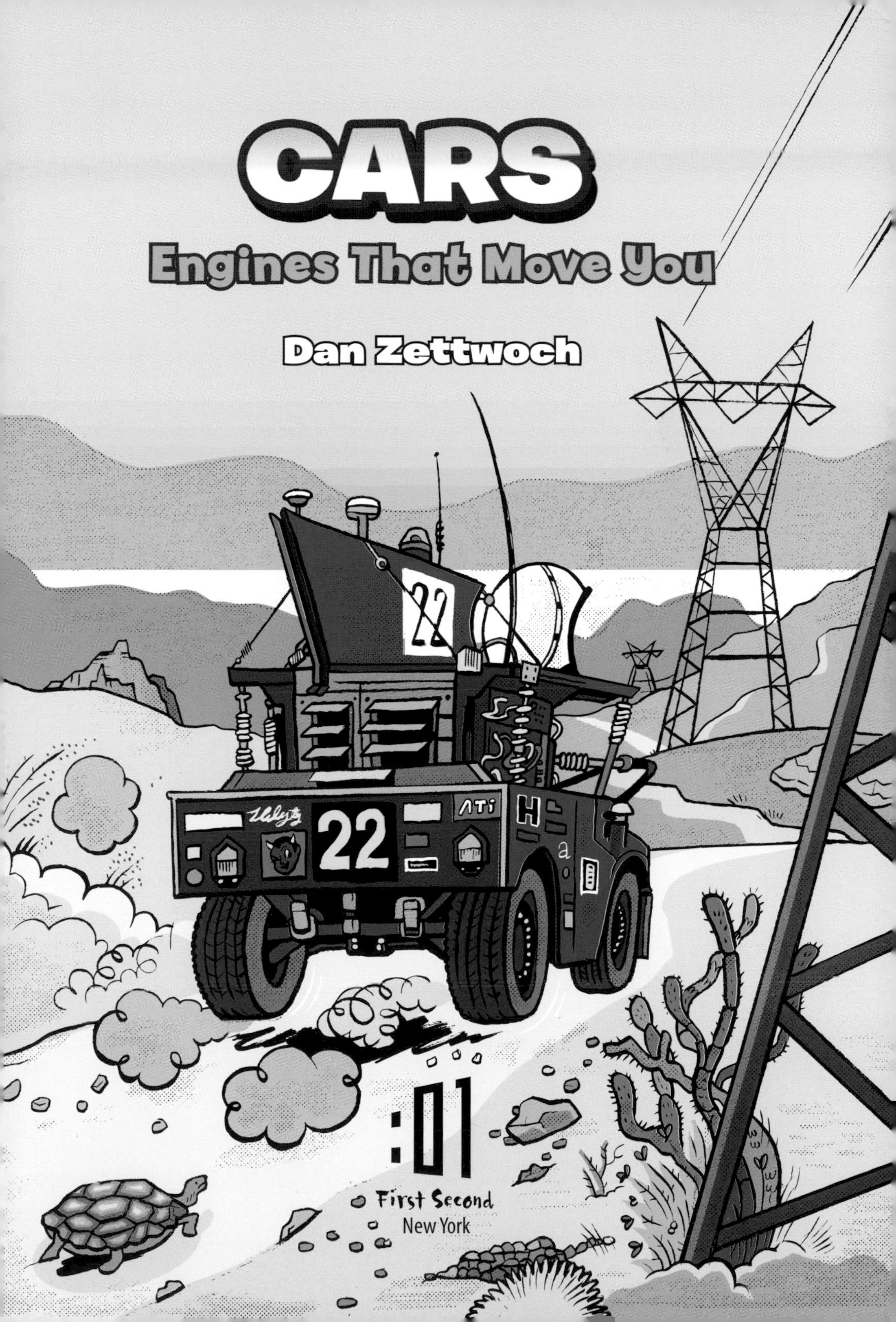
22
22
ATi
H

:01 First Second
New York

Left title page: Komanosuke Uchiyama's *Takuri*, the first gasoline-powered car built in Japan, rolls through 1907 Tokyo.
Right title page: Red Team Racing's *Sandstorm*, an autonomous robot vehicle, competes in the 2004 DARPA Grand Challenge for driverless cars (and crashes after 7 miles).

First Second

Copyright © 2019 by Dan Zettwoch

Published by First Second
First Second is an imprint of Roaring Brook Press,
a division of Holtzbrinck Publishing Holdings Limited Partnership
120 Broadway, New York, NY 10271

Don't miss your next favorite book from First Second!
For the latest updates go to firstsecondnewsletter.com and sign up for our enewsletter.

Library of Congress Control Number: 2018944912

Paperback ISBN: 978-1-62672-822-6
Hardcover ISBN: 978-1-62672-821-9

Our books may be purchased in bulk for promotional, educational, or business use.
Please contact your local bookseller or the Macmillan Corporate and Premium Sales Department at
(800) 221-7945 ext. 5442 or by e-mail at MacmillanSpecialMarkets@macmillan.com.

First edition, 2019

Edited by Dave Roman
Book design by Dan Zettwoch and Rob Steen
Automotive consultant: Louis Fourie

Created using Strathmore 400 series recycled drawing paper with Prismacolor Col-Erase non-photo blue pencil, inked with Kuretake pocket double-sided brush pen and various black colored pencils. Halftoned in Adobe Photoshop and colored in Adobe Illustrator. Lettered with Comicrazy font by Comicraft.

Printed in China by Toppan Leefung Printing Ltd., Dongguan City, Guangdong Province

Paperback: 10 9 8 7 6
Hardcover: 10 9 8 7 6 5 4

What pops into your head when you think "science"? Beakers and test tubes? Quarks and black holes? Maybe rocks and volcanos?

When I think "science," I think cars.

As you're about to find out, a car is a science lab on wheels. A car demonstrates everything from chemical reactions and simple machines to (these days) electronics and computers.

My first car was the world's ugliest, most beat-up, mud-brown-and-rust 1969 Buick LeSabre. That car played a big part in why I became a scientist.

How?

It was an old junker, so it broke—a lot. But because it was an old junker, no one minded when I tried to fix it myself. I learned a lot about how cars worked that way. I got very good at taking things apart. (I had to work slightly harder at getting them back together correctly.) When you take something apart and put it back together again, you learn how it works.

Science is all about figuring out how things work. In college, I got interested in physics. I started researching nanomaterials: very small materials that are a thousandth the diameter of a human hair in size. I worked on ways to attach chemotherapy drugs to nanoparticles to better treat cancer. Cars became mostly a way to get to and from the lab.

One Sunday afternoon, I was flipping through television channels and I happened on a NASCAR race. Normally, I would have flipped right past it, but something happened . . .

A group of six cars were going around a turn. With no warning, one of the cars wiggled, then went *wham!*—right into the wall. The driver was fine, but I wasn't. I was annoyed. I couldn't understand why a car would suddenly veer off into a wall.

The driver was one of the best in the series. He didn't hit any of the other cars. There were no tire problems or engine problems . . . or any problems, as far as I could tell. I watched replay after replay, trying to figure out how it happened.

Why? Because I'm a scientist. And when you're a scientist, it drives you crazy when you see something that you can't explain.

So I did what all scientists do when they don't understand something: I started asking questions. Those questions took me on a great adventure. I followed a NASCAR race team from their race shop to the track. I learned how race cars are built and why they're so fast. I learned how they design the cars (and the tracks and the drivers' equipment) so they can walk away from crashes.

And I was reminded of something I'd sort of forgotten: There's a lot of science in cars!

Today's cars are a lot more complicated than my old '69 Buick—but that doesn't mean you can't understand them. In fact, it's even more important that you understand them, because we've learned so much about how our cars impact the rest of the world. That new knowledge has prompted us to invent many new types of cars, some of which you'll learn about here. By the time you buy your first car, you'll have a lot of choices: hybrids, electric vehicles, maybe even hydrogen-fuel-cell or solar-powered cars.

Your choices matter. You may never fix your car yourself, but you should know how it works, because that will let you understand how your car affects the environment. Cars using petroleum fuels emit greenhouse gases and contribute to climate change. An electric car may not produce pollution from its tailpipe, but if the electricity used to charge it comes from a coal-fired power plant, it's still contributing to greenhouse gas emissions and climate change. There are around 260 million cars in the United States. We all have to make smart, informed choices. This book is a great place to start.

—Diandra Leslie-Pelecky, PhD,
author, *The Physics of NASCAR*

P.S. Oops! I almost forgot to tell you why that race car crashed. Going fast requires grip. In racing, high-speed air rushing over the car helps push the car's wheels into the track, which gives the car more grip. Stock cars have spoilers (a straight piece of metal sticking up) on their trunks specifically to catch more air and give the car more grip.

The airflow around a car changes when it gets near other cars. You can feel it when your car gets up next to a big semi truck on the expressway. If a race car gets in just the right position, it can actually take away grip from another race car just by changing how air flows over the car. In NASCAR, it's called "taking air off the spoiler."

CONTENTS

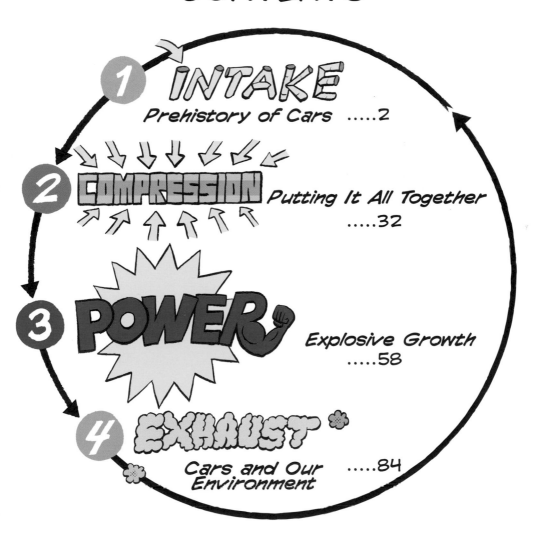

STROKE 1: INTAKE

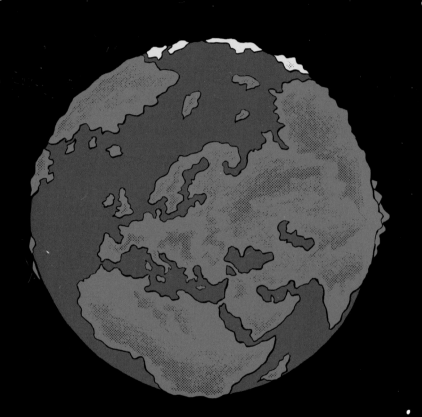

Prehistory of Cars

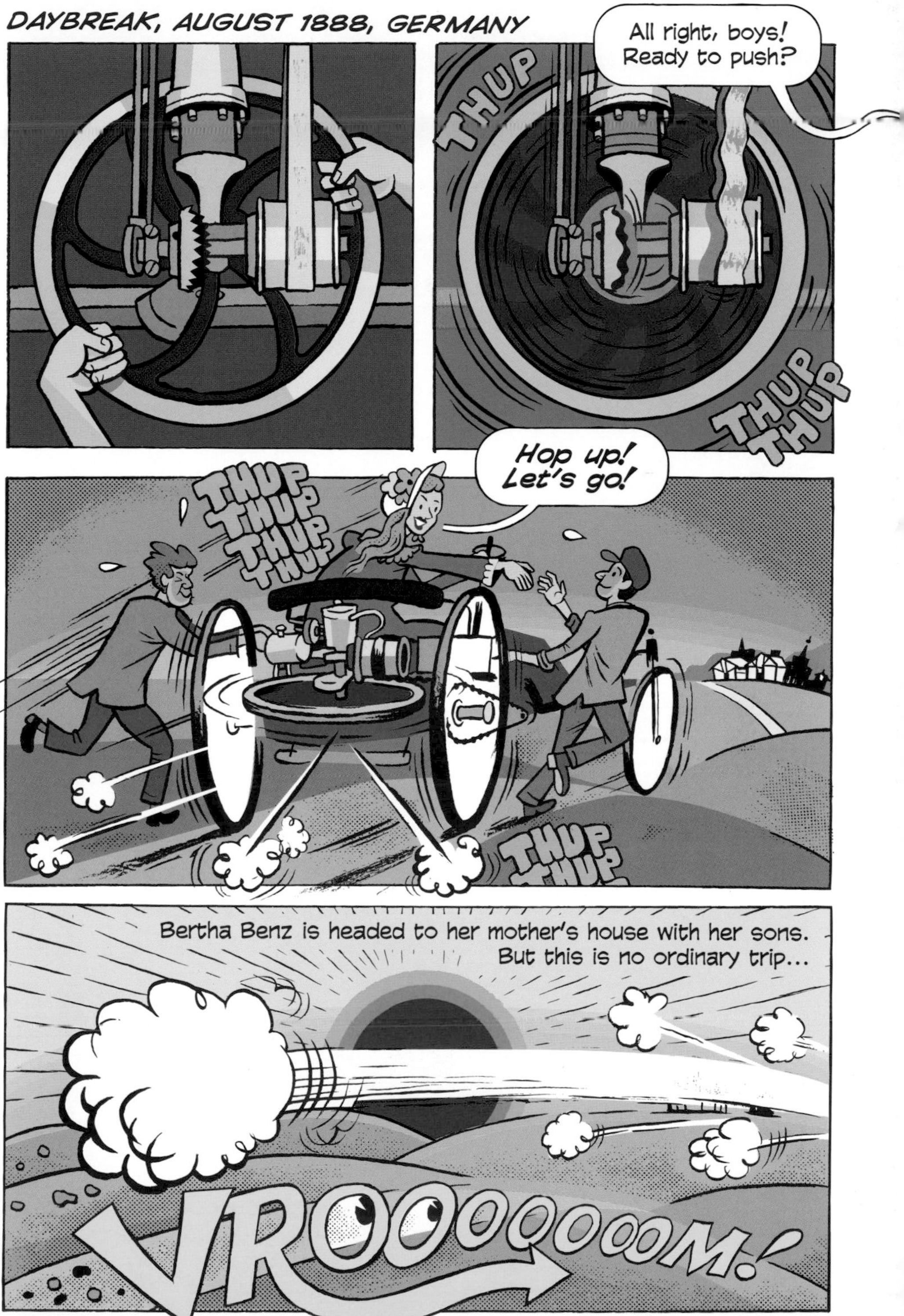
DAYBREAK, AUGUST 1888, GERMANY
All right, boys! Ready to push?
THUP
THUP THUP
THUP THUP THUP THUP
Hop up! Let's go!
THUP THUP
Bertha Benz is headed to her mother's house with her sons. But this is no ordinary trip...
VROOOOOOOM!

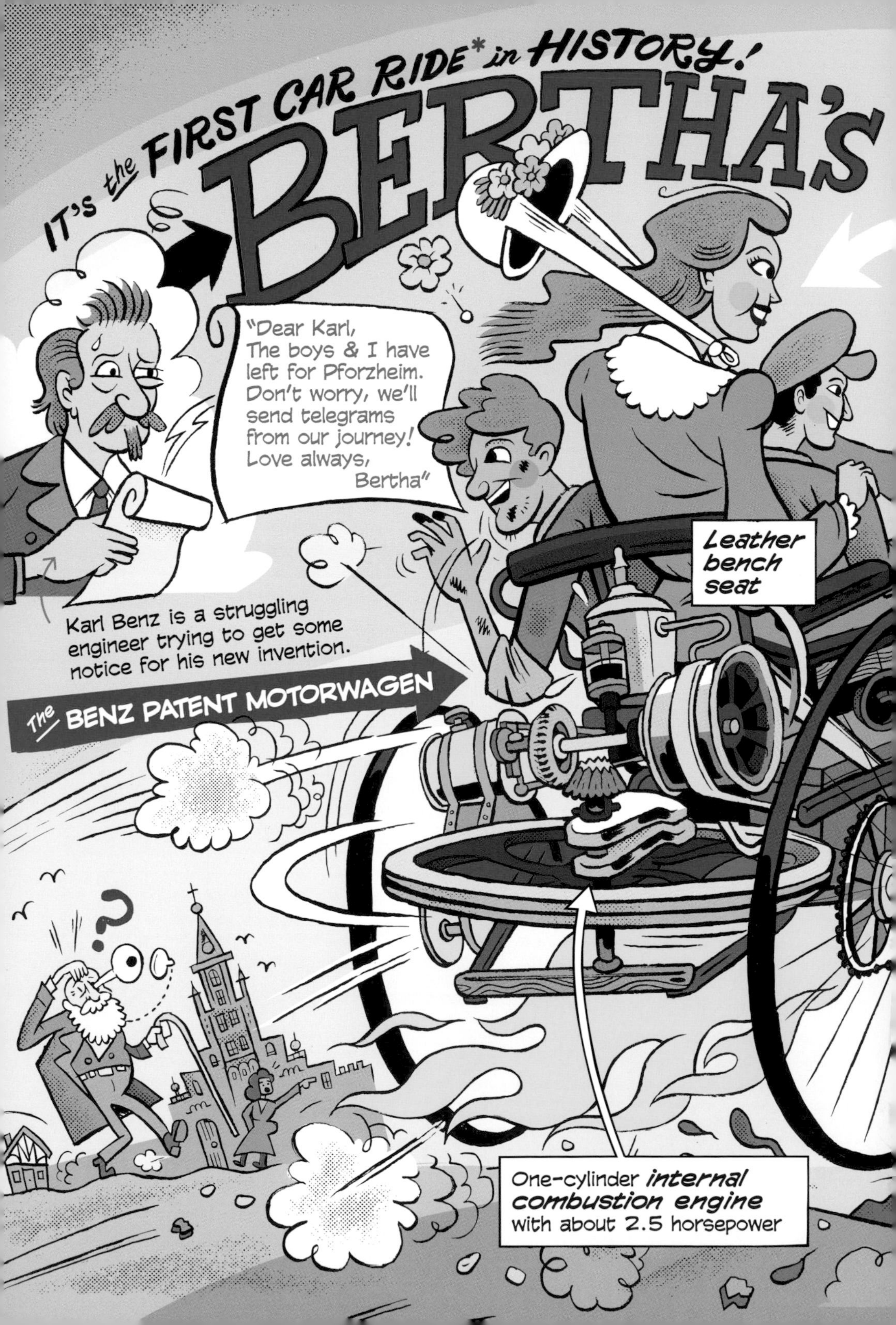

IT'S the FIRST CAR RIDE* in HISTORY!
BERTHA'S
"Dear Karl,
The boys & I have left for Pforzheim. Don't worry, we'll send telegrams from our journey!
Love always,
Bertha"
Karl Benz is a struggling engineer trying to get some notice for his new invention.
The BENZ PATENT MOTORWAGEN
Leather bench seat
One-cylinder internal combustion engine with about 2.5 horsepower

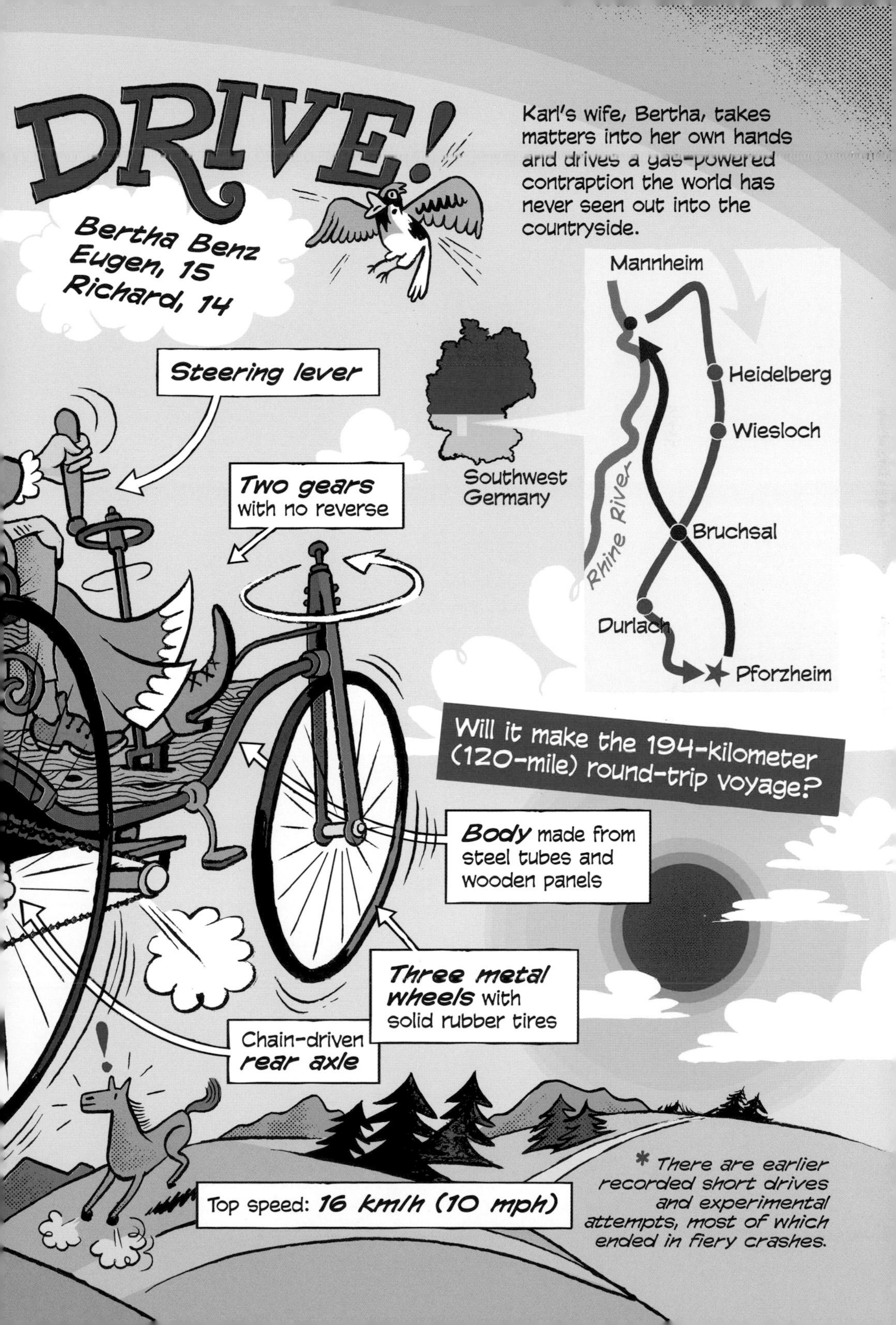
DRIVE!
Bertha Benz
Eugen, 15
Richard, 14
Karl's wife, Bertha, takes matters into her own hands and drives a gas-powered contraption the world has never seen out into the countryside.
Mannheim
Heidelberg
Wiesloch
Southwest Germany
Rhine River
Bruchsal
Durlach
Pforzheim
Steering lever
Two gears with no reverse
Will it make the 194-kilometer (120-mile) round-trip voyage?
Body made from steel tubes and wooden panels
Three metal wheels with solid rubber tires
Chain-driven rear axle
Top speed: 16 km/h (10 mph)
* There are earlier recorded short drives and experimental attempts, most of which ended in fiery crashes.

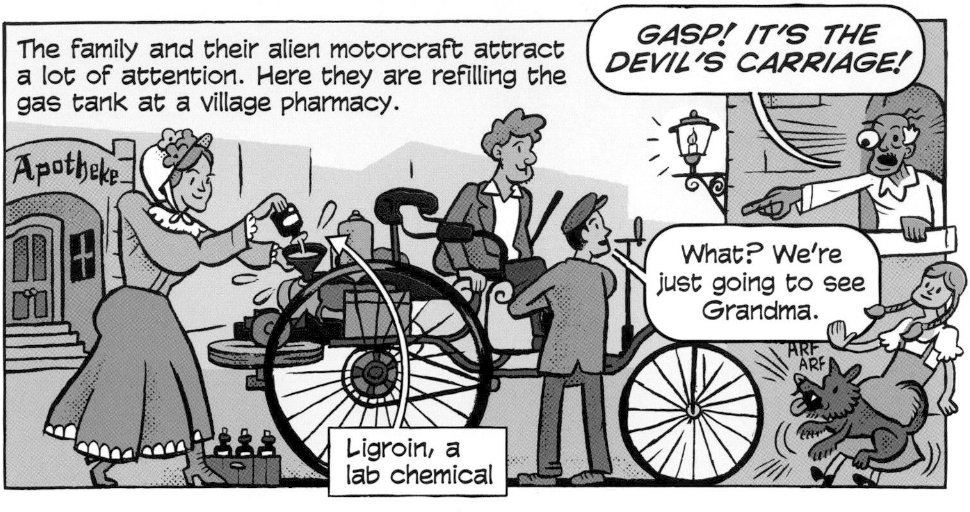
The family and their alien motorcraft attract a lot of attention. Here they are refilling the gas tank at a village pharmacy.
GASP! IT'S THE DEVIL'S CARRIAGE!
Apotheke
What? We're just going to see Grandma.
ARF ARF
Ligroin, a lab chemical

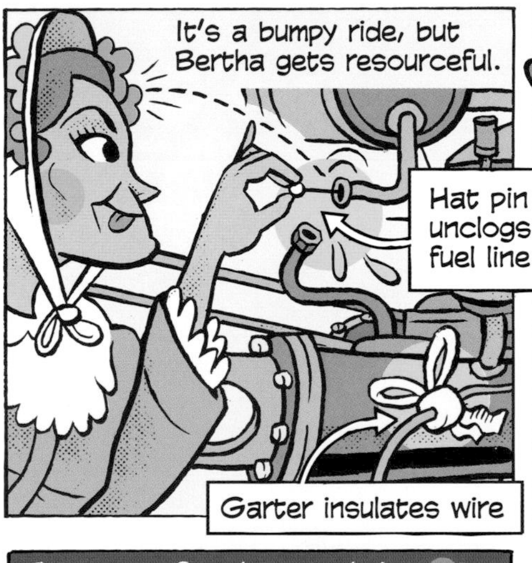
It's a bumpy ride, but Bertha gets resourceful.
Hat pin unclogs fuel line
Garter insulates wire

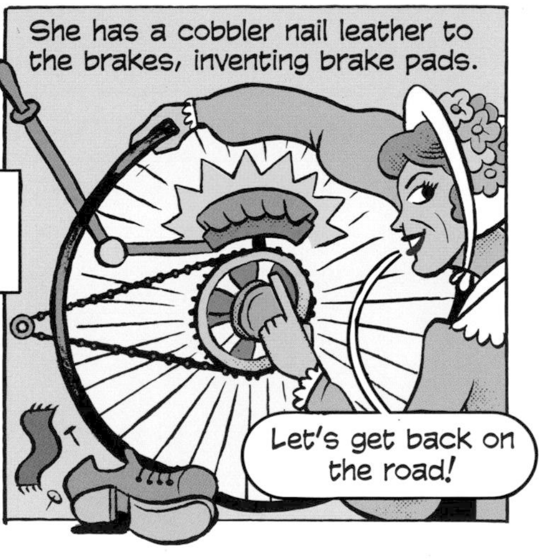
She has a cobbler nail leather to the brakes, inventing brake pads.
Let's get back on the road!

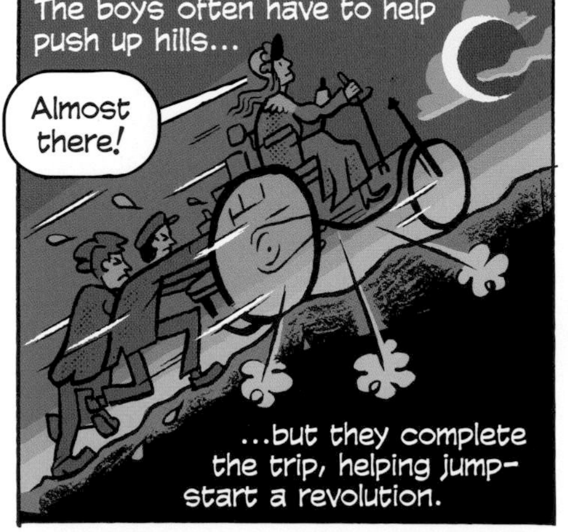
The boys often have to help push up hills...
Almost there!
...but they complete the trip, helping jump-start a revolution.

Benz will become one of the biggest names in car manufacturing.

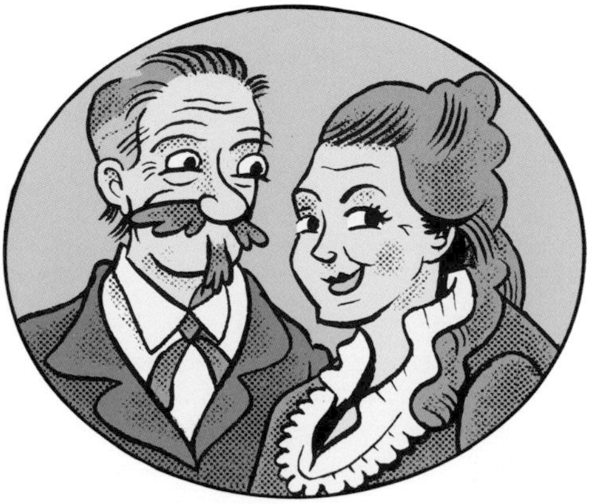

Let's put it in reverse...

MILLIONS OF YEARS AGO

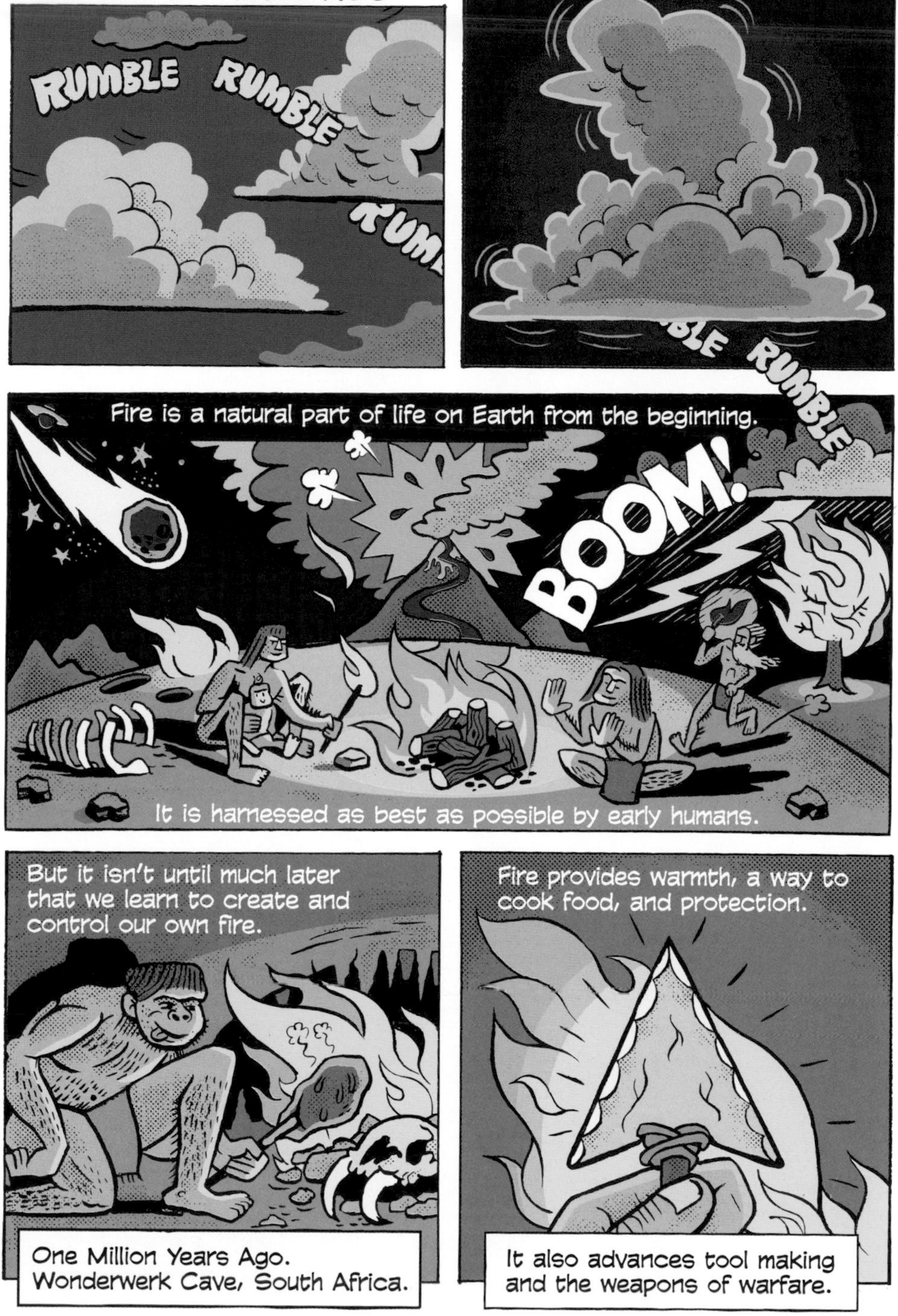
RUMBLE RUMBLE
RUMBLE
RUMBLE RUMBLE
Fire is a natural part of life on Earth from the beginning.
BOOM!
It is harnessed as best as possible by early humans.
But it isn't until much later that we learn to create and control our own fire.
One Million Years Ago. Wonderwerk Cave, South Africa.
Fire provides warmth, a way to cook food, and protection.
It also advances tool making and the weapons of warfare.

What Exactly Is Fire?

Fire is the visible effect of ***combustion.*** It occurs when oxygen and fuel meet at a really high temperature. A chain reaction that creates heat, flame, and smoke is ignited. A way to visualize combustion is the...

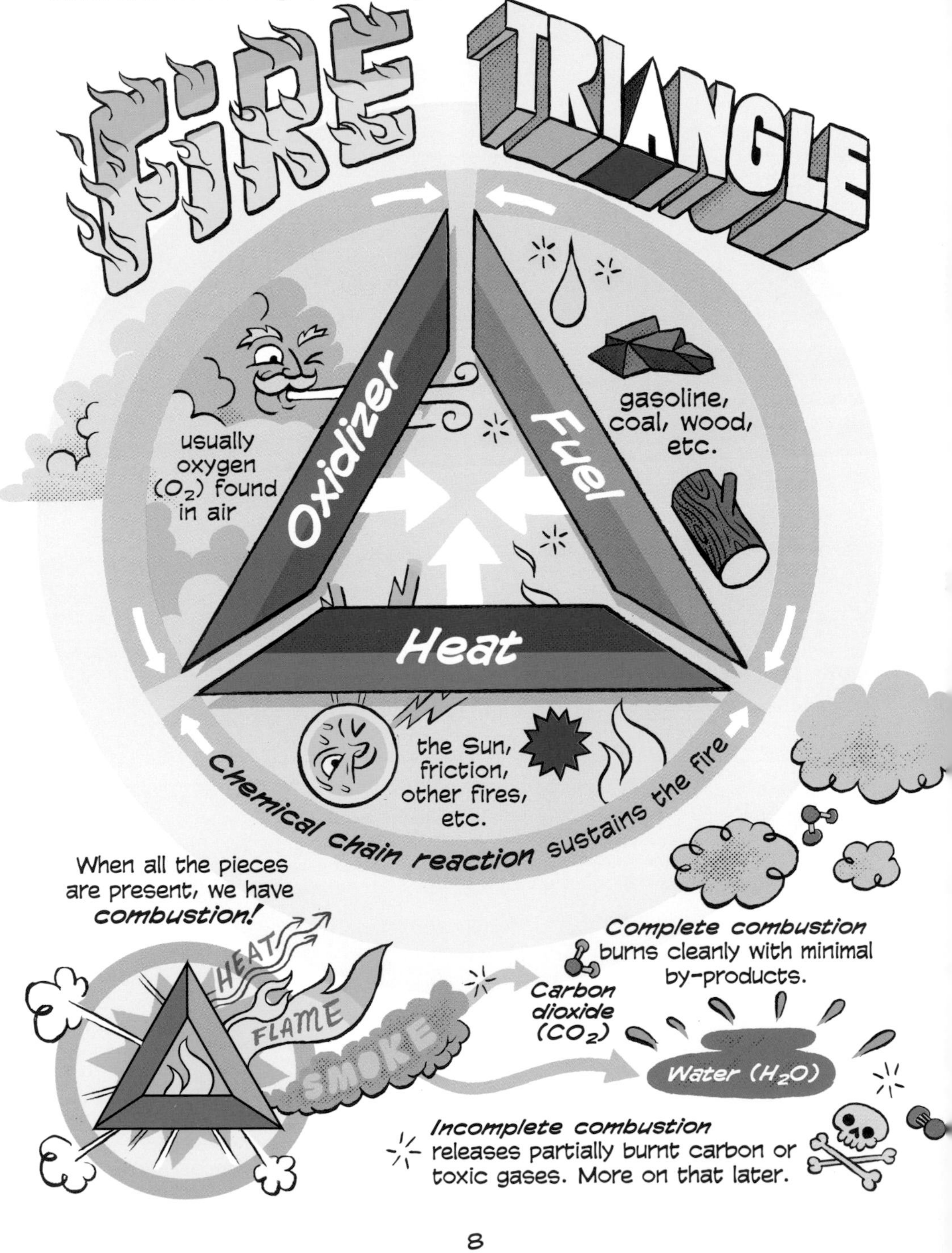

FIRE TRIANGLE
Oxidizer
usually oxygen (O_2) found in air
Fuel
gasoline, coal, wood, etc.
Heat
the Sun, friction, other fires, etc.
Chemical chain reaction sustains the fire
When all the pieces are present, we have combustion!
HEAT
FLAME
SMOKE
Complete combustion burns cleanly with minimal by-products.
Carbon dioxide (CO_2)
Water (H_2O)
Incomplete combustion releases partially burnt carbon or toxic gases. More on that later.

Switching gears from chemistry to phsyics, let's talk about the

SIX SIMPLE MACHINES

Originated in ancient Greece and fine-tuned during the Renaissance, these devices use mechanical advantage to move the world.

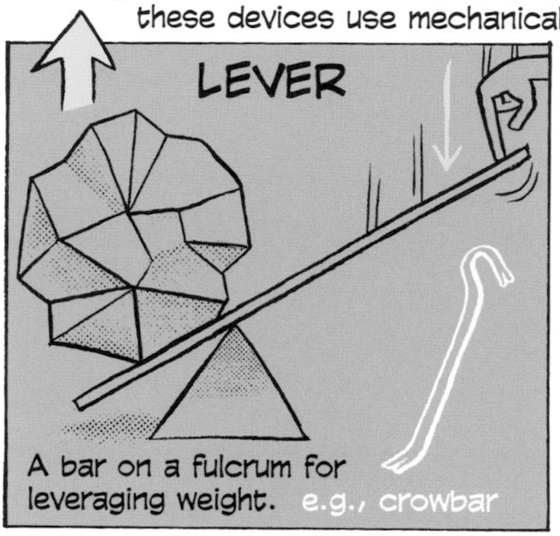
LEVER
A bar on a fulcrum for leveraging weight. e.g., crowbar

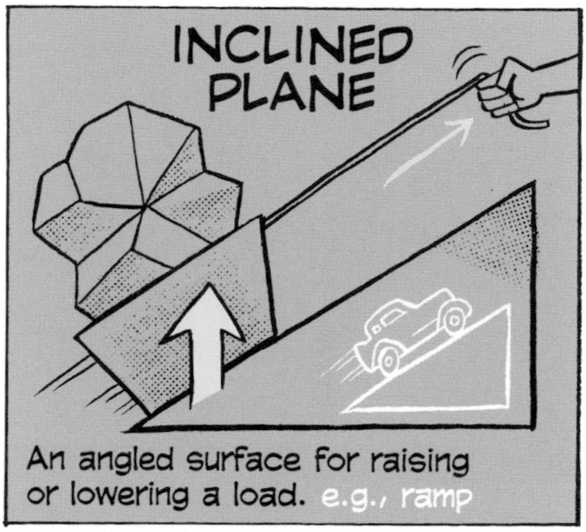
INCLINED PLANE
An angled surface for raising or lowering a load. e.g., ramp

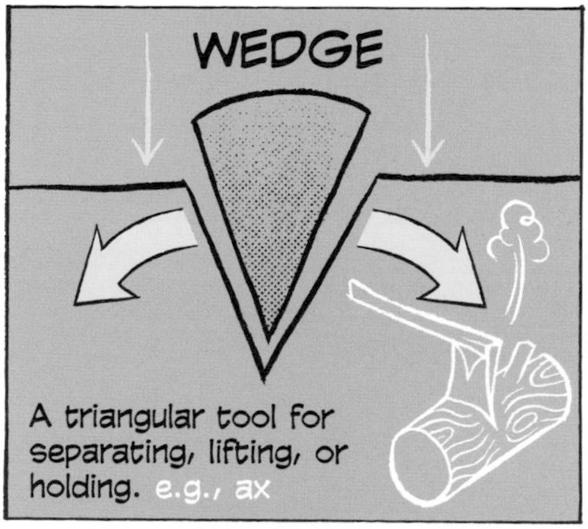
WEDGE
A triangular tool for separating, lifting, or holding. e.g., ax

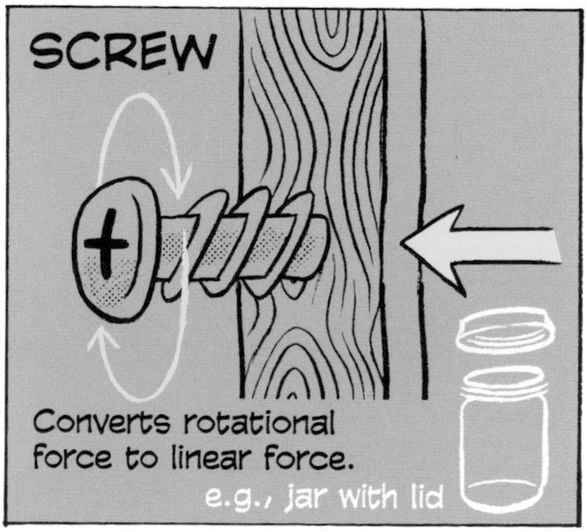
SCREW
Converts rotational force to linear force.
e.g., jar with lid

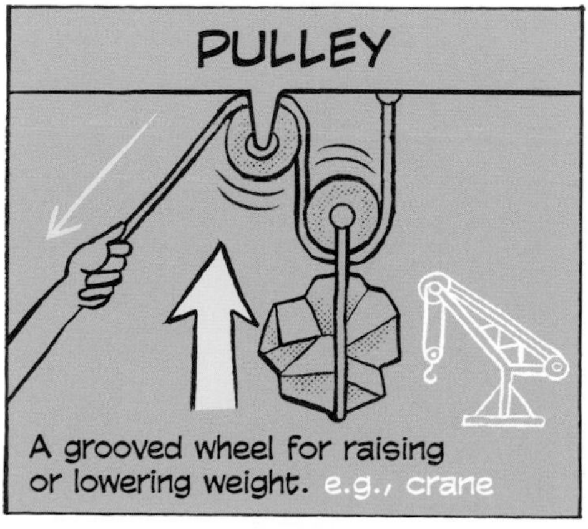
PULLEY
A grooved wheel for raising or lowering weight. e.g., crane

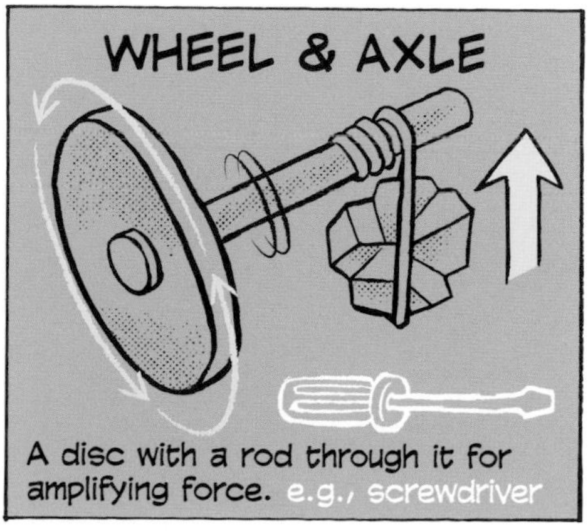
WHEEL & AXLE
A disc with a rod through it for amplifying force. e.g., screwdriver

Which brings us to the HISTORY of
The wheel is not found in nature. It had to be invented.
(There are microscopic bacteria with tiny spinning flagella, but those are more like corkscrews.)
Rotary motor
We think of the wheel as a primitive invention, but it comes along fairly late, well *after* things like:
The canoe
Bronze
The flute
Silk shirts
The first-known wheel dates from 3500 BCE, but it isn't even used for transport.
Mesopotamian potter's wheel
Then there's the *Ljubljana Marshes Wheel,* c. 3000 BCE.
Large wooden wheel and axle from a pushcart
Which brings us to another prehistoric artifact from central Europe, ***the Bronocice pot!***

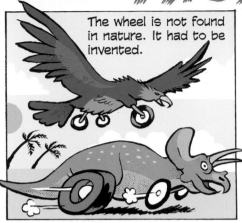

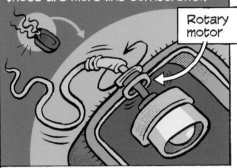

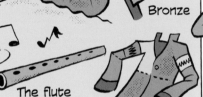

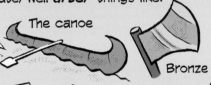

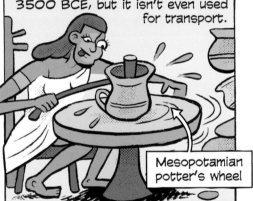

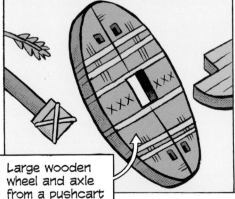

the WHEEL!

The Bronocice Pot, c. 3400 BCE, appears to depict a four-wheeled cart led by animals hauling a load. It's the earliest-known image of a wheeled vehicle.

Inscribed on the pot is a poem written in code. It reads:

Cart: "Into the grove to woo I drive, wizard of our enclosure."
Driver: "Escort, Cart, the food...haul these on virtuous ground."

Wheels have had prominent roles in religions throughout history:

| Sun Cross | Buddhist Wheel of Dharma | Winged Wheel | Native American Sacred Hoop | Wheel of Fortune |

Wheels are made lighter weight (and faster!) around 2000 BCE with the invention of spokes.

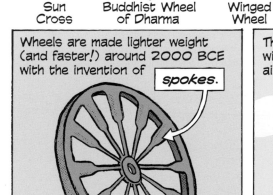

The smooth-riding pneumatic tire, with its inner tube inflated with air, is popularized in 1888.

11

HORSE-POWER!

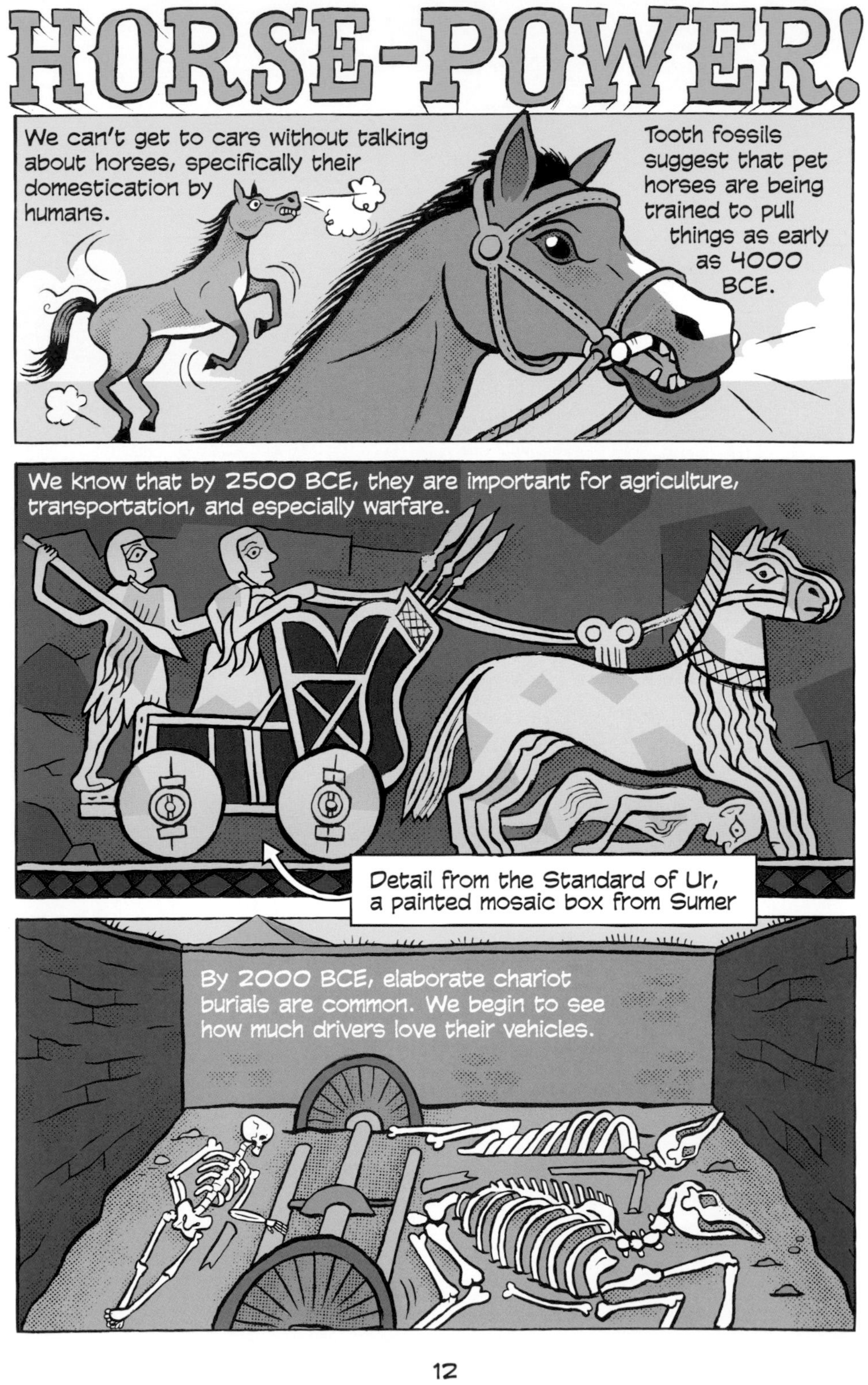

We can't get to cars without talking about horses, specifically their domestication by humans.
Tooth fossils suggest that pet horses are being trained to pull things as early as 4000 BCE.
We know that by 2500 BCE, they are important for agriculture, transportation, and especially warfare.
Detail from the Standard of Ur, a painted mosaic box from Sumer
By 2000 BCE, elaborate chariot burials are common. We begin to see how much drivers love their vehicles.

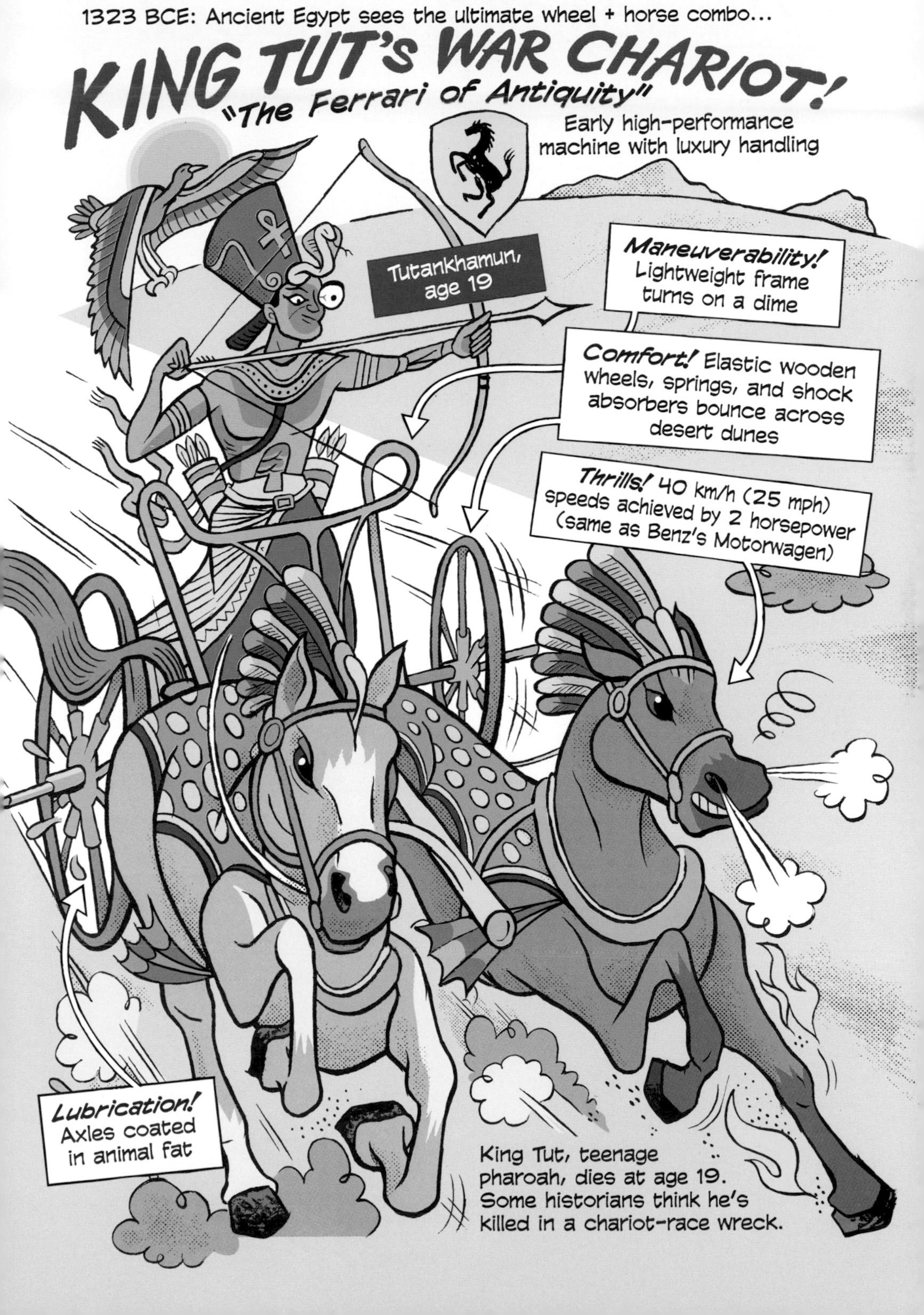
1323 BCE: Ancient Egypt sees the ultimate wheel + horse combo...
KING TUT'S WAR CHARIOT!
"The Ferrari of Antiquity"
Early high-performance machine with luxury handling
Tutankhamun, age 19
Maneuverability! Lightweight frame turns on a dime
Comfort! Elastic wooden wheels, springs, and shock absorbers bounce across desert dunes
Thrills! 40 km/h (25 mph) speeds achieved by 2 horsepower (same as Benz's Motorwagen)
Lubrication! Axles coated in animal fat
King Tut, teenage pharoah, dies at age 19. Some historians think he's killed in a chariot-race wreck.

Personal Transport

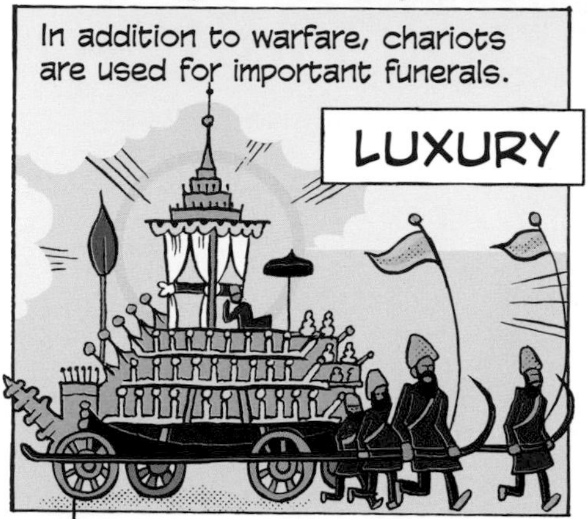
In addition to warfare, chariots are used for important funerals.
LUXURY

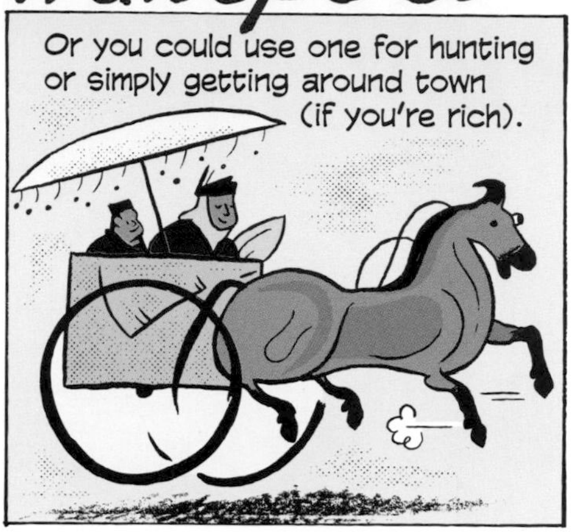
Or you could use one for hunting or simply getting around town (if you're rich).

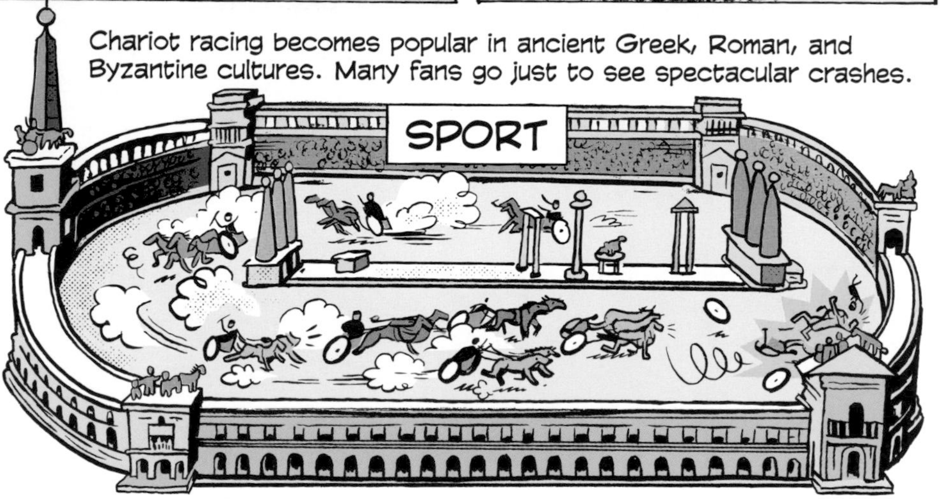
Chariot racing becomes popular in ancient Greek, Roman, and Byzantine cultures. Many fans go just to see spectacular crashes.
SPORT

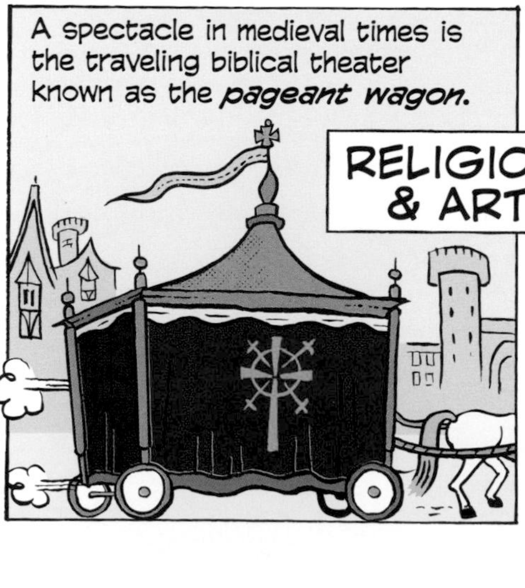
A spectacle in medieval times is the traveling biblical theater known as the ***pageant wagon.***
RELIGION & ART

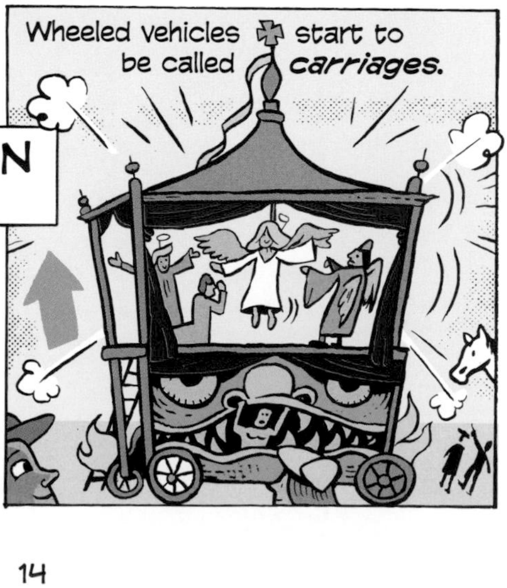
Wheeled vehicles start to be called ***carriages.***

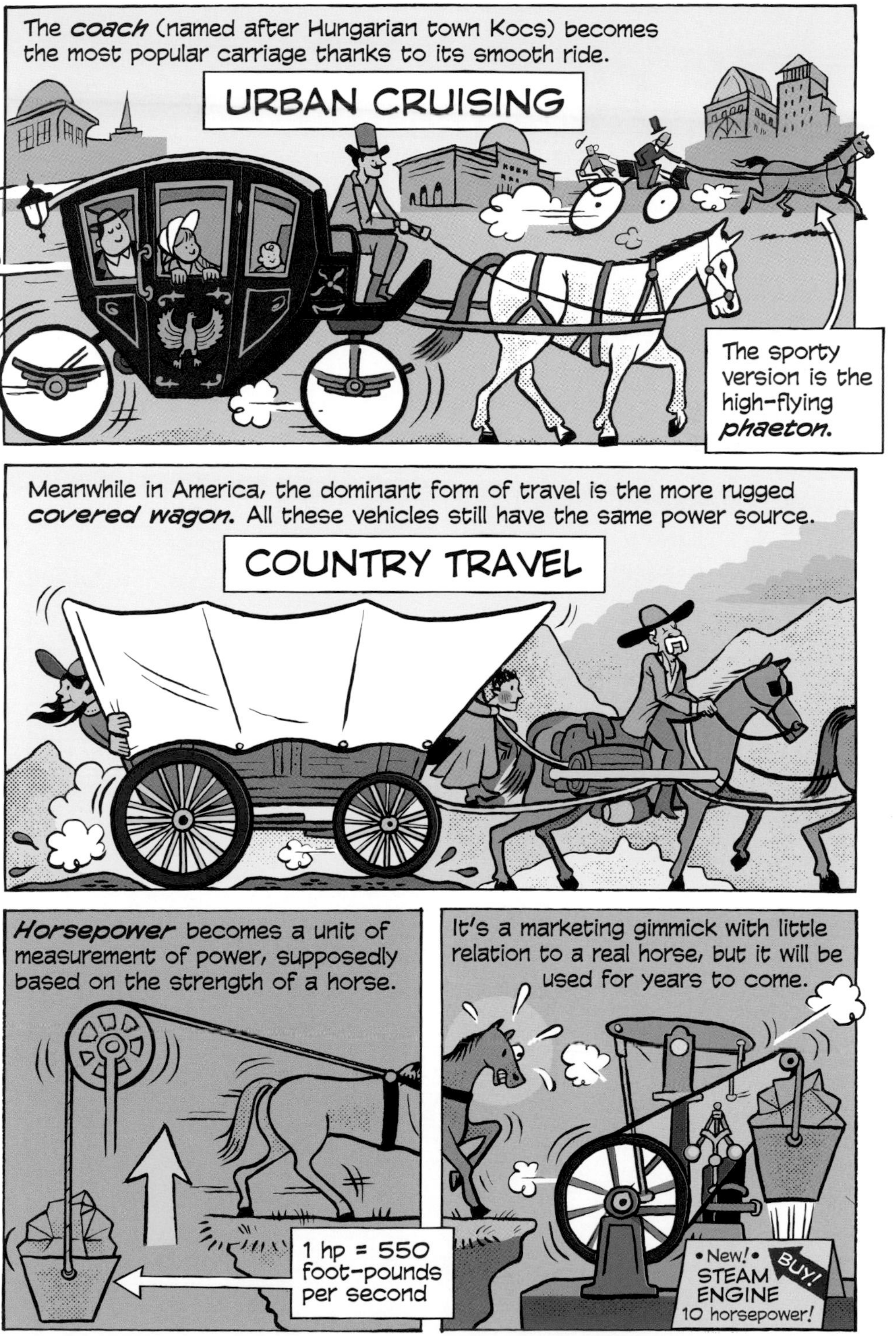
The *coach* (named after Hungarian town Kocs) becomes the most popular carriage thanks to its smooth ride.
URBAN CRUISING
The sporty version is the high-flying *phaeton*.
Meanwhile in America, the dominant form of travel is the more rugged *covered wagon*. All these vehicles still have the same power source.
COUNTRY TRAVEL
Horsepower becomes a unit of measurement of power, supposedly based on the strength of a horse.
1 hp = 550 foot-pounds per second
It's a marketing gimmick with little relation to a real horse, but it will be used for years to come.
•New!• STEAM ENGINE 10 horsepower!
BUY!

Combining chemical reactions and mechanical movements, it's...

THE AGE of STEAM POWERED VEHICLES!

1670s: Father Ferdinand Verbiest, a priest in China, designs* a steam-powered toy that many call

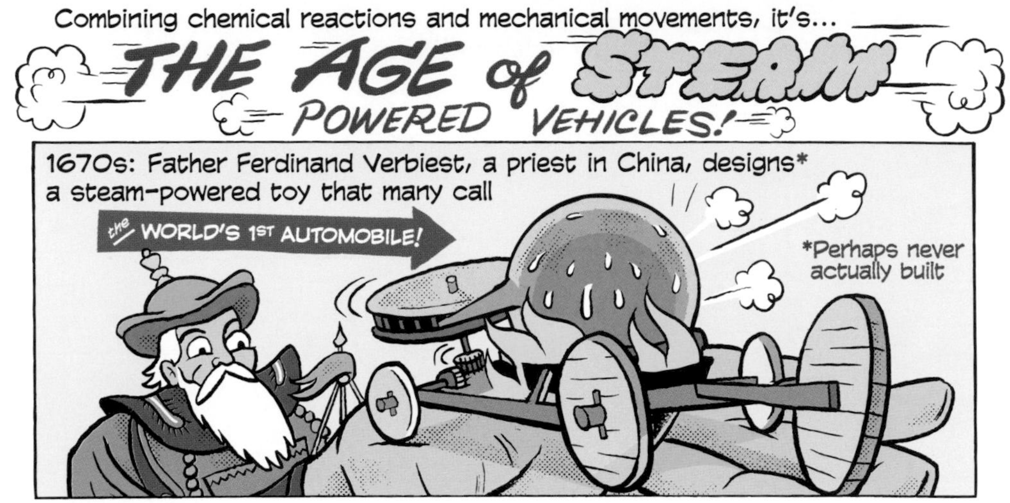
the WORLD'S 1ST AUTOMOBILE!
*Perhaps never actually built

1769: French army captain Nicolas-Joseph Cugnot's *fardier à vapeur,* a big slow tricycle, is the first "working" steam-powered vehicle.
It's also history's first car wreck.

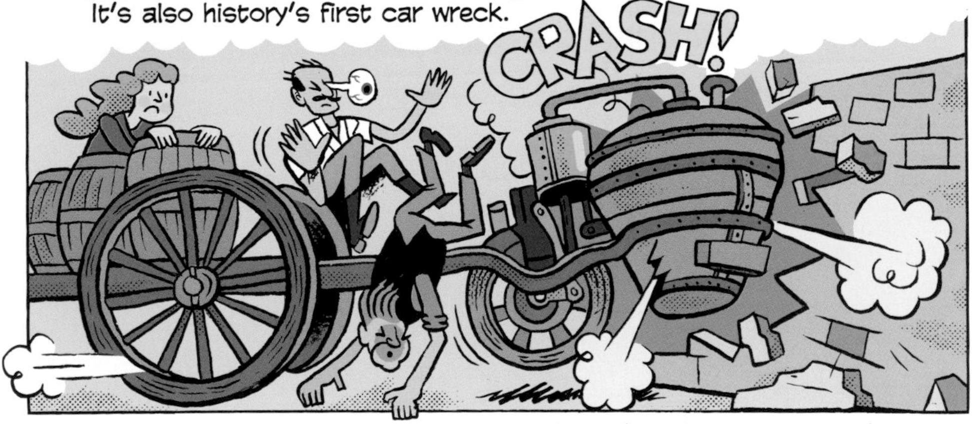
CRASH!

1801: British engineer Richard Trevithick's *Puffing Devil* is the first "road locomotive" to carry a passenger. It pioneers dangerous high-pressure steam.

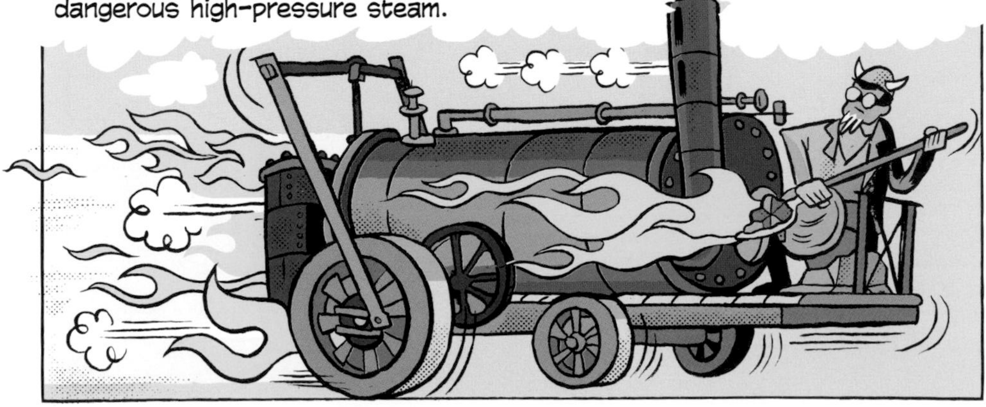

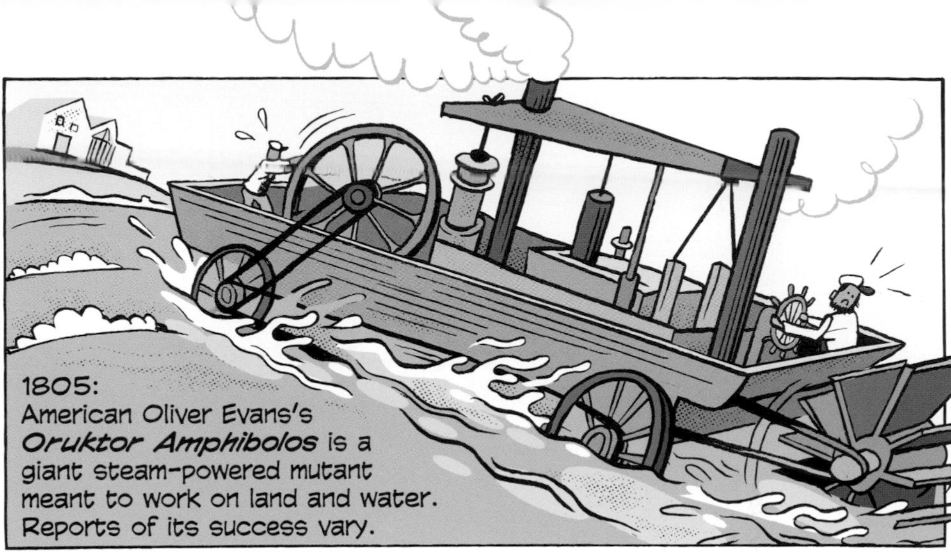
1805:
American Oliver Evans's *Oruktor Amphibolos* is a giant steam-powered mutant meant to work on land and water. Reports of its success vary.

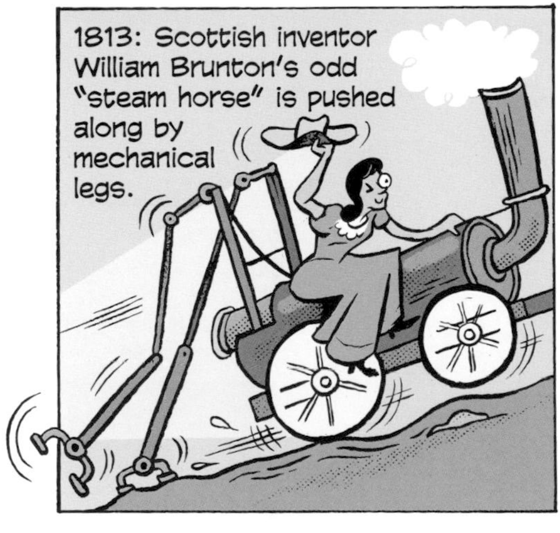
1813: Scottish inventor William Brunton's odd "steam horse" is pushed along by mechanical legs.

1829: Englishman Robert Stephenson's ***Rocket*** is the first major steam train.

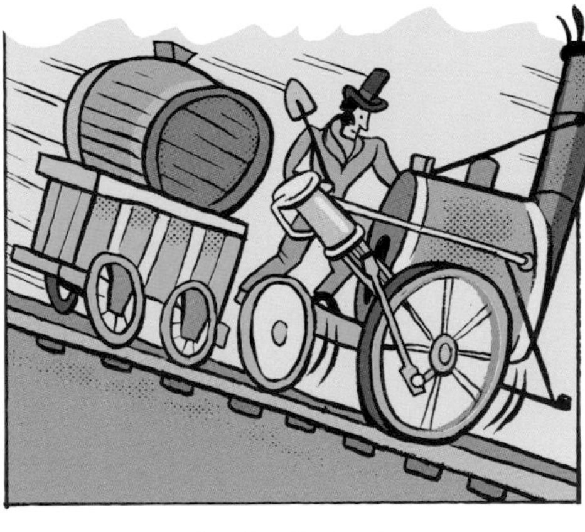

1860s–1910s: Steam-powered cars become mechanically and commercially viable and seem ready to take over the world.

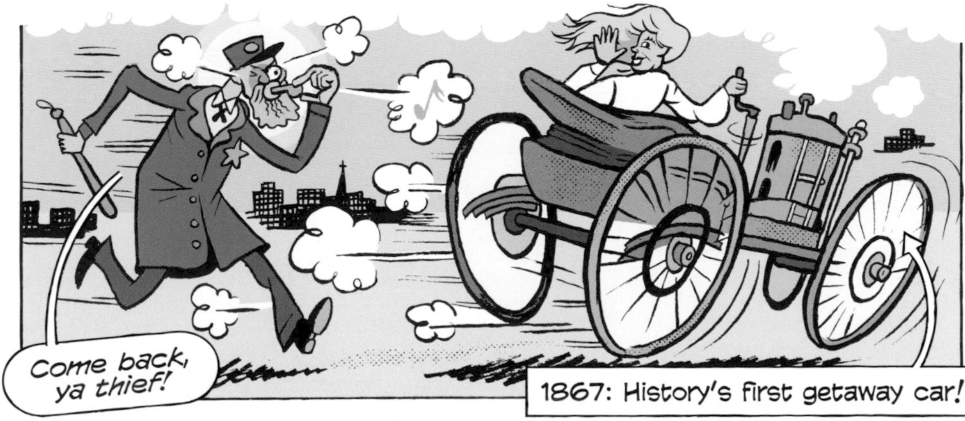
Come back, ya thief!
1867: History's first getaway car!

BOILING POINT!

Here's how a typical steam-powered car works:

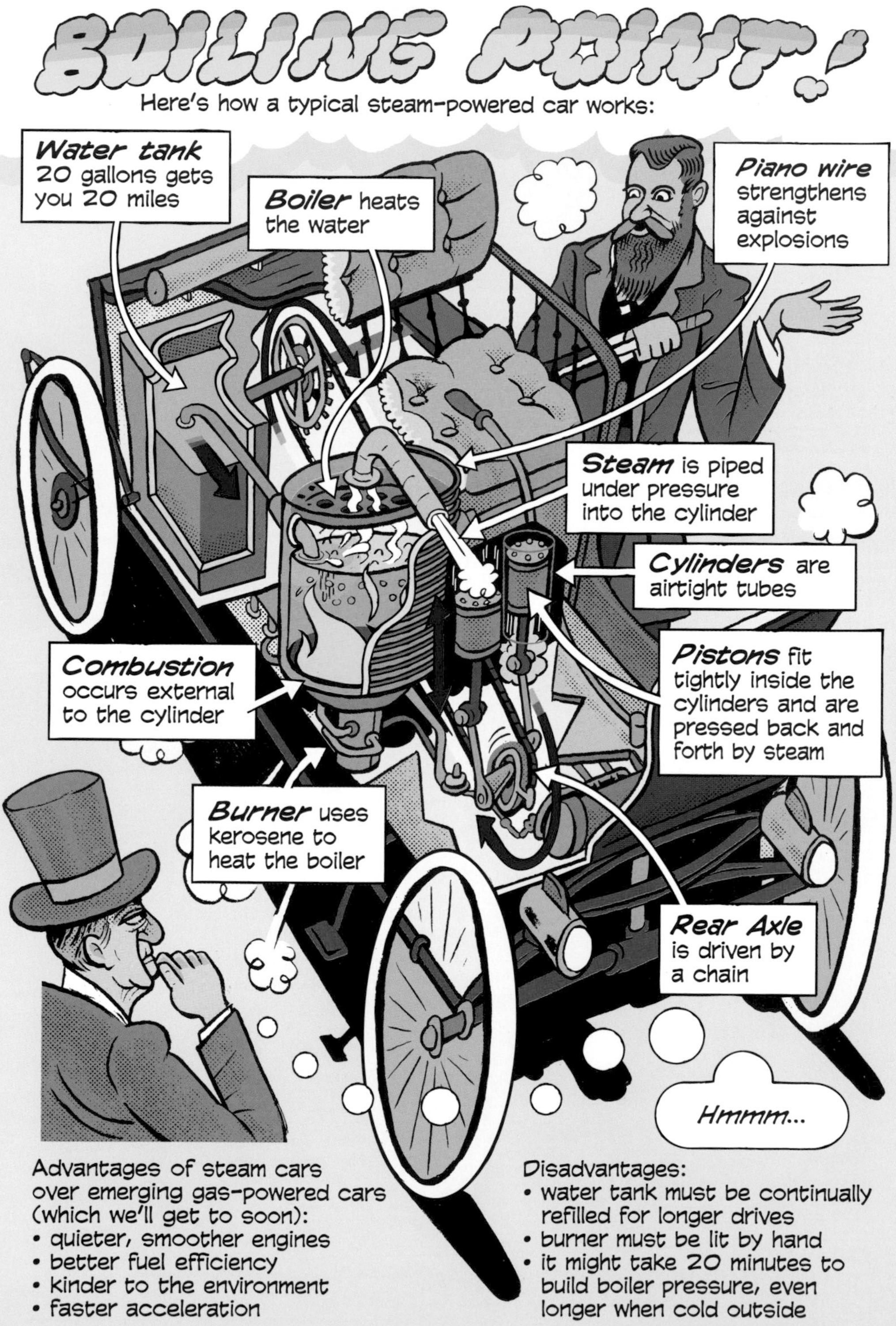
Water tank 20 gallons gets you 20 miles
Boiler heats the water
Piano wire strengthens against explosions
Steam is piped under pressure into the cylinder
Cylinders are airtight tubes
Combustion occurs external to the cylinder
Pistons fit tightly inside the cylinders and are pressed back and forth by steam
Burner uses kerosene to heat the boiler
Rear Axle is driven by a chain
Hmmm...

Advantages of steam cars over emerging gas-powered cars (which we'll get to soon):

- quieter, smoother engines
- better fuel efficiency
- kinder to the environment
- faster acceleration

Disadvantages:

- water tank must be continually refilled for longer drives
- burner must be lit by hand
- it might take 20 minutes to build boiler pressure, even longer when cold outside

1899: William McKinley is the first US president to ride in a car, a *Locomobile Steamer*. He expresses some hesitation.

I appreciate the invitation, Mr. Stanley, but are you sure the contraption is safe?

You have my word there will not be the slightest danger.

Afterward, he remarks:

Stanley is overoptimistic, I think, when he says those things will someday replace horses.

But it won't be McKinley's last car ride; after being shot in 1901, he is transported by an electric ambulance.

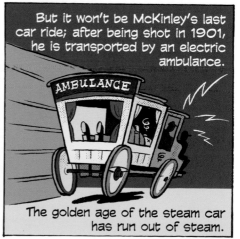

The golden age of the steam car has run out of steam.

Let's back up a bit. "Engines" are defined as *a machine that produces movement*. But how do they work in theory?

Nicolas Léonard Sadi Carnot

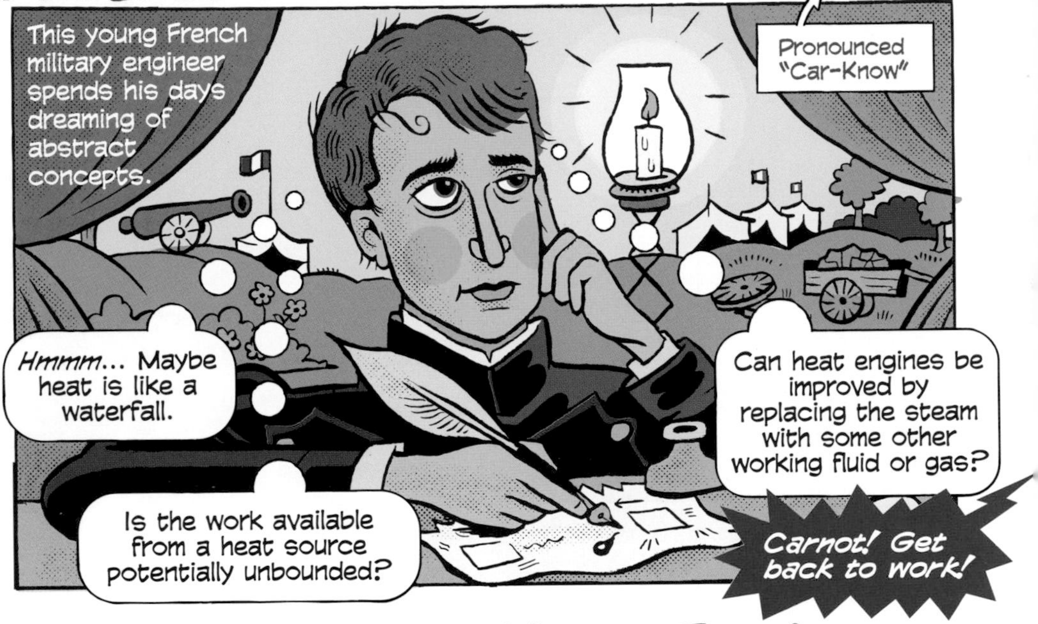

Pronounced "Car-Know"
This young French military engineer spends his days dreaming of abstract concepts.
Hmmm... Maybe heat is like a waterfall.
Can heat engines be improved by replacing the steam with some other working fluid or gas?
Is the work available from a heat source potentially unbounded?
Carnot! Get back to work!

The Carnot Heat Engine

He develops a model showing that when heat is moved from a hot place to a cool place, some of it can be turned into work. It just needs to pass through an ***engine***.

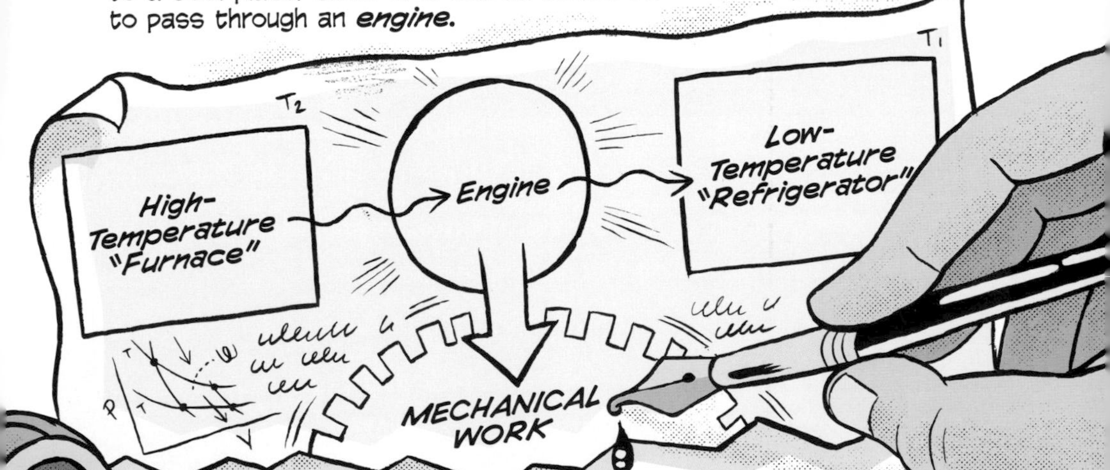

T_2
T_1
High-Temperature "Furnace"
Engine
Low-Temperature "Refrigerator"
MECHANICAL WORK

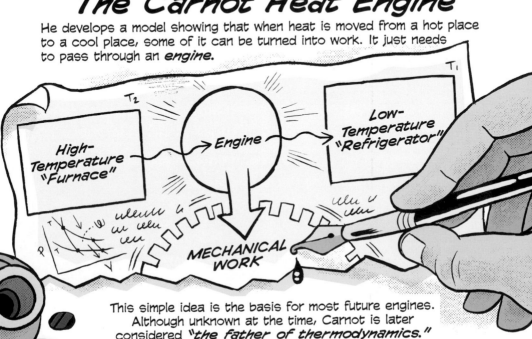

This simple idea is the basis for most future engines. Although unknown at the time, Carnot is later considered ***"the father of thermodynamics."***

Energy is the invisible fuel that drives the universe. *Thermodynamics* is the branch of science that deals with energy and its products: *heat, work,* and *power*.

The important **2nd law of thermodynamics** states:

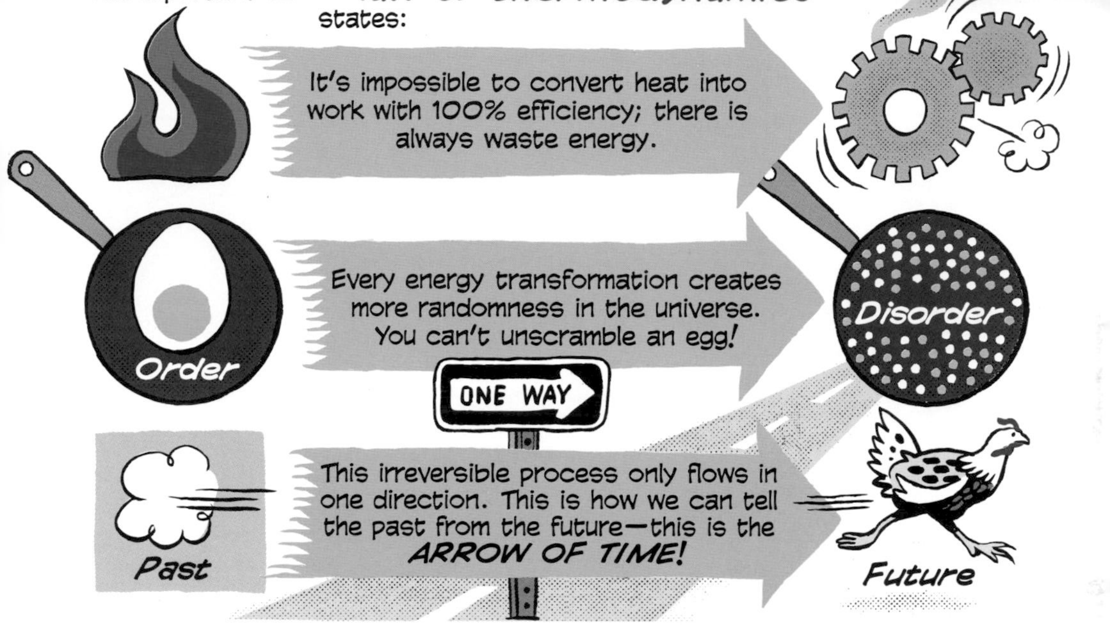
It's impossible to convert heat into work with 100% efficiency; there is always waste energy.
Order
Every energy transformation creates more randomness in the universe. You can't unscramble an egg!
Disorder
ONE WAY
Past
This irreversible process only flows in one direction. This is how we can tell the past from the future—this is the ARROW OF TIME!
Future

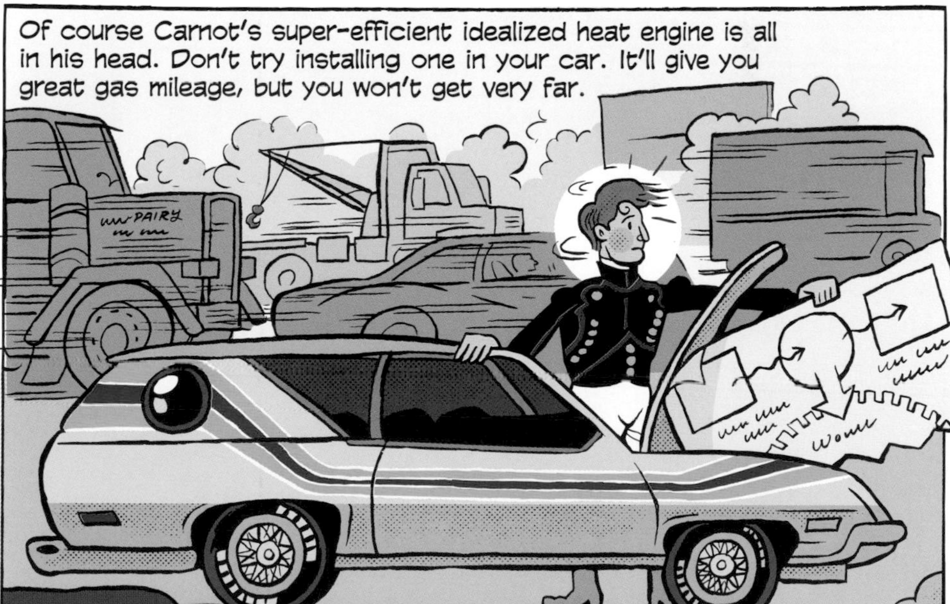
Of course Carnot's super-efficient idealized heat engine is all in his head. Don't try installing one in your car. It'll give you great gas mileage, but you won't get very far.
Next let's move from theoretical engines to real ones—loud, filthy, stinky, and gigantic.

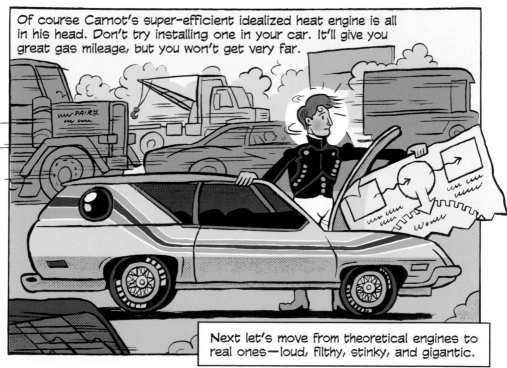

Whether you're racing a fire-breathing hot rod down a drag strip or cruising a minivan through the suburbs, you've got one engine to thank:

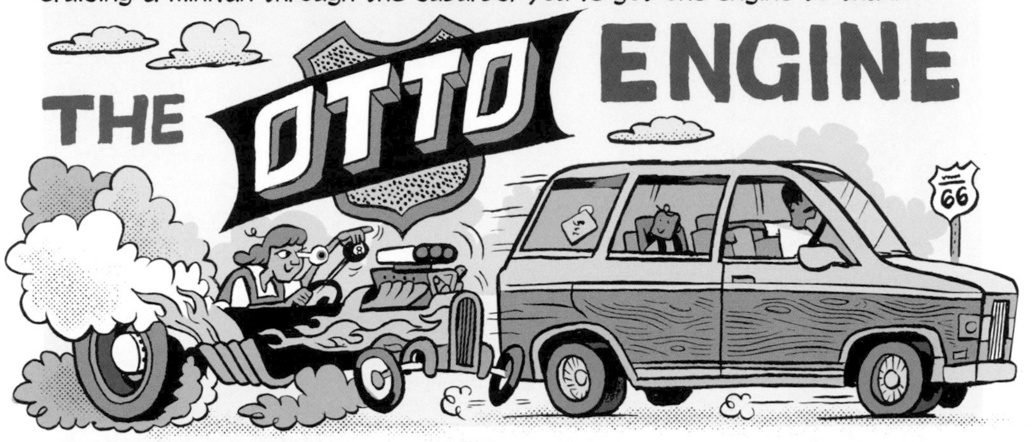
THE OTTO ENGINE
66

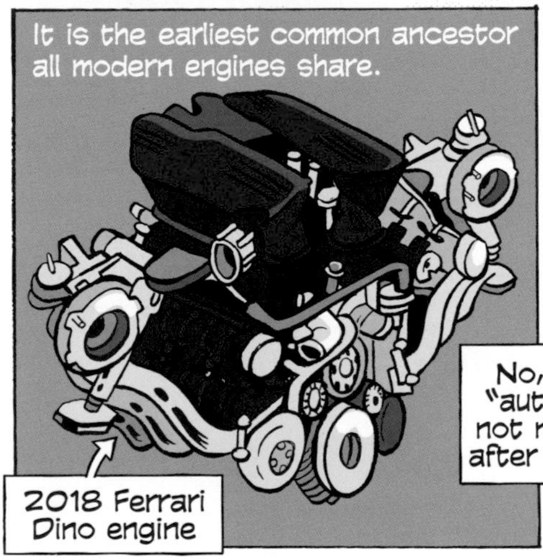
It is the earliest common ancestor all modern engines share.
2018 Ferrari Dino engine

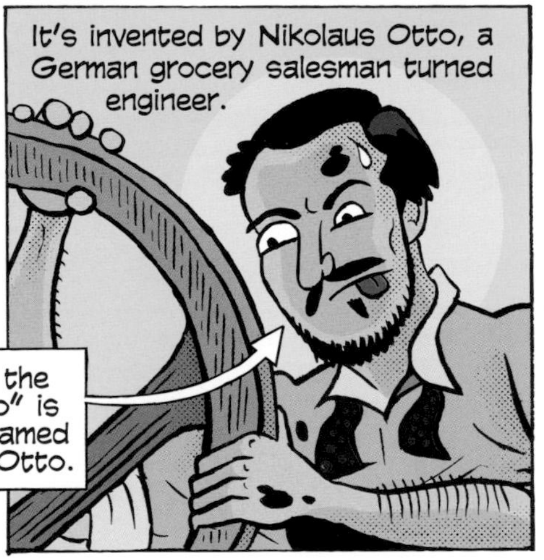
It's invented by Nikolaus Otto, a German grocery salesman turned engineer.
No, the "auto" is not named after Otto.

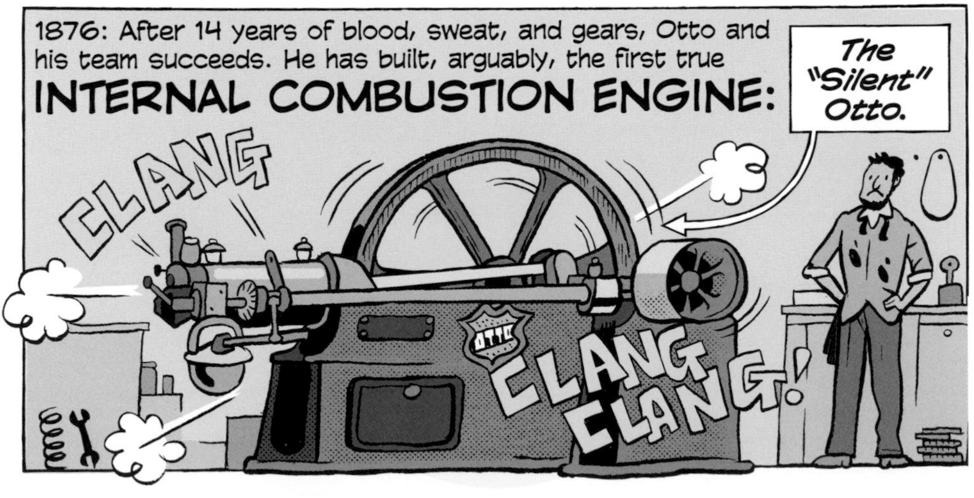
1876: After 14 years of blood, sweat, and gears, Otto and his team succeeds. He has built, arguably, the first true
INTERNAL COMBUSTION ENGINE:
The "Silent" Otto.
CLANG
OTTO
CLANG CLANG CLANG!

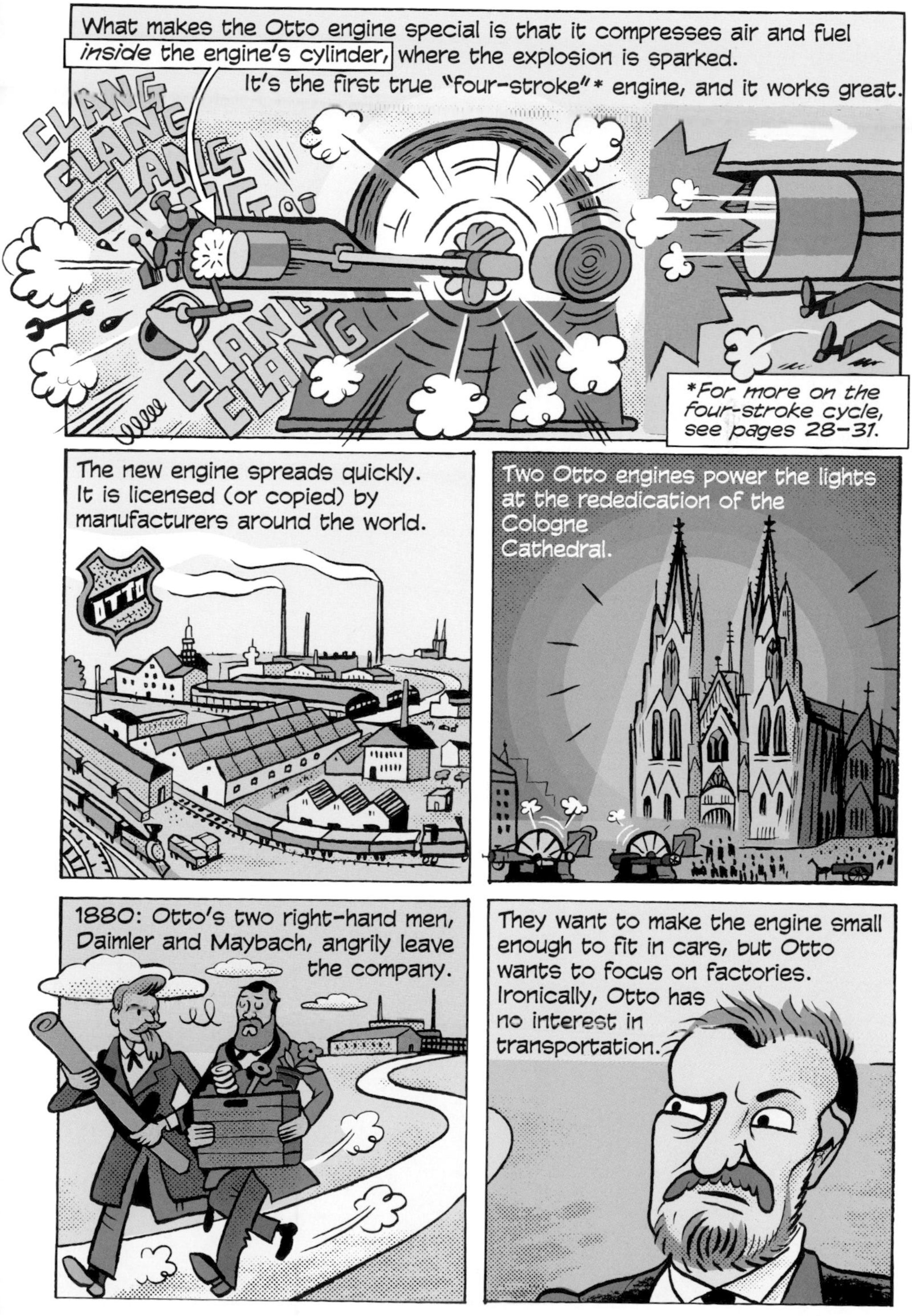

What makes the Otto engine special is that it compresses air and fuel
inside the engine's cylinder, where the explosion is sparked.
It's the first true "four-stroke"* engine, and it works great.
CLANG CLANG CLANG
CLANG CLANG
*For more on the four-stroke cycle, see pages 28–31.
The new engine spreads quickly. It is licensed (or copied) by manufacturers around the world.
OTTO
Two Otto engines power the lights at the rededication of the Cologne Cathedral.
1880: Otto's two right-hand men, Daimler and Maybach, angrily leave the company.
They want to make the engine small enough to fit in cars, but Otto wants to focus on factories. Ironically, Otto has no interest in transportation.

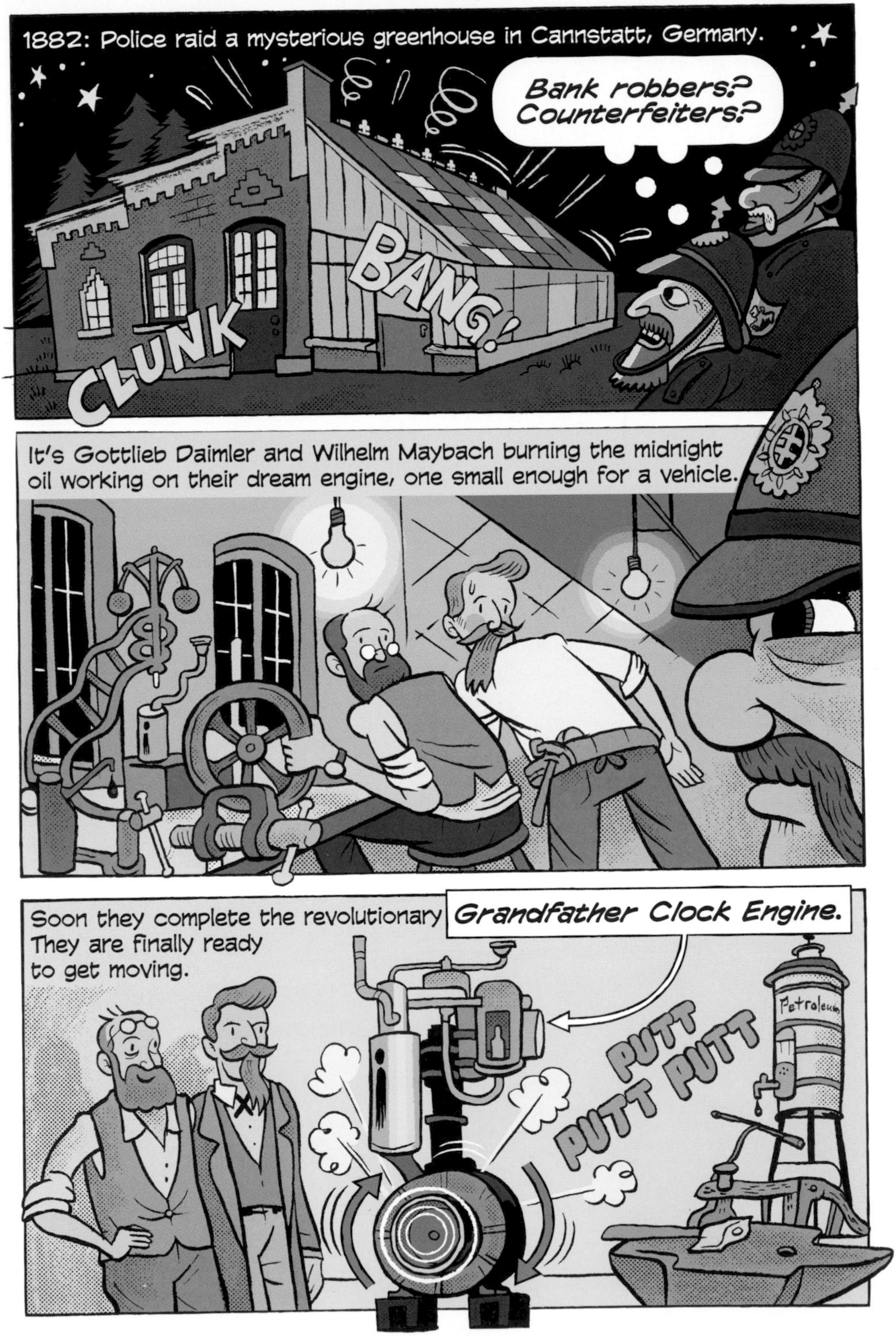
1882: Police raid a mysterious greenhouse in Cannstatt, Germany.
Bank robbers? Counterfeiters?
CLUNK
BANG!
It's Gottlieb Daimler and Wilhelm Maybach burning the midnight oil working on their dream engine, one small enough for a vehicle.
Soon they complete the revolutionary
Grandfather Clock Engine.
They are finally ready to get moving.
PUTT PUTT PUTT
Petroleum

1885: **The DAIMLER PETROLEUM REITWAGEN** ("riding car") is built. Daimler is often called "the father of the motorcycle" for this gnarly invention, though Maybach is surely co-inventor.

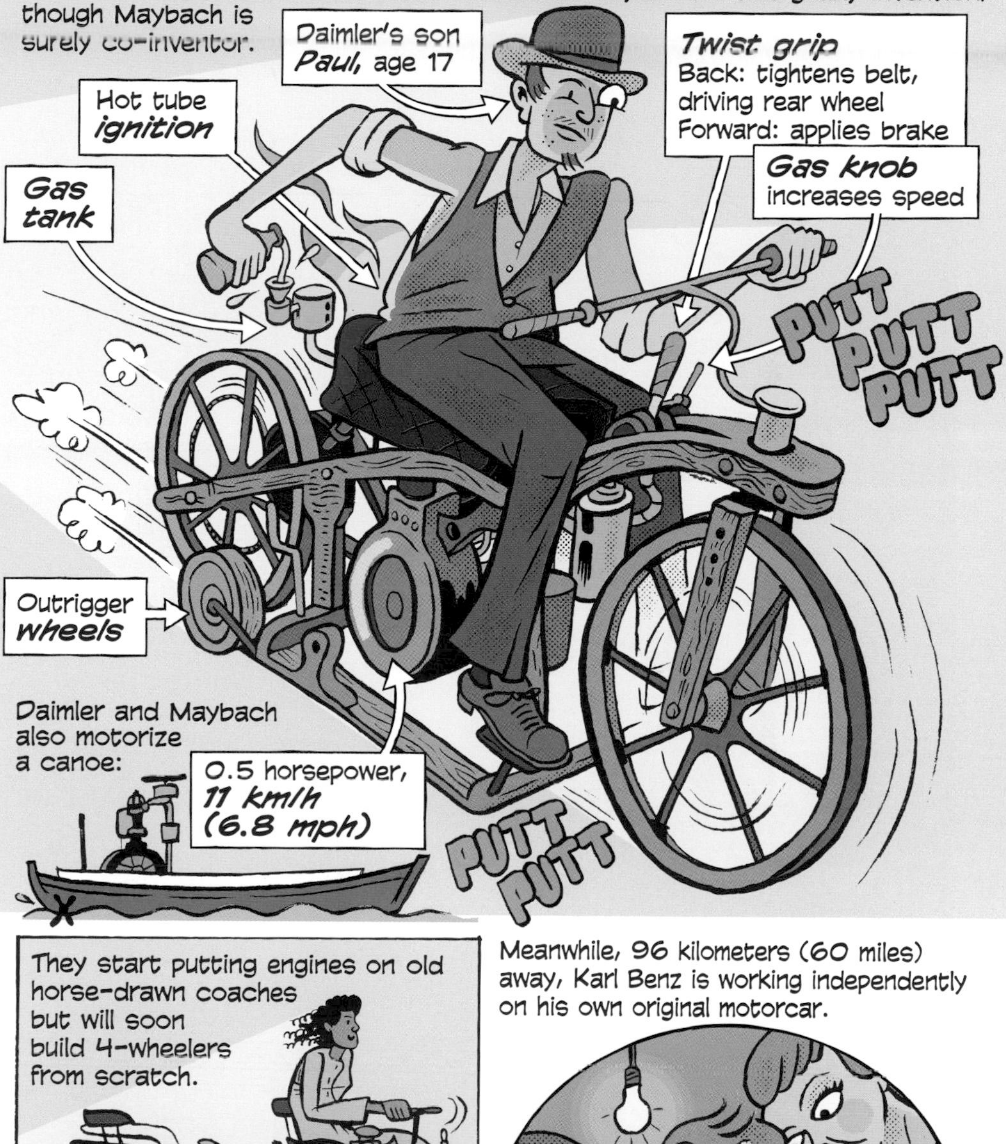

Daimler's son *Paul,* age 17
Twist grip
Back: tightens belt, driving rear wheel
Forward: applies brake
Hot tube *ignition*
Gas tank
Gas knob increases speed
PUTT PUTT PUTT
Outrigger *wheels*
Daimler and Maybach also motorize a canoe:
0.5 horsepower, *11 km/h (6.8 mph)*
PUTT PUTT

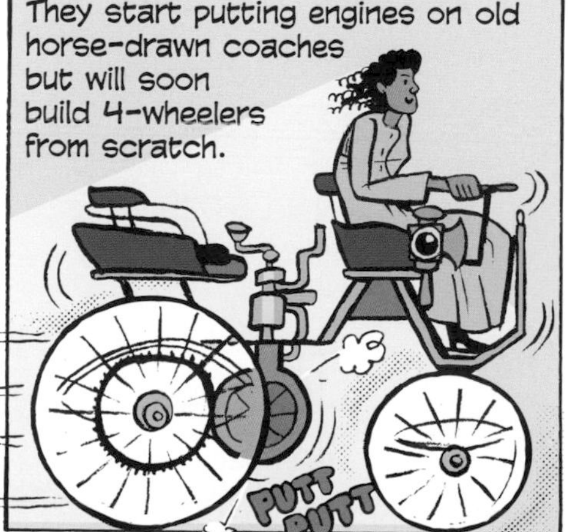

They start putting engines on old horse-drawn coaches but will soon build 4-wheelers from scratch.
PUTT PUTT

Meanwhile, 96 kilometers (60 miles) away, Karl Benz is working independently on his own original motorcar.

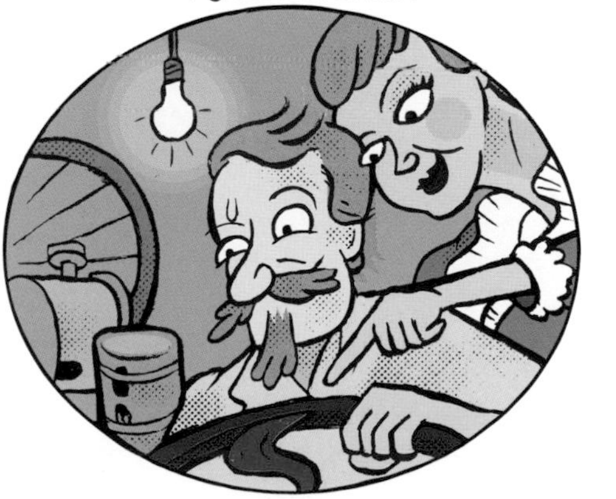

Not To Be FORGOTTEN!

Obscure Antecedents and Evolutionary Dead Ends in Early Car Making

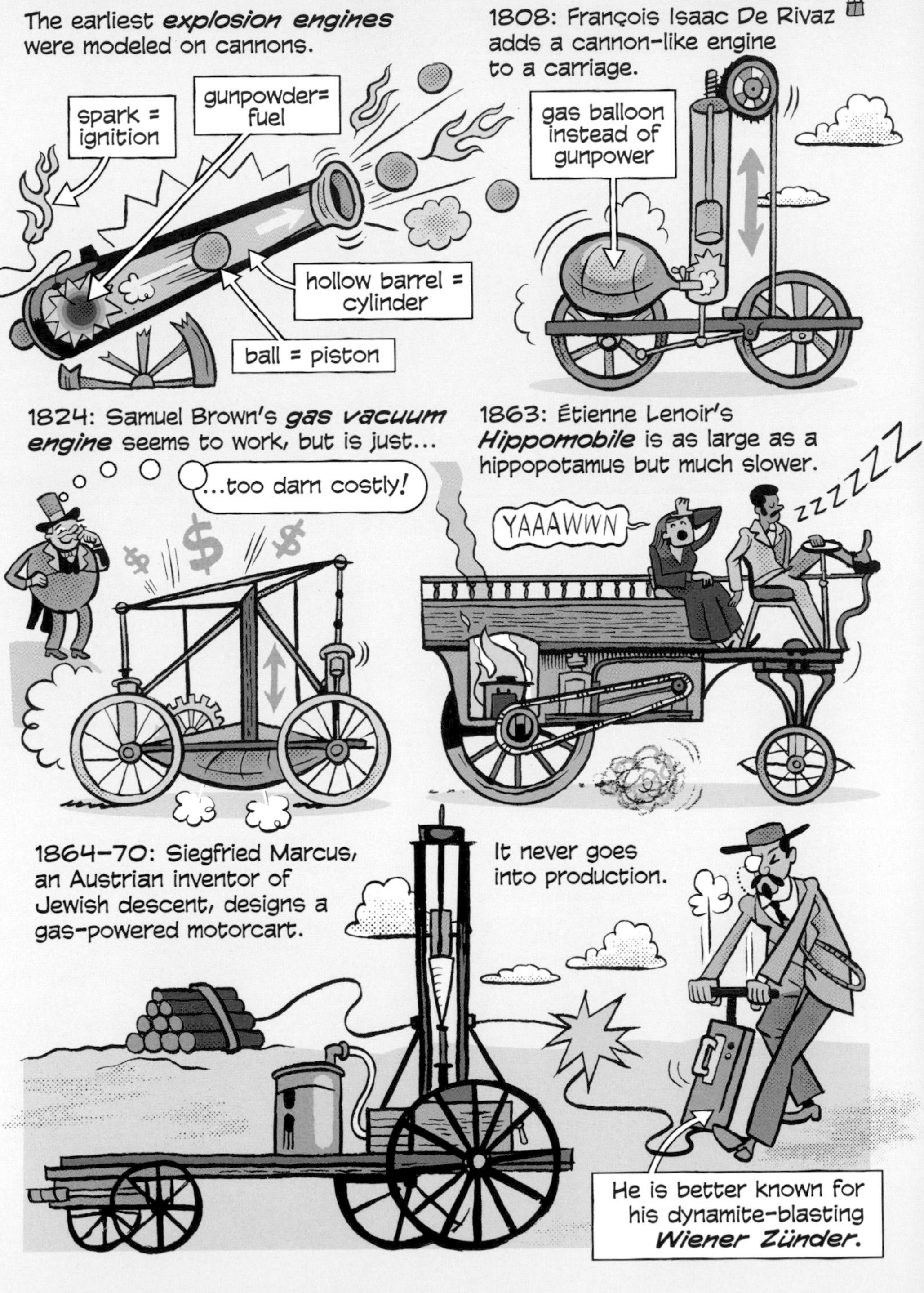

The earliest explosion engines were modeled on cannons.
spark = ignition
gunpowder= fuel
hollow barrel = cylinder
ball = piston
1808: François Isaac De Rivaz adds a cannon-like engine to a carriage.
gas balloon instead of gunpower
1824: Samuel Brown's gas vacuum engine seems to work, but is just…
…too darn costly!
1863: Étienne Lenoir's Hippomobile is as large as a hippopotamus but much slower.
YAAAWWN
ZZZZZZZ
1864–70: Siegfried Marcus, an Austrian inventor of Jewish descent, designs a gas-powered motorcart.
It never goes into production.
He is better known for his dynamite-blasting Wiener Zünder.

1872: George Brayton's ***Ready Motor*** starts quickly and runs on constant pressure.

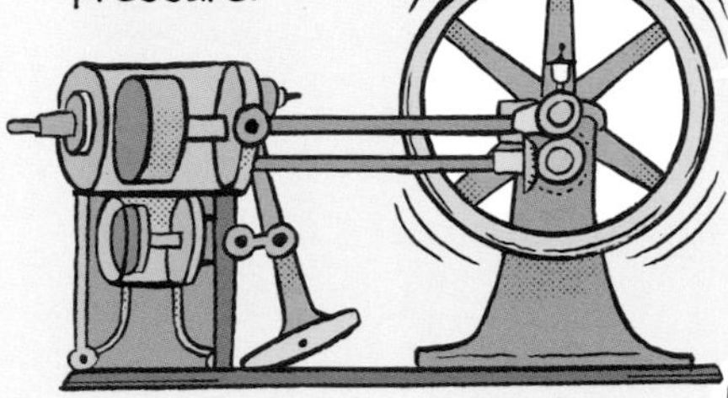

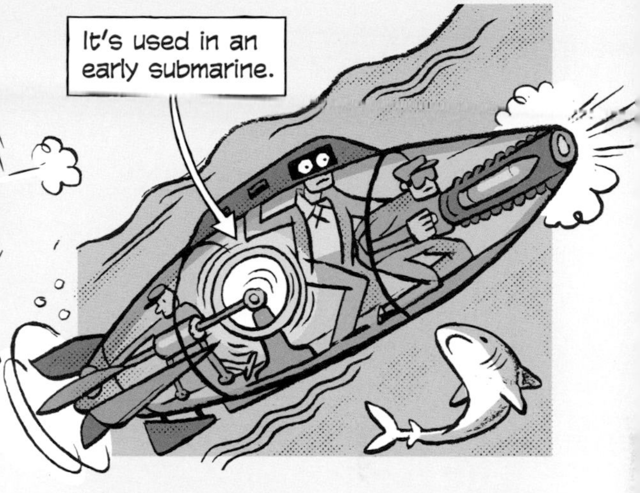
It's used in an early submarine.

1879–95: George B. Selden patents the automobile in the US, starting legal wars that would last decades.

Selden never builds a single car.

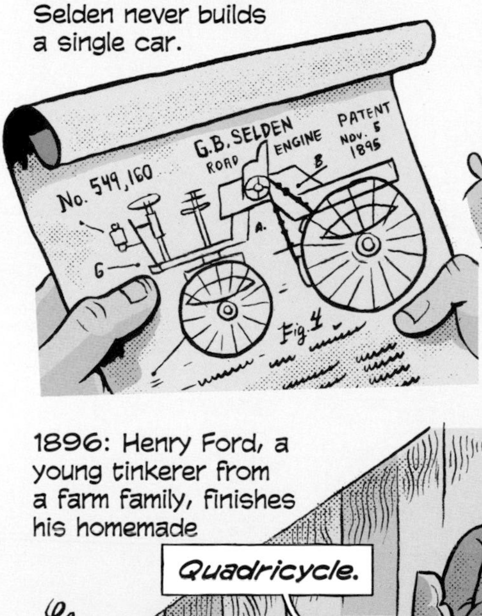
G.B. SELDEN
ROAD ENGINE
PATENT NOV. 5 1895
No. 549,160
Fig. 4

1893: The Duryea brothers build the first American cars and later loan one to the Barnum & Bailey Circus.

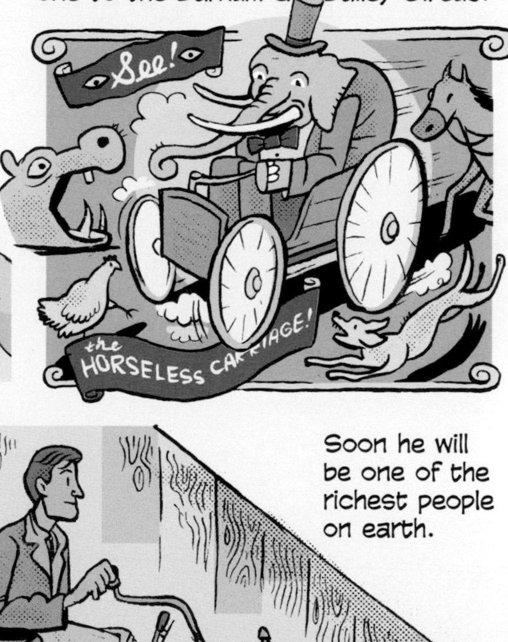
See!
the HORSELESS CARRIAGE!

1896: Henry Ford, a young tinkerer from a farm family, finishes his homemade

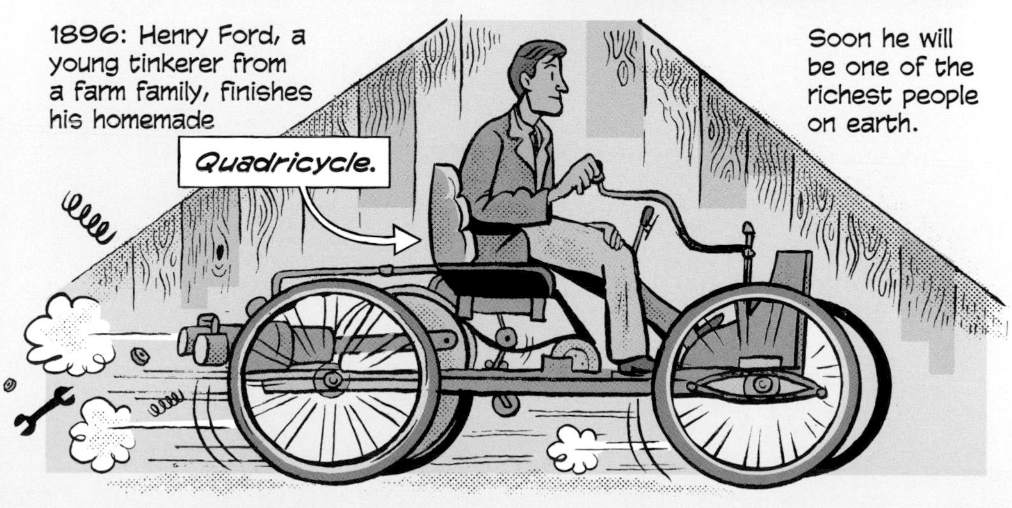
Quadricycle.

Soon he will be one of the richest people on earth.

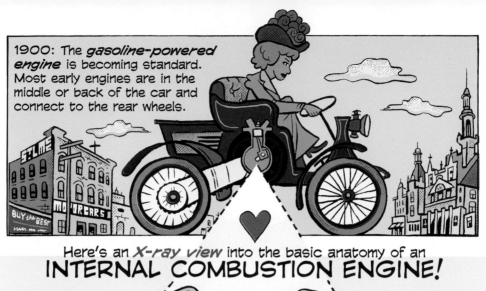

1900: The *gasoline-powered engine* is becoming standard. Most early engines are in the middle or back of the car and connect to the rear wheels.

Here's an *X-ray view* into the basic anatomy of an

INTERNAL COMBUSTION ENGINE!

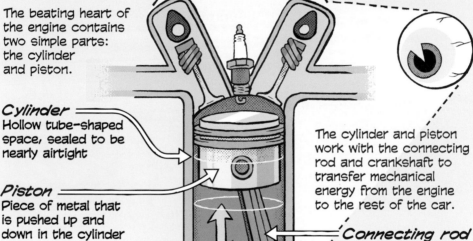

The beating heart of the engine contains two simple parts: the cylinder and piston.

Cylinder
Hollow tube-shaped space, sealed to be nearly airtight

Piston
Piece of metal that is pushed up and down in the cylinder

The cylinder and piston work with the connecting rod and crankshaft to transfer mechanical energy from the engine to the rest of the car.

Connecting rod
Connects the piston to the crankshaft

Early cars like Benz's and Daimler's have just one cylinder. The Quadricycle has two. Future cars will have several more (e.g., Inline-4 or V8.)

Crankshaft
Rotating shaft that turns the piston's up-and-down motion into rotational motion, like bicycle pedals

But without air, fuel, and heat, the engine is just a bunch of interconnected hunks of useless metal. Here's how we get moving!

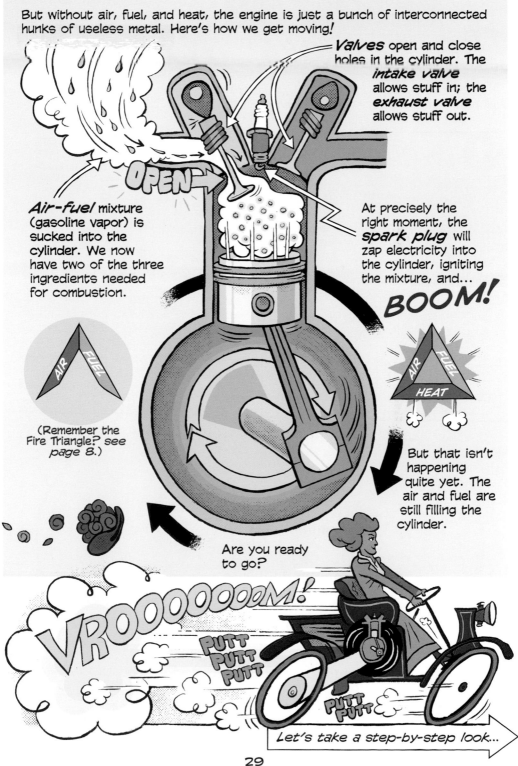

Valves open and close holes in the cylinder. The **intake valve** allows stuff in; the **exhaust valve** allows stuff out.

OPEN

Air-fuel mixture (gasoline vapor) is sucked into the cylinder. We now have two of the three ingredients needed for combustion.

At precisely the right moment, the **spark plug** will zap electricity into the cylinder, igniting the mixture, and...

BOOM!

AIR FUEL

(Remember the Fire Triangle? see page 8.)

AIR FUEL HEAT

But that isn't happening quite yet. The air and fuel are still filling the cylinder.

Are you ready to go?

VROOOOOOM!

PUTT PUTT PUTT

PUTT PUTT

Let's take a step-by-step look...

The (4-STROKE) INTERNAL

One explosion won't get you very far. You'll need thousands of explosions happening repeatedly in sequence just to drive down the street to grab lunch. Here are the four steps (or "strokes") in the engine's cycle:

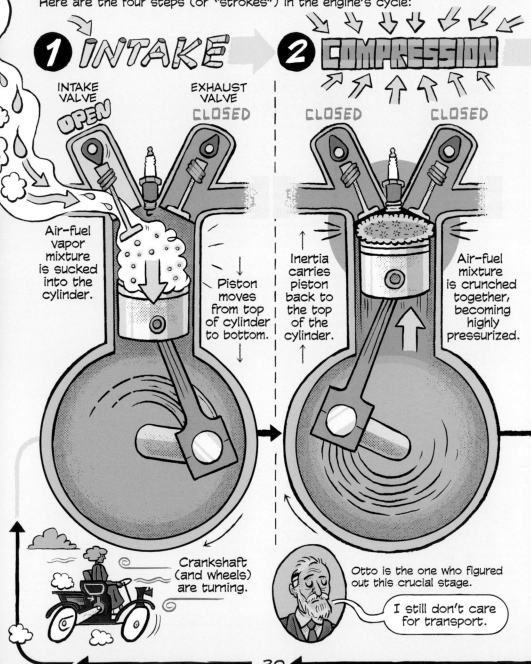

1 INTAKE

INTAKE VALVE **OPEN**

EXHAUST VALVE **CLOSED**

Air-fuel vapor mixture is sucked into the cylinder.

↓ Piston moves from top of cylinder to bottom. ↓

Crankshaft (and wheels) are turning.

2 COMPRESSION

CLOSED   **CLOSED**

↑ Inertia carries piston back to the top of the cylinder. ↑

Air-fuel mixture is crunched together, becoming highly pressurized.

Otto is the one who figured out this crucial stage.

I still don't care for transport.

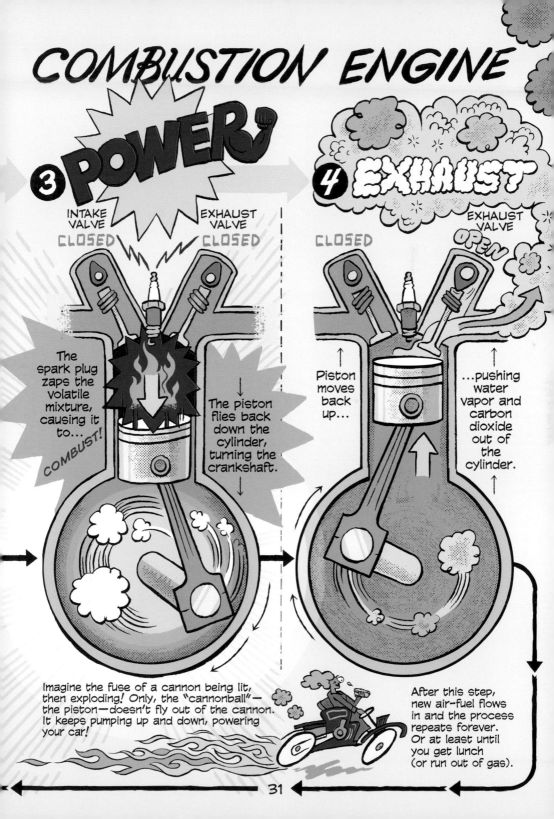

COMBUSTION ENGINE

③ POWER!

INTAKE VALVE **CLOSED**   EXHAUST VALVE **CLOSED**

The spark plug zaps the volatile mixture, causing it to... *COMBUST!*

The piston flies back down the cylinder, turning the crankshaft.

Imagine the fuse of a cannon being lit, then exploding! Only, the "cannonball"— the piston—doesn't fly out of the cannon. It keeps pumping up and down, powering your car!

④ EXHAUST

CLOSED   EXHAUST VALVE **OPEN**

Piston moves back up...

...pushing water vapor and carbon dioxide out of the cylinder.

After this step, new air-fuel flows in and the process repeats forever. Or at least until you get lunch (or run out of gas).

31

STROKE 2:
COMPRESSION

Putting It All Together

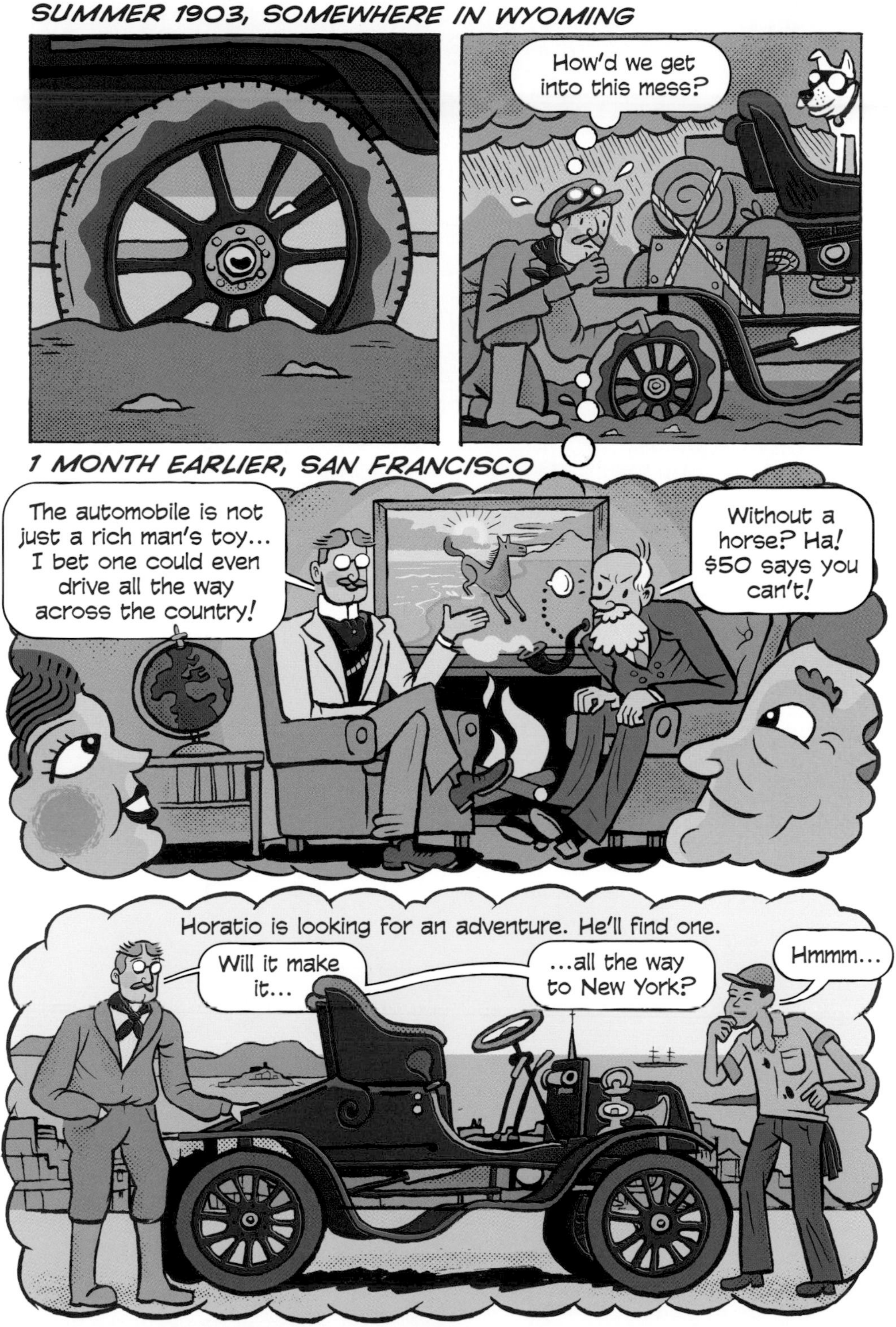
SUMMER 1903, SOMEWHERE IN WYOMING
How'd we get into this mess?
1 MONTH EARLIER, SAN FRANCISCO
The automobile is not just a rich man's toy... I bet one could even drive all the way across the country!
Without a horse? Ha! $50 says you can't!
Horatio is looking for an adventure. He'll find one.
Will it make it...
...all the way to New York?
Hmmm...

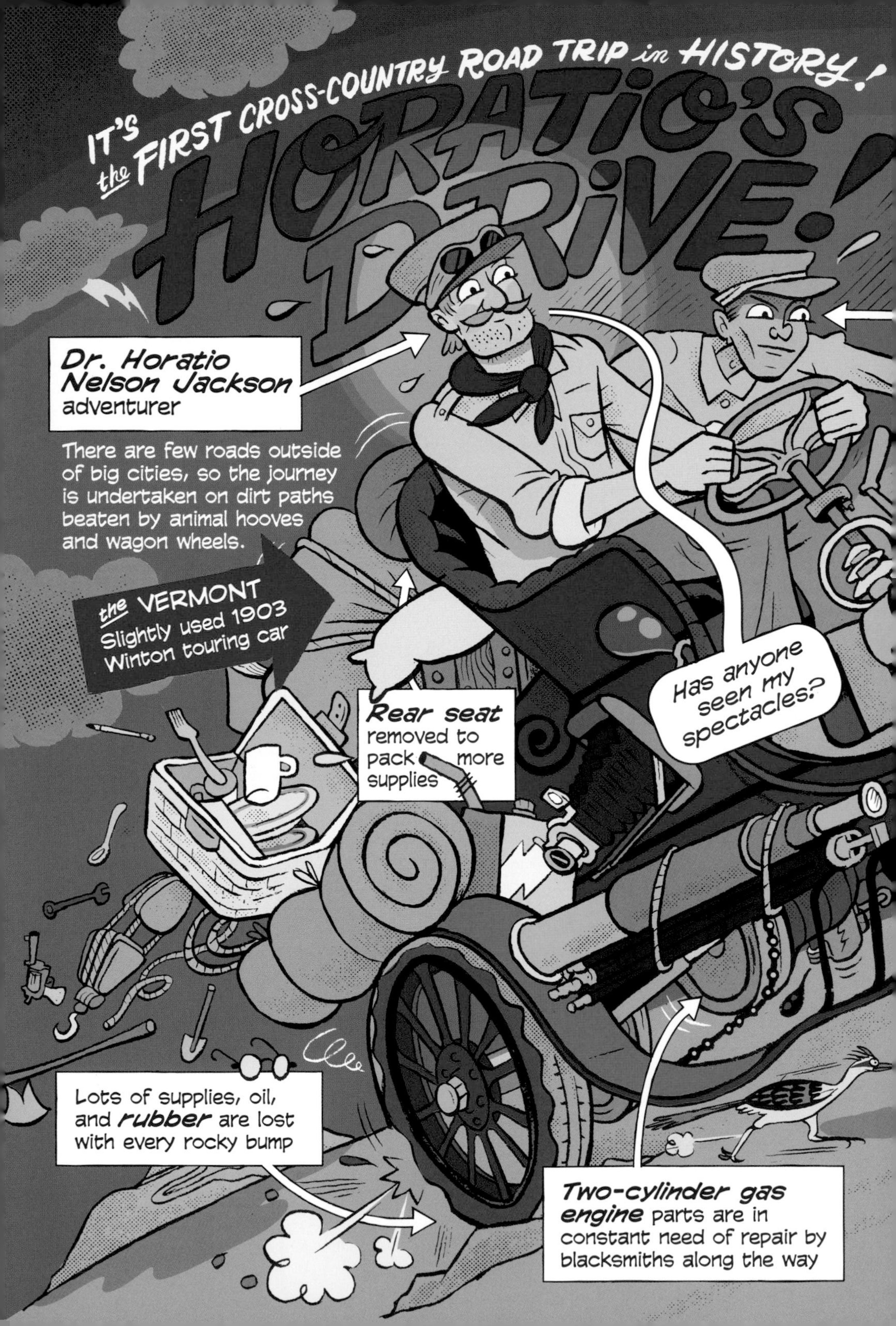

IT'S the FIRST CROSS-COUNTRY ROAD TRIP in HISTORY!
HORATIO'S DRIVE!
Dr. Horatio Nelson Jackson adventurer
There are few roads outside of big cities, so the journey is undertaken on dirt paths beaten by animal hooves and wagon wheels.
the VERMONT Slightly used 1903 Winton touring car
Rear seat removed to pack more supplies
Has anyone seen my spectacles?
Lots of supplies, oil, and rubber are lost with every rocky bump
Two-cylinder gas engine parts are in constant need of repair by blacksmiths along the way

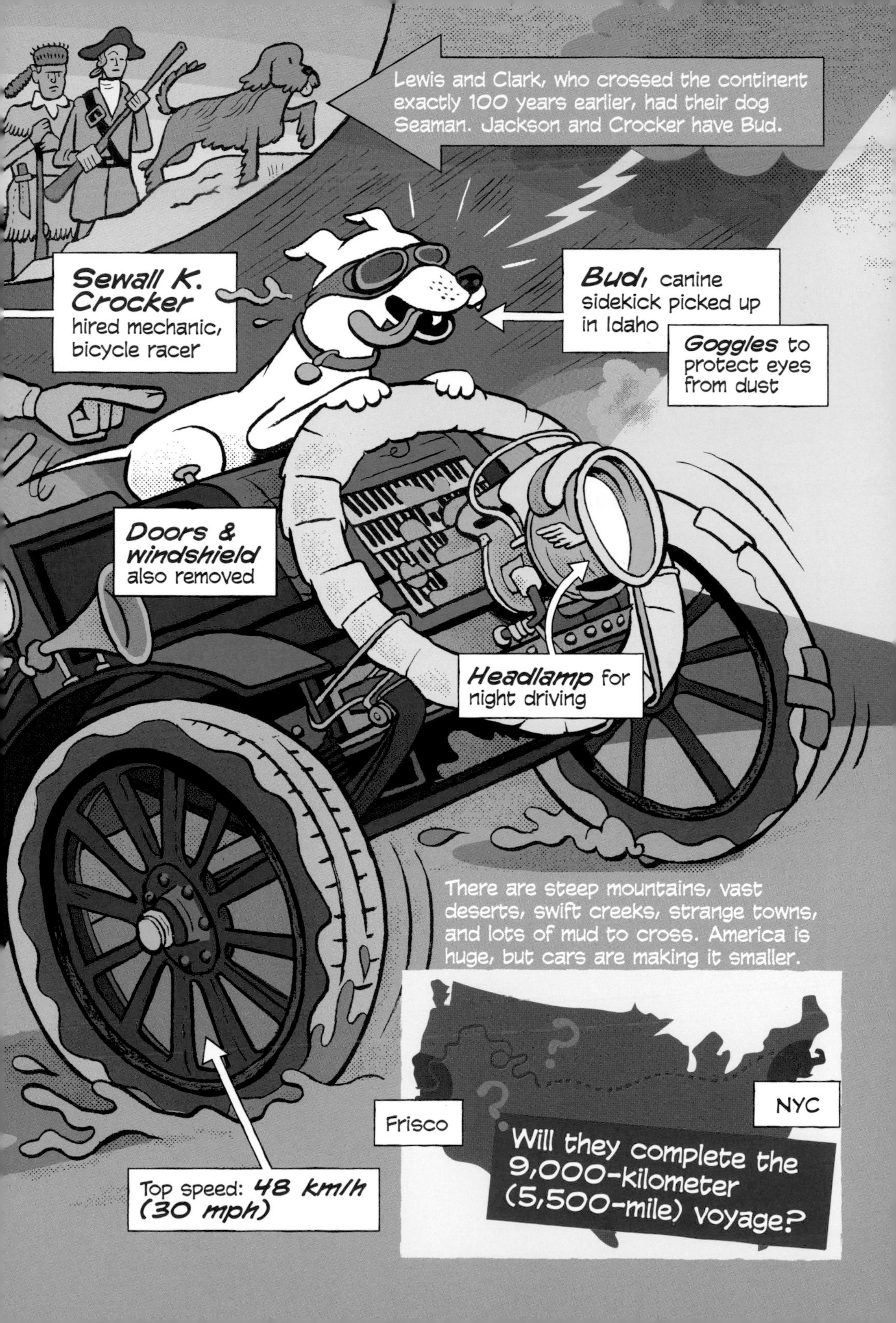

Lewis and Clark, who crossed the continent exactly 100 years earlier, had their dog Seaman. Jackson and Crocker have Bud.
Sewall K. Crocker hired mechanic, bicycle racer
Bud, canine sidekick picked up in Idaho
Goggles to protect eyes from dust
Doors & windshield also removed
Headlamp for night driving
There are steep mountains, vast deserts, swift creeks, strange towns, and lots of mud to cross. America is huge, but cars are making it smaller.
Top speed: *48 km/h (30 mph)*
Frisco
NYC
Will they complete the 9,000-kilometer (5,500-mile) voyage?

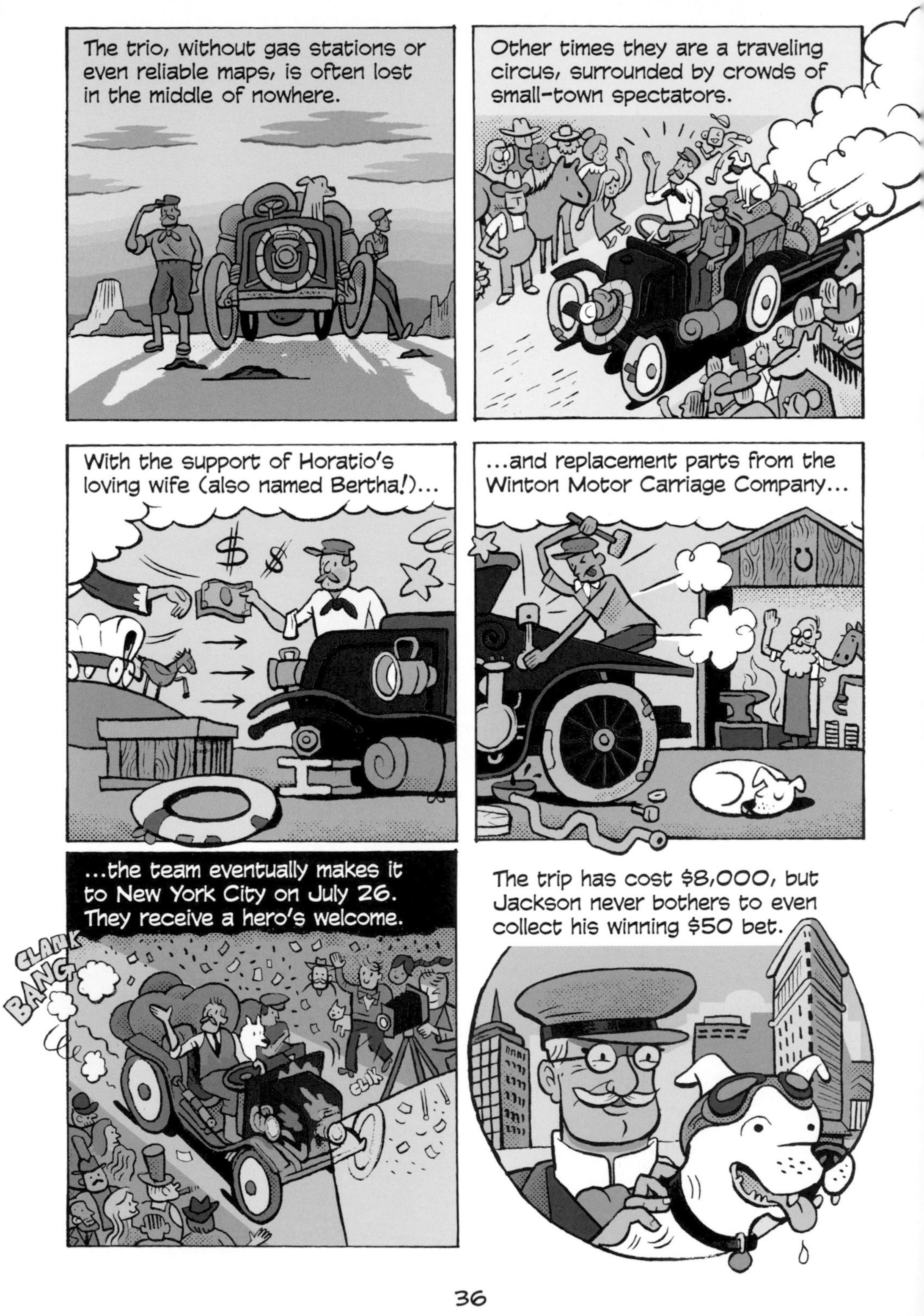
The trio, without gas stations or even reliable maps, is often lost in the middle of nowhere.
Other times they are a traveling circus, surrounded by crowds of small-town spectators.
With the support of Horatio's loving wife (also named Bertha!)...
$ $
...and replacement parts from the Winton Motor Carriage Company...
...the team eventually makes it to New York City on July 26. They receive a hero's welcome.
CLANK
BANG
CLIK
The trip has cost $8,000, but Jackson never bothers to even collect his winning $50 bet.

HIGHWAYS & ByWAYS!
Road Culture from the Silk Road to Route 66

The earliest prehistoric trails are formed by animals and humans that hunt them.

CLOMP

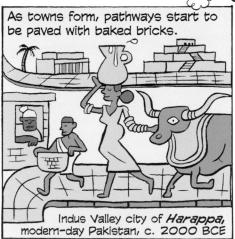

As towns form, pathways start to be paved with baked bricks.

Indus Valley city of *Harappa,* modern-day Pakistan, c. 2000 BCE

Roman roads are really straight, allowing efficient travel.

The Appian Way, "Queen of the Long Roads," c. 300 BCE

Trade networks between cities turn into primitive "highways."

The *Silk Road* connecting the ancient world, c. 100 BCE

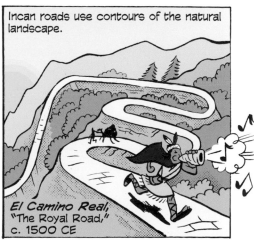

Incan roads use contours of the natural landscape.

El Camino Real, "The Royal Road," c. 1500 CE

When cars take over, roads themselves are the landscape.

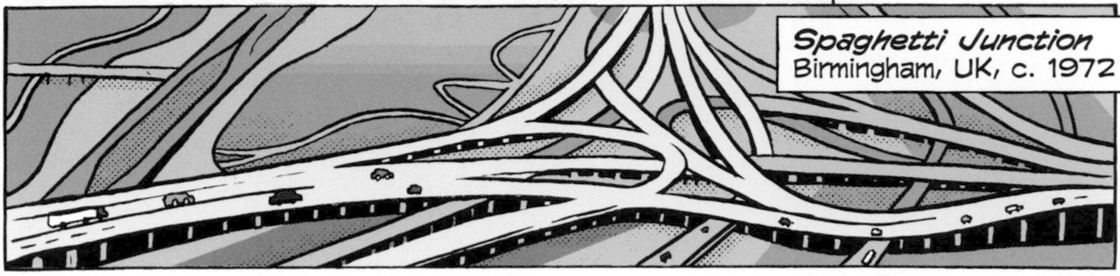

Spaghetti Junction
Birmingham, UK, c. 1972

STREET VIEW!

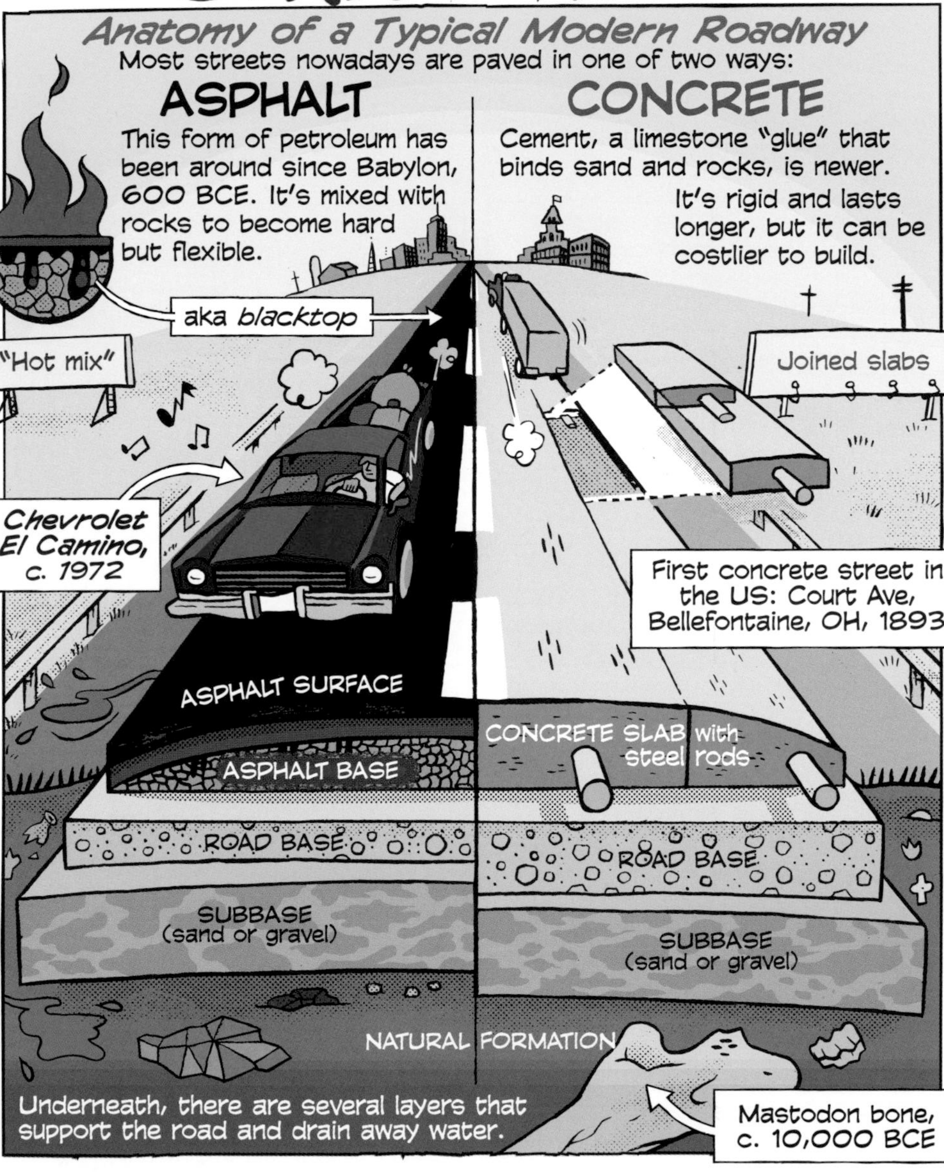

Anatomy of a Typical Modern Roadway
Most streets nowadays are paved in one of two ways:
ASPHALT
This form of petroleum has been around since Babylon, 600 BCE. It's mixed with rocks to become hard but flexible.
CONCRETE
Cement, a limestone "glue" that binds sand and rocks, is newer.
It's rigid and lasts longer, but it can be costlier to build.
aka blacktop
"Hot mix"
Joined slabs
Chevrolet El Camino, c. 1972
First concrete street in the US: Court Ave, Bellefontaine, OH, 1893
ASPHALT SURFACE
ASPHALT BASE
CONCRETE SLAB with steel rods
ROAD BASE
ROAD BASE
SUBBASE (sand or gravel)
SUBBASE (sand or gravel)
NATURAL FORMATION
Underneath, there are several layers that support the road and drain away water.
Mastodon bone, c. 10,000 BCE

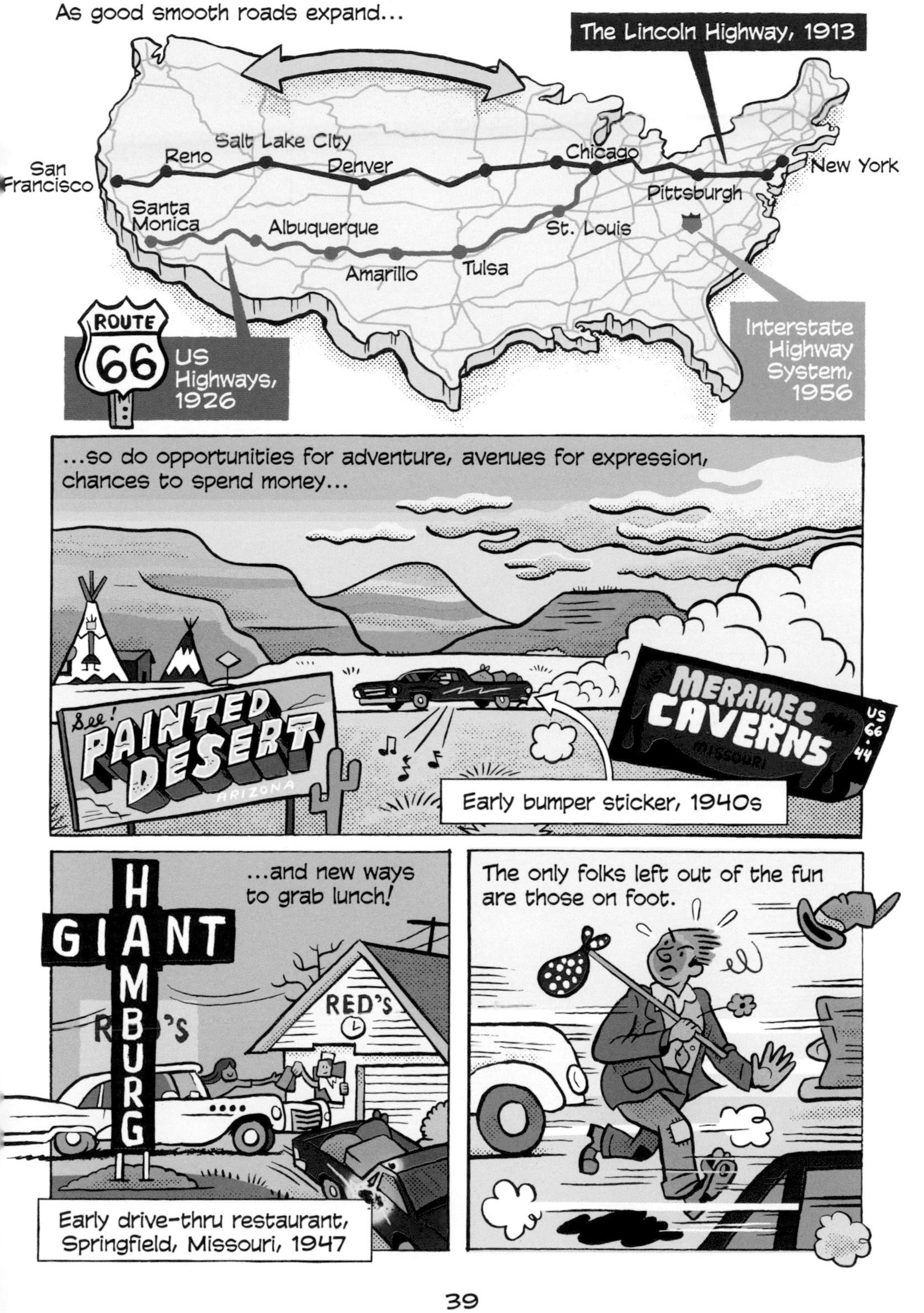

As good smooth roads expand...
The Lincoln Highway, 1913
San Francisco
Reno
Salt Lake City
Denver
Chicago
New York
Pittsburgh
Santa Monica
Albuquerque
St. Louis
Amarillo
Tulsa
ROUTE 66
US Highways, 1926
Interstate Highway System, 1956
...so do opportunities for adventure, avenues for expression, chances to spend money...
See! PAINTED DESERT ARIZONA
VISIT MERAMEC CAVERNS MISSOURI US 66 • 44
Early bumper sticker, 1940s
GIANT HAMBURG
...and new ways to grab lunch!
RED'S
Early drive-thru restaurant, Springfield, Missouri, 1947
The only folks left out of the fun are those on foot.

SUMMER 1896, DETROIT

Henry Ford's homemade ***Quadricycle*** is ready to hit the streets, but there's one problem.

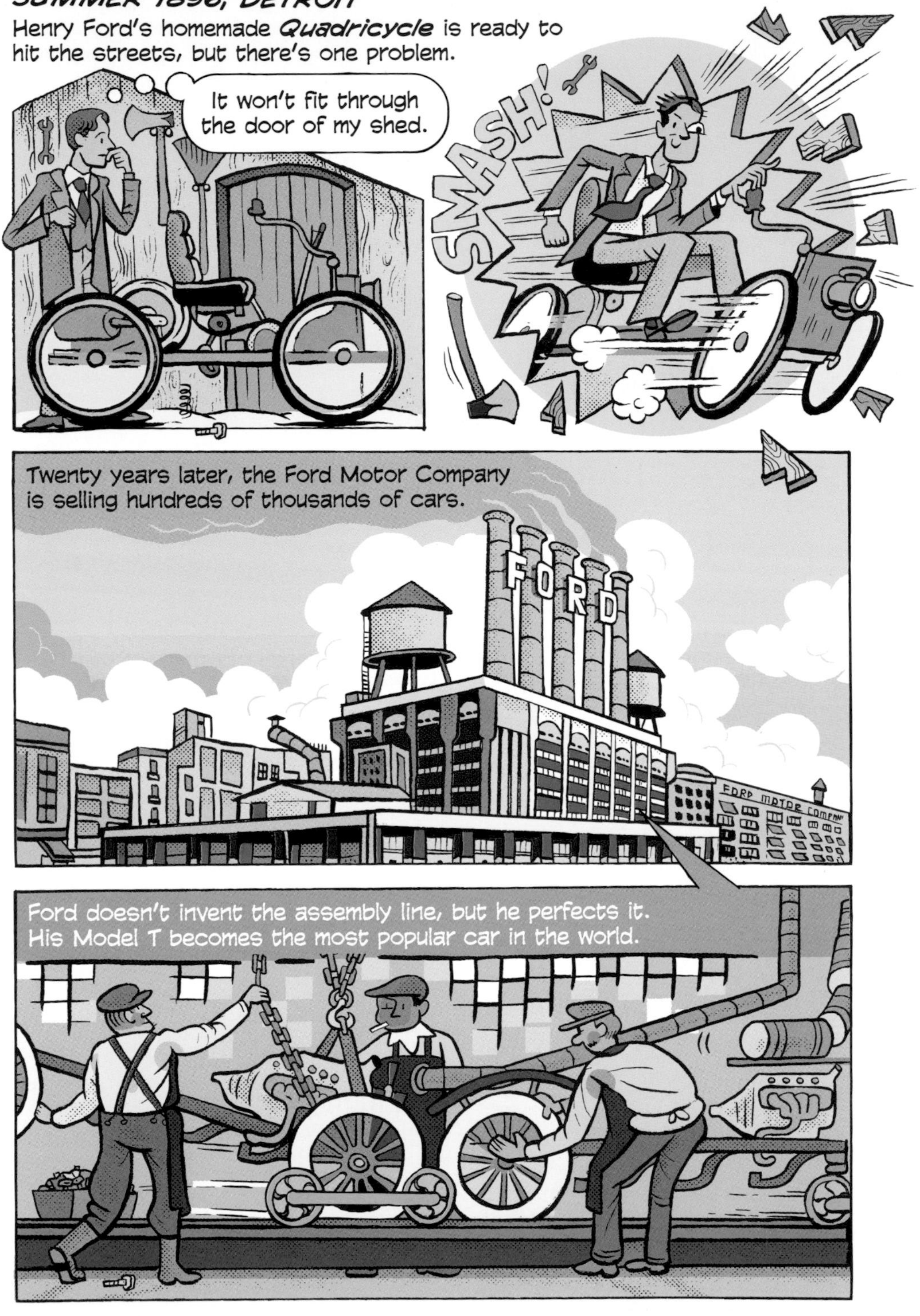
It won't fit through the door of my shed.
SMASH!
Twenty years later, the Ford Motor Company is selling hundreds of thousands of cars.
FORD
Ford doesn't invent the assembly line, but he perfects it. His Model T becomes the most popular car in the world.

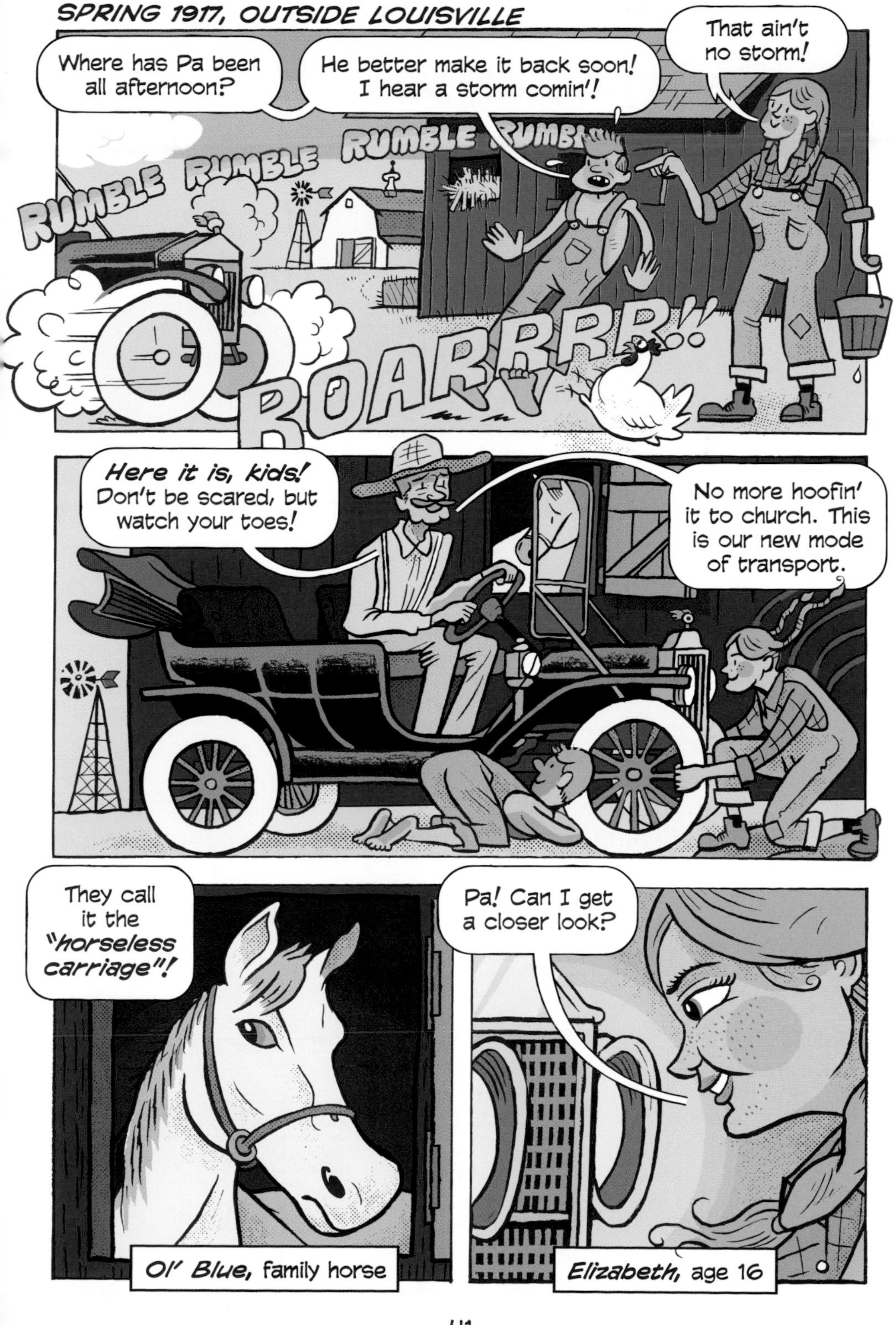
SPRING 1917, OUTSIDE LOUISVILLE
Where has Pa been all afternoon?
He better make it back soon! I hear a storm comin'!
That ain't no storm!
RUMBLE RUMBLE RUMBLE RUMBLE
ROARRRR!!
Here it is, kids! Don't be scared, but watch your toes!
No more hoofin' it to church. This is our new mode of transport.
They call it the "horseless carriage"!
Ol' Blue, family horse
Pa! Can I get a closer look?
Elizabeth, age 16

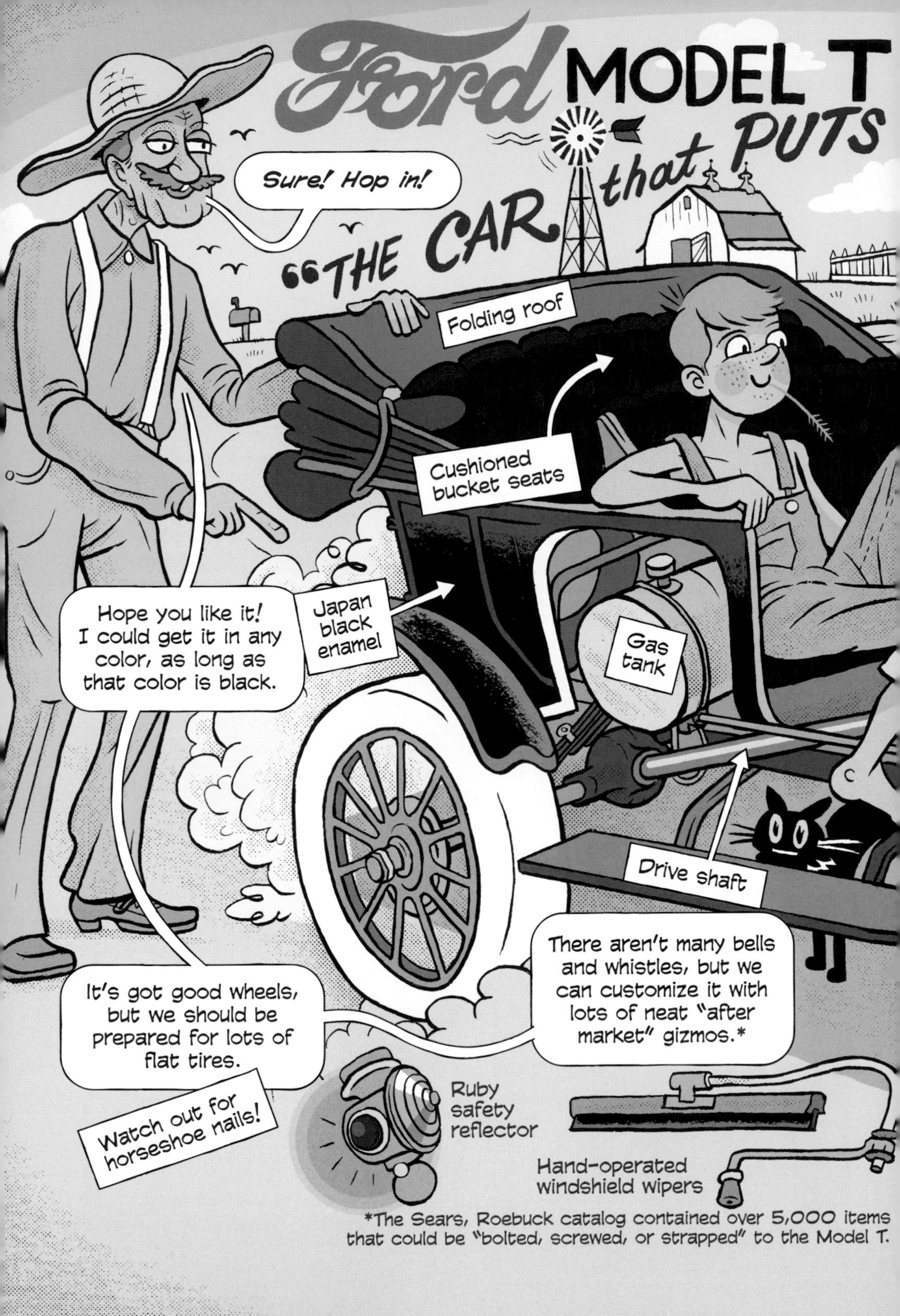
Ford MODEL T
"THE CAR that PUTS
Sure! Hop in!
Folding roof
Cushioned bucket seats
Japan black enamel
Gas tank
Hope you like it! I could get it in any color, as long as that color is black.
Drive shaft
There aren't many bells and whistles, but we can customize it with lots of neat "after market" gizmos.*
It's got good wheels, but we should be prepared for lots of flat tires.
Watch out for horseshoe nails!
Ruby safety reflector
Hand-operated windshield wipers

*The Sears, Roebuck catalog contained over 5,000 items that could be "bolted, screwed, or strapped" to the Model T.

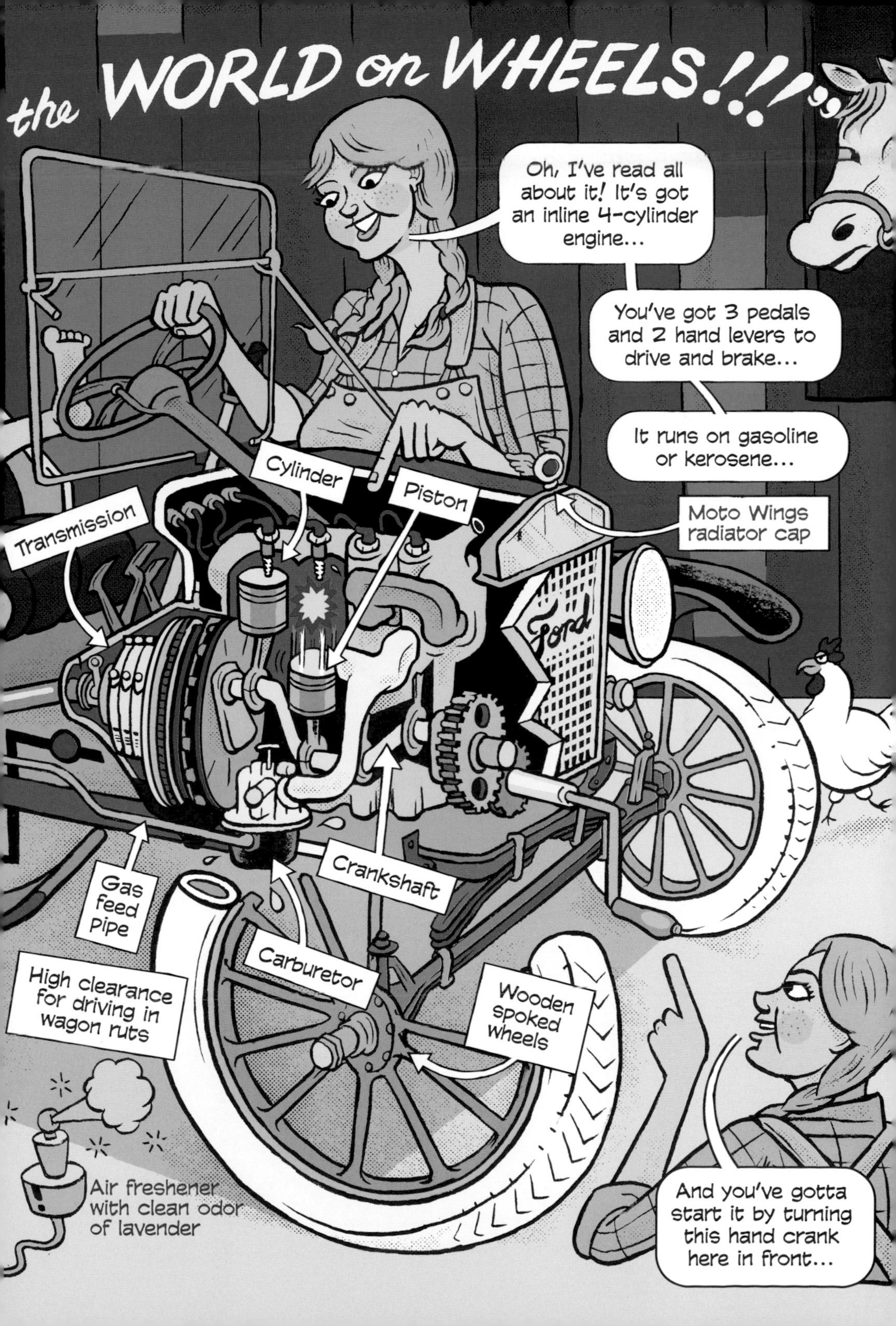
the WORLD on WHEELS!!!"
Oh, I've read all about it! It's got an inline 4-cylinder engine...
You've got 3 pedals and 2 hand levers to drive and brake...
It runs on gasoline or kerosene...
Moto Wings radiator cap
Cylinder
Piston
Transmission
Ford
Crankshaft
Gas feed pipe
Carburetor
High clearance for driving in wagon ruts
Wooden spoked wheels
Air freshener with clean odor of lavender
And you've gotta start it by turning this hand crank here in front...

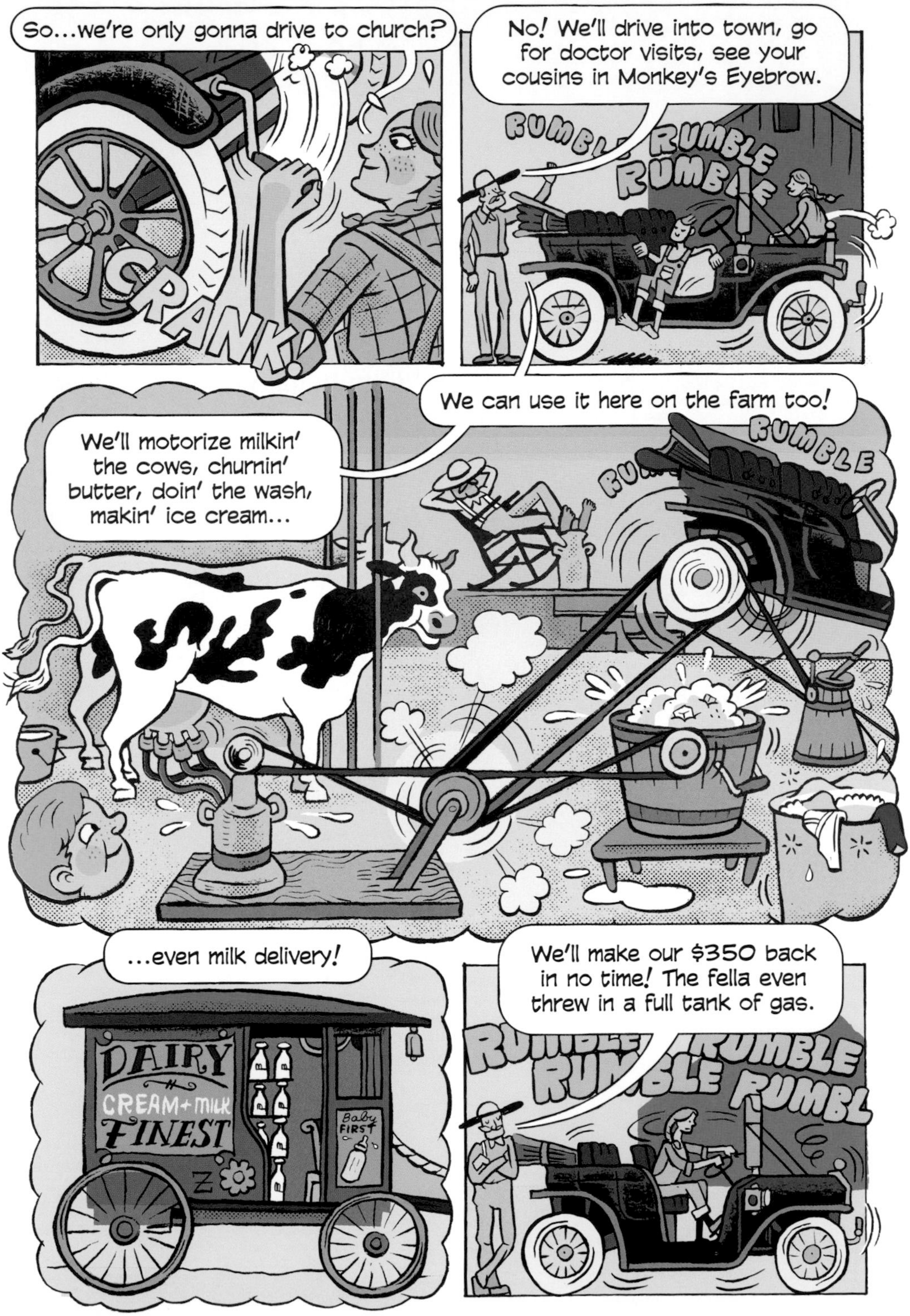
So...we're only gonna drive to church?
CRANK!
No! We'll drive into town, go for doctor visits, see your cousins in Monkey's Eyebrow.
RUMBLE RUMBLE RUMBLE
We can use it here on the farm too!
We'll motorize milkin' the cows, churnin' butter, doin' the wash, makin' ice cream...
RUMBLE
...even milk delivery!
DAIRY
CREAM + MILK
FINEST
Baby FIRST
We'll make our $350 back in no time! The fella even threw in a full tank of gas.
RUMBLE RUMBLE RUMBLE RUMBL

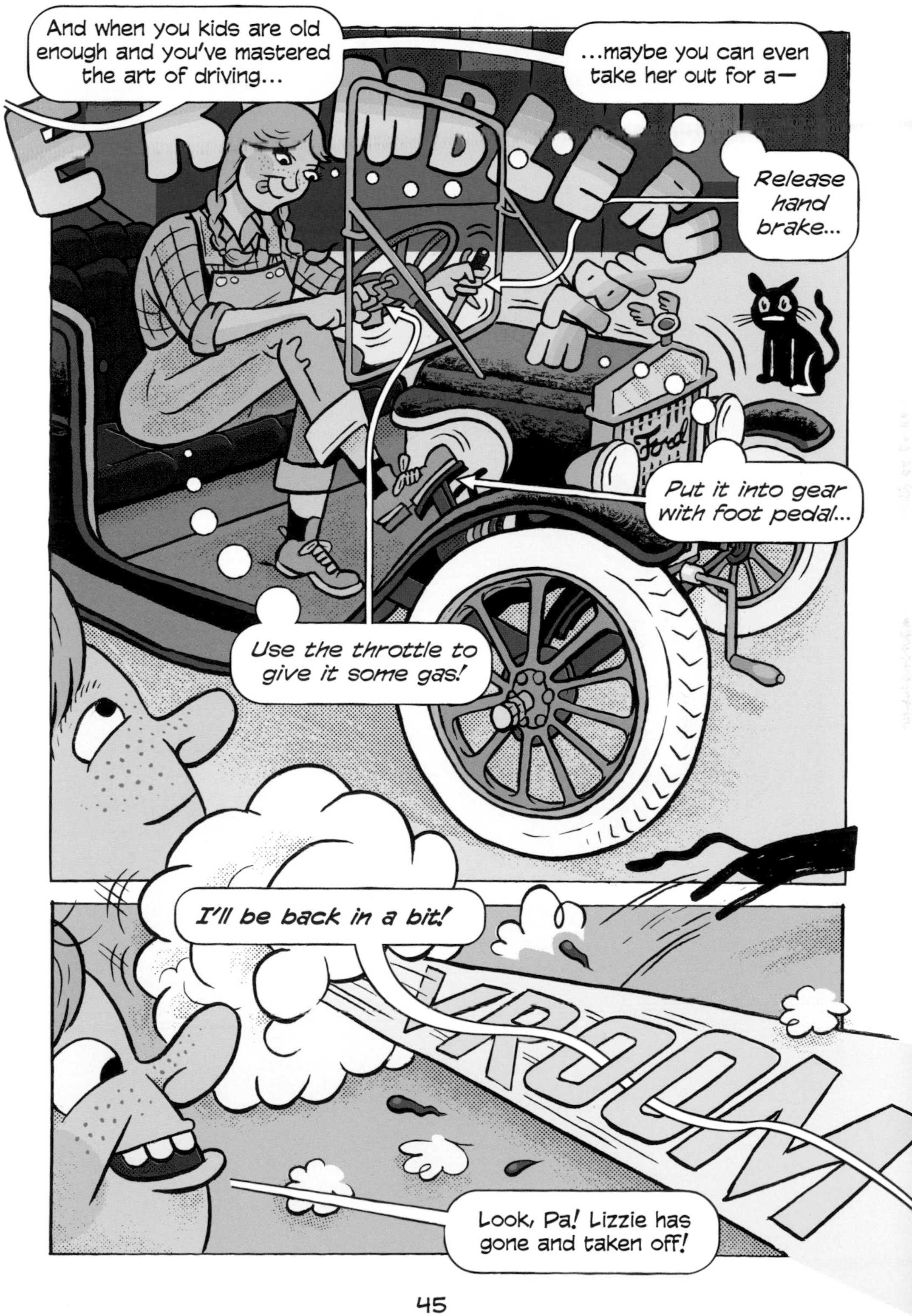
And when you kids are old enough and you've mastered the art of driving...
...maybe you can even take her out for a—
RUMBLE RUMBLE
Release hand brake...
Put it into gear with foot pedal...
Use the throttle to give it some gas!
I'll be back in a bit!
VROOM
Look, Pa! Lizzie has gone and taken off!

TRANSFORMING

The automobile constantly mutates, both inside and out. Here's a chart* showing how its most visible part, the body, has changed over time.

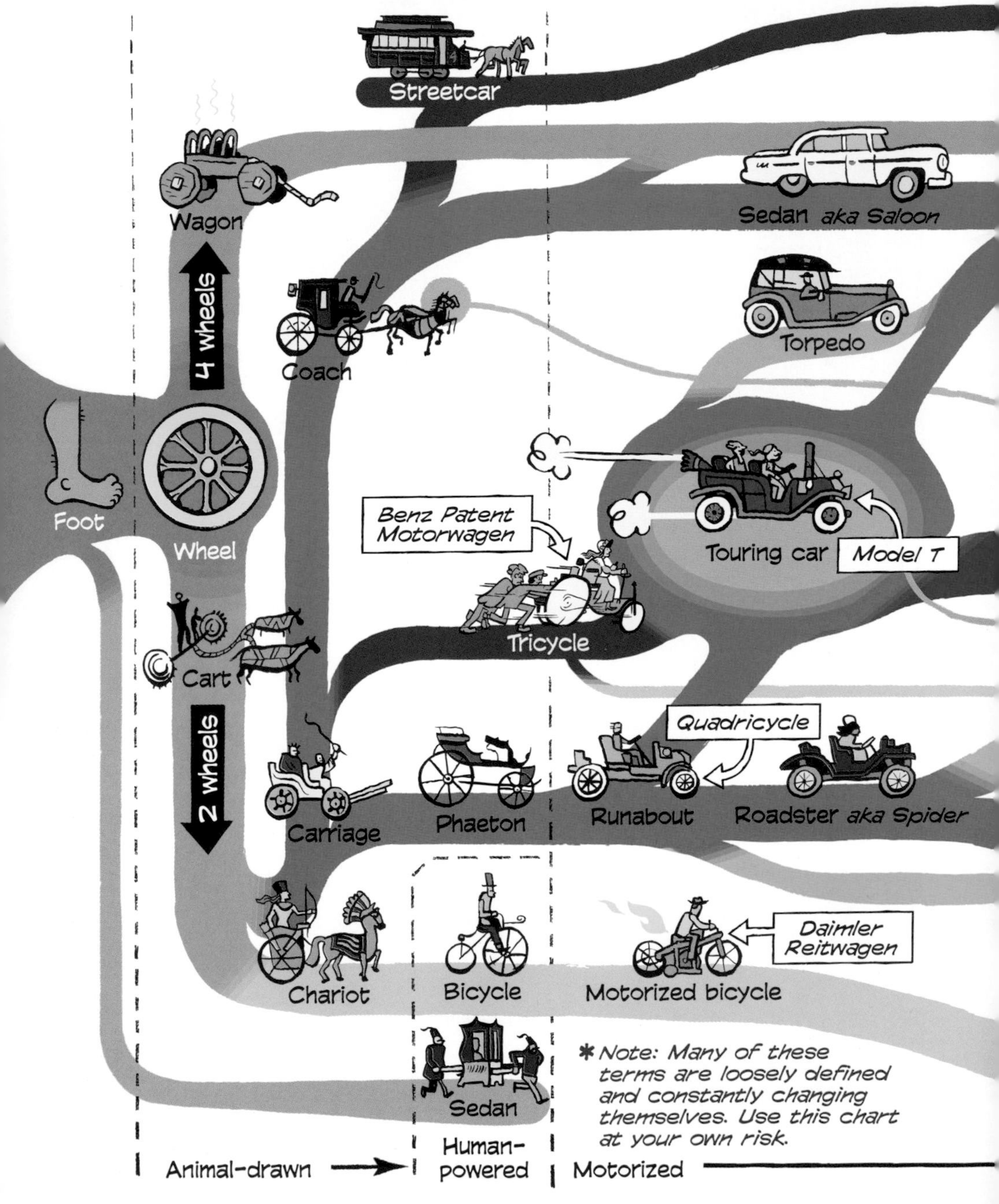

Streetcar
Sedan aka Saloon
Wagon
4 wheels
Torpedo
Coach
Foot
Wheel
Benz Patent Motorwagen
Touring car
Model T
Tricycle
Cart
2 wheels
Quadricycle
Carriage
Phaeton
Runabout
Roadster aka Spider
Daimler Reitwagen
Chariot
Bicycle
Motorized bicycle
Sedan
Animal-drawn
Human-powered
Motorized

*Note: Many of these terms are loosely defined and constantly changing themselves. Use this chart at your own risk.

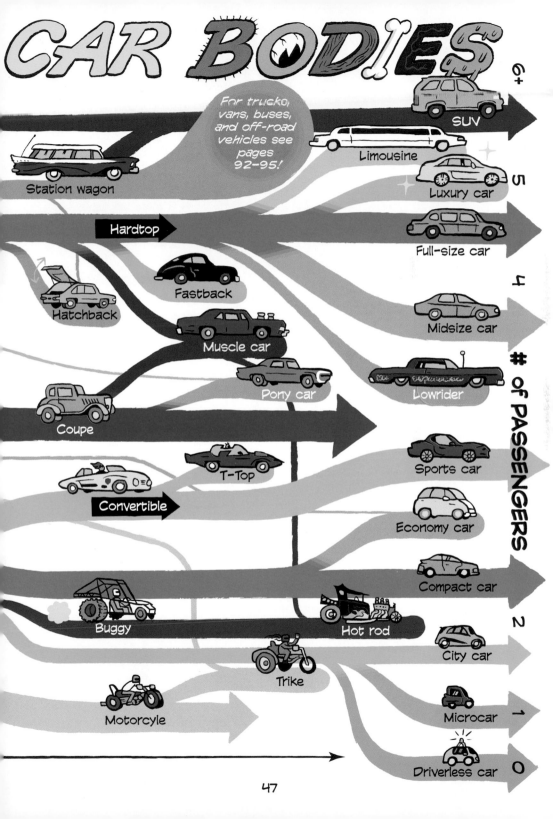

CAR BODIES

For trucks, vans, buses, and off-road vehicles see pages 92-95!

SUV

Station wagon

Limousine

Luxury car

Hardtop

Full-size car

Fastback

Hatchback

Midsize car

Muscle car

Coupe

Pony car

Lowrider

T-Top

Sports car

Convertible

Economy car

Compact car

Buggy

Hot rod

City car

Trike

Motorcyle

Microcar

Driverless car

# of PASSENGERS

6+

5

4

2

1

0

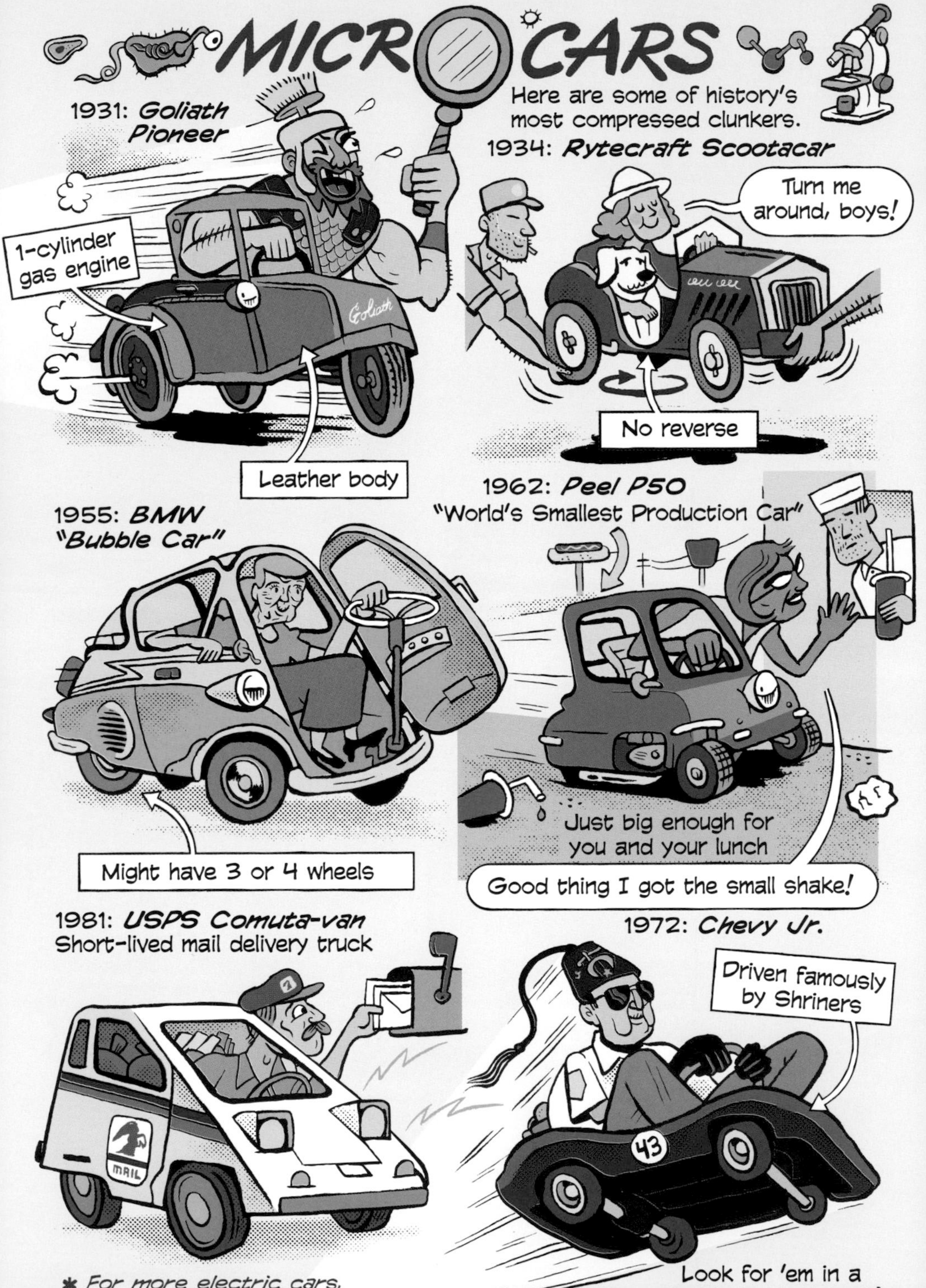
MICRO CARS
Here are some of history's most compressed clunkers.
1931: *Goliath Pioneer*
1-cylinder gas engine
Goliath
Leather body
1934: *Rytecraft Scootacar*
Turn me around, boys!
No reverse
1955: *BMW "Bubble Car"*
Might have 3 or 4 wheels
1962: *Peel P50*
"World's Smallest Production Car"
Just big enough for you and your lunch
Good thing I got the small shake!
1981: *USPS Comuta-van*
Short-lived mail delivery truck
MAIL
1972: *Chevy Jr.*
Driven famously by Shriners
43
Look for 'em in a parade in your town!

* *For more electric cars, see pages 109–1110!*

SKY'S the LIMIT!
The Golden Age of Car Design

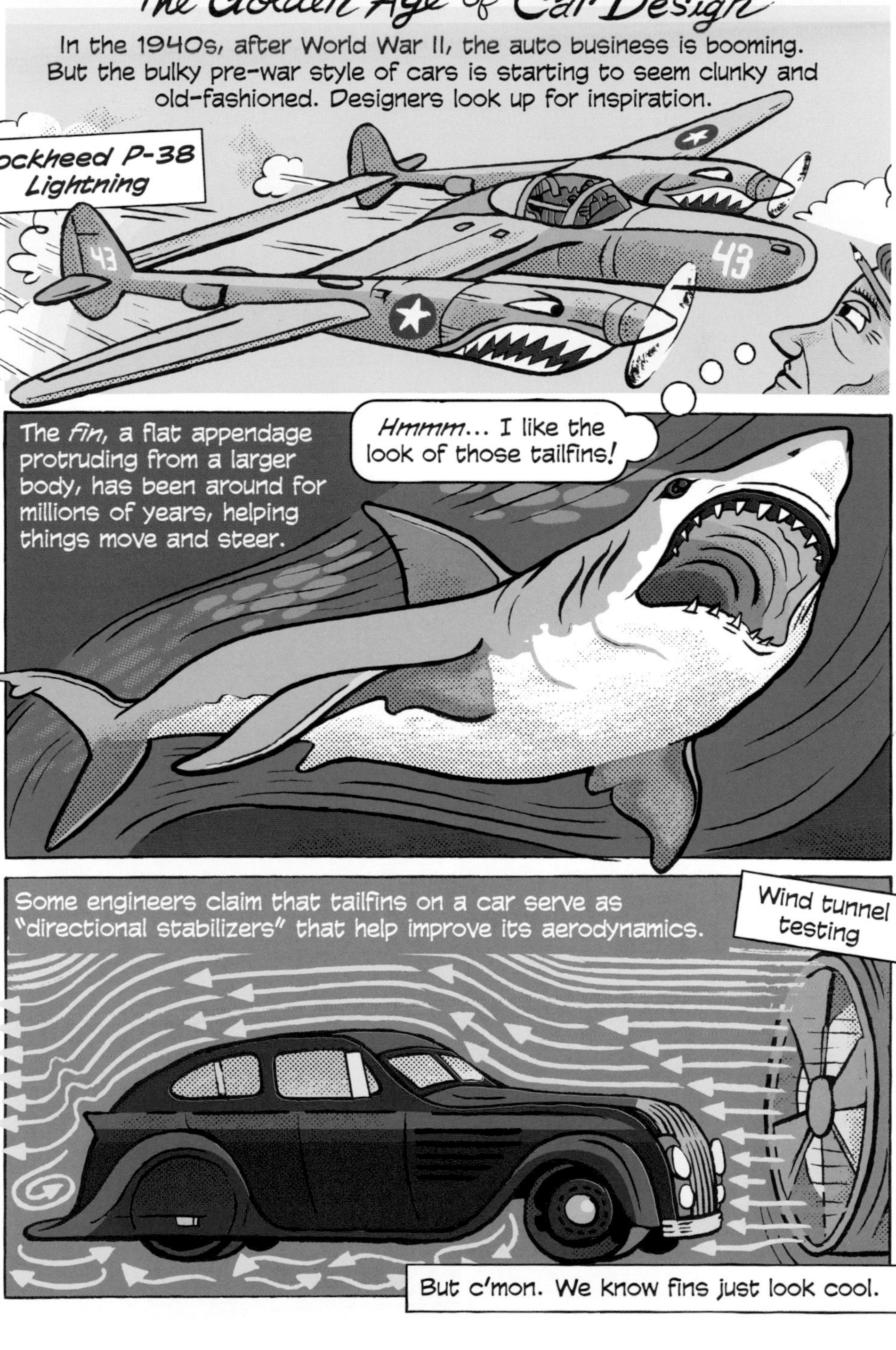
In the 1940s, after World War II, the auto business is booming. But the bulky pre-war style of cars is starting to seem clunky and old-fashioned. Designers look up for inspiration.
Lockheed P-38 Lightning
43
43
The *fin*, a flat appendage protruding from a larger body, has been around for millions of years, helping things move and steer.
Hmmm... I like the look of those tailfins!
Some engineers claim that tailfins on a car serve as "directional stabilizers" that help improve its aerodynamics.
Wind tunnel testing
But c'mon. We know fins just look cool.

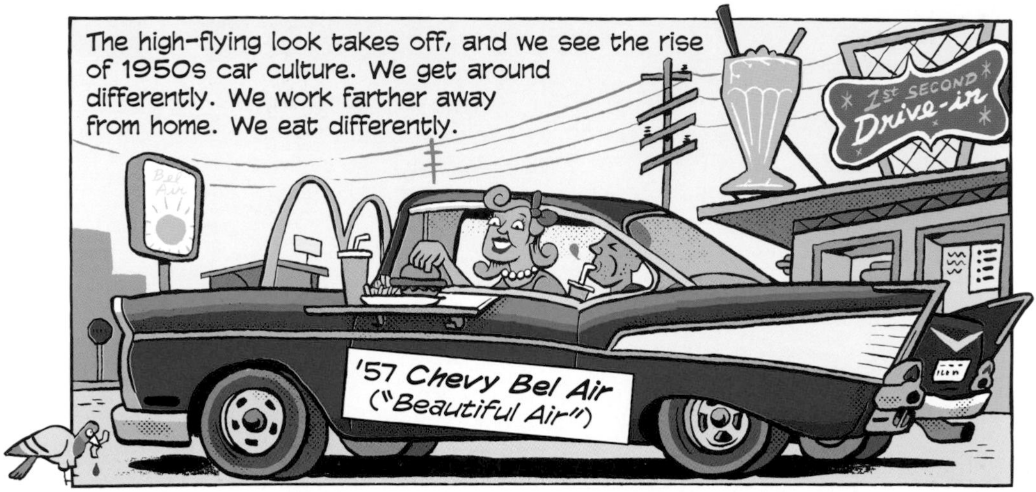
The high-flying look takes off, and we see the rise of 1950s car culture. We get around differently. We work farther away from home. We eat differently.
1st SECOND Drive-in
Bel Air
'57 Chevy Bel Air ("Beautiful Air")

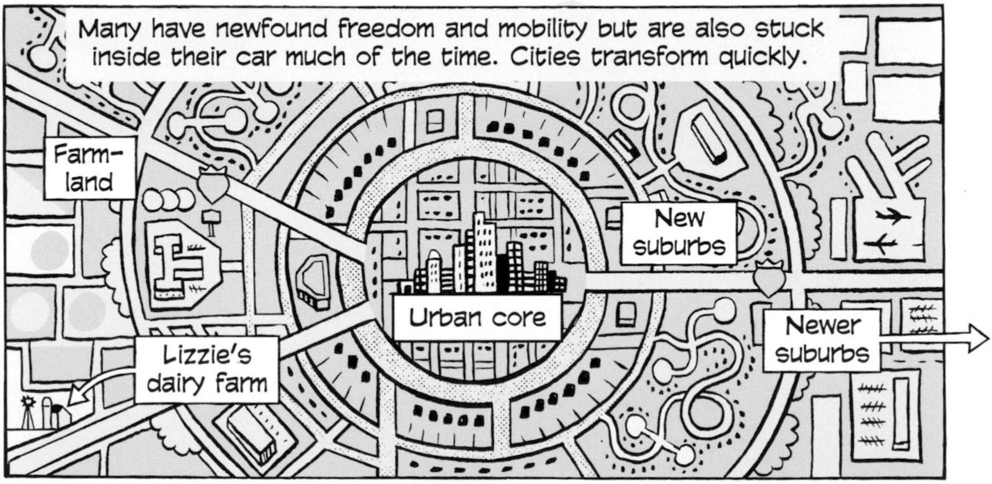
Many have newfound freedom and mobility but are also stuck inside their car much of the time. Cities transform quickly.
Farm-land
New suburbs
Urban core
Newer suburbs
Lizzie's dairy farm

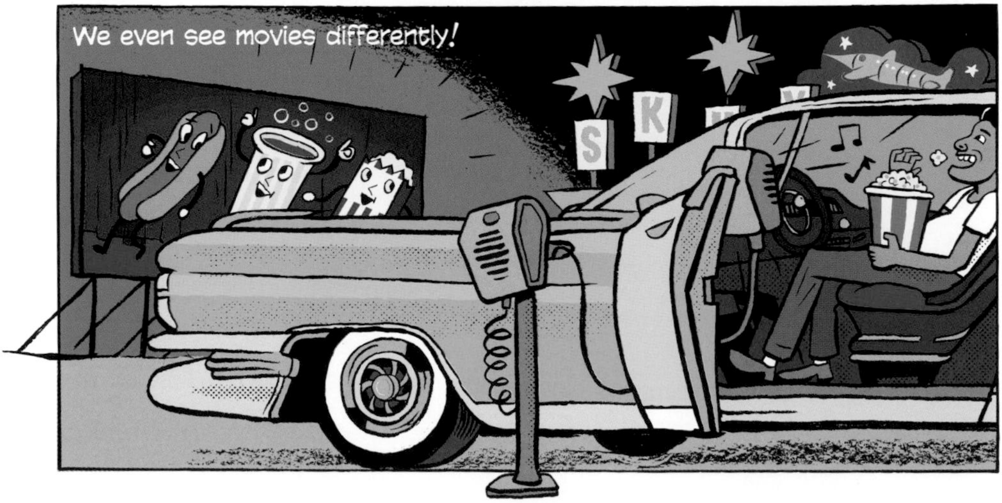
We even see movies differently!
S
K

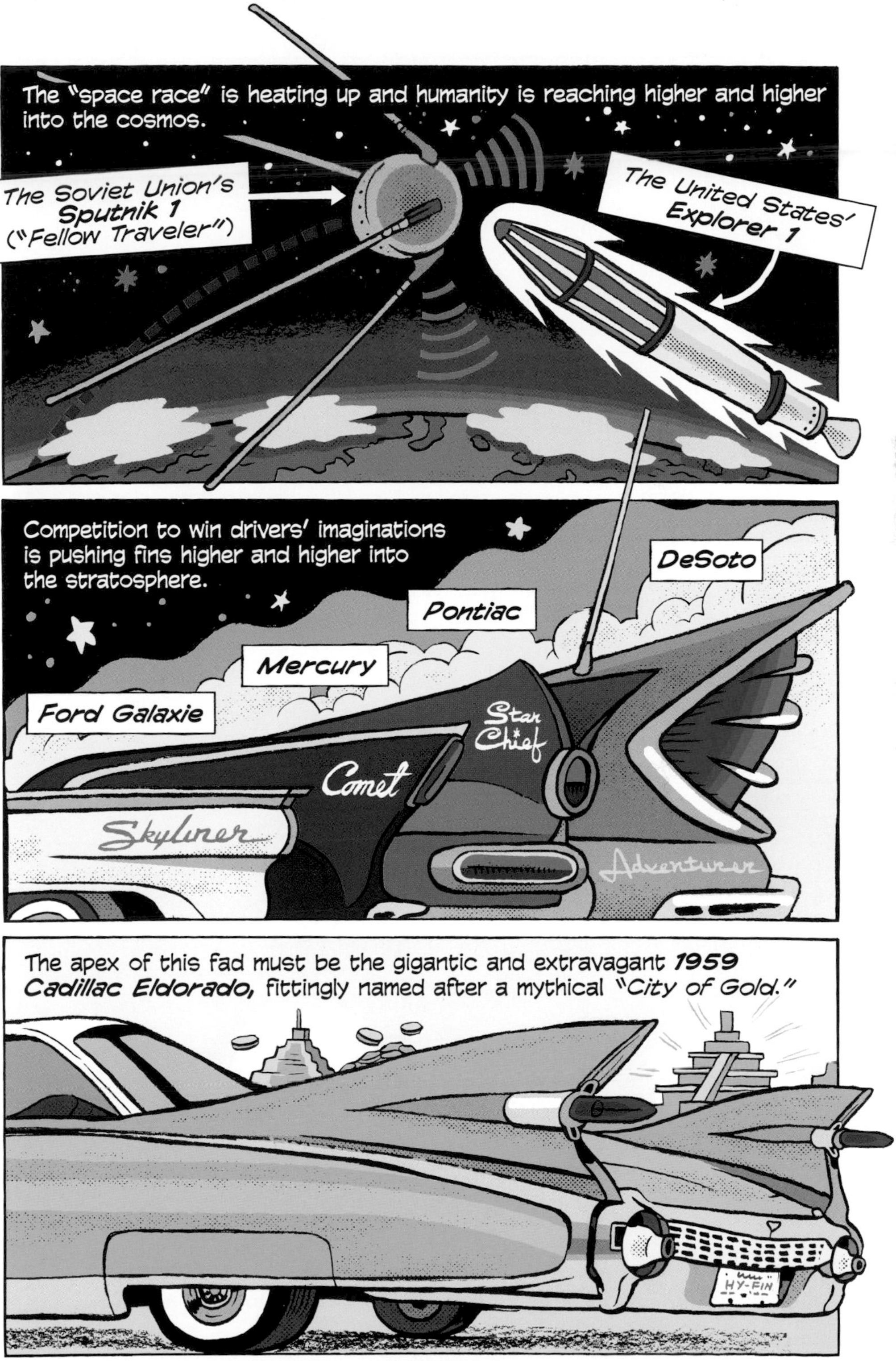
The "space race" is heating up and humanity is reaching higher and higher into the cosmos.
The Soviet Union's **Sputnik 1** ("Fellow Traveler")
The United States' **Explorer 1**
Competition to win drivers' imaginations is pushing fins higher and higher into the stratosphere.
DeSoto
Pontiac
Mercury
Ford Galaxie
Star Chief
Comet
Skyliner
Adventurer
The apex of this fad must be the gigantic and extravagant ***1959 Cadillac Eldorado,*** fittingly named after a mythical *"City of Gold."*
HY-FIN

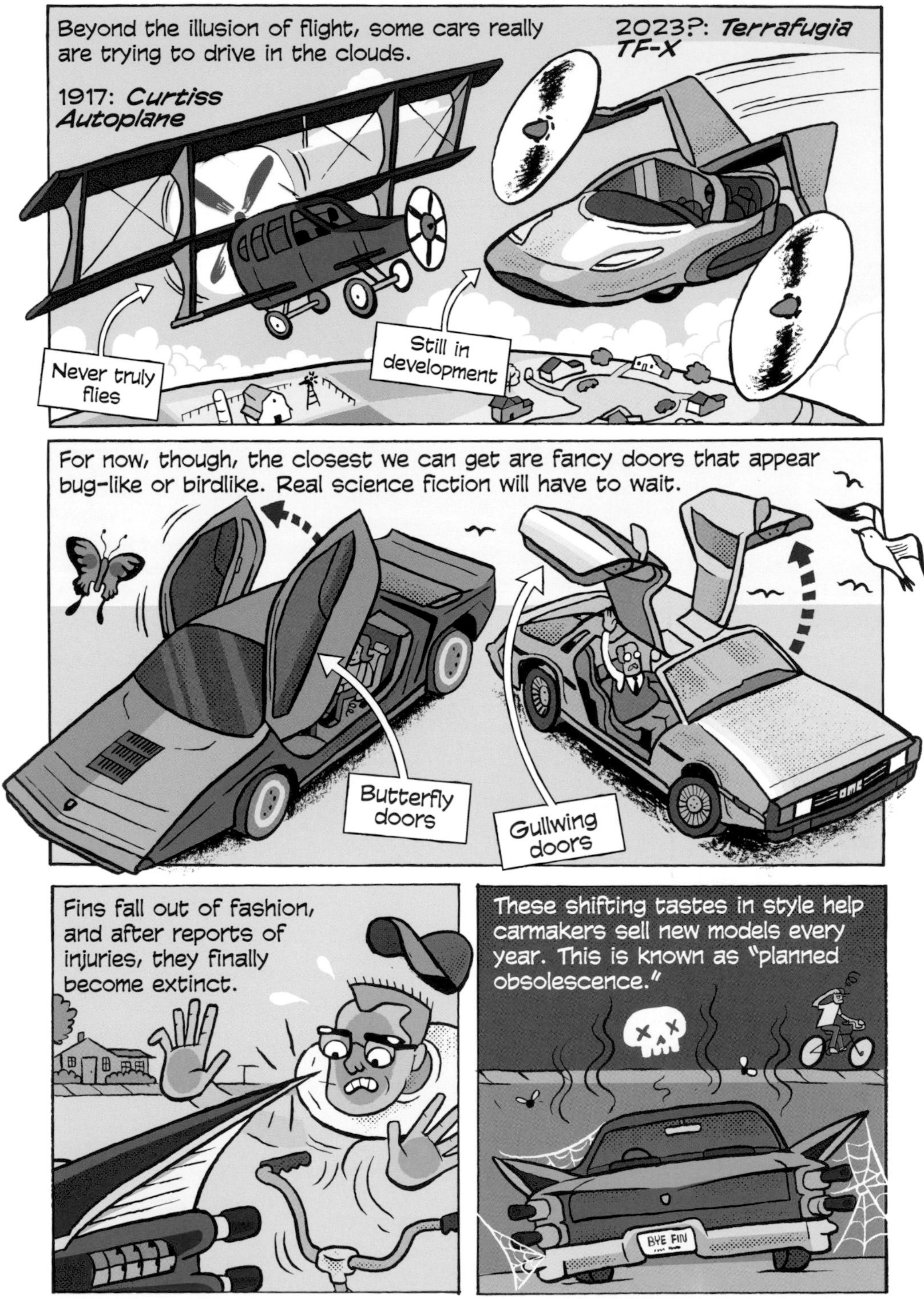
Beyond the illusion of flight, some cars really are trying to drive in the clouds.
1917: *Curtiss Autoplane*
2023?: *Terrafugia TF-X*
Never truly flies
Still in development
For now, though, the closest we can get are fancy doors that appear bug-like or birdlike. Real science fiction will have to wait.
Butterfly doors
Gullwing doors
Fins fall out of fashion, and after reports of injuries, they finally become extinct.
These shifting tastes in style help carmakers sell new models every year. This is known as "planned obsolescence."
BYE FIN

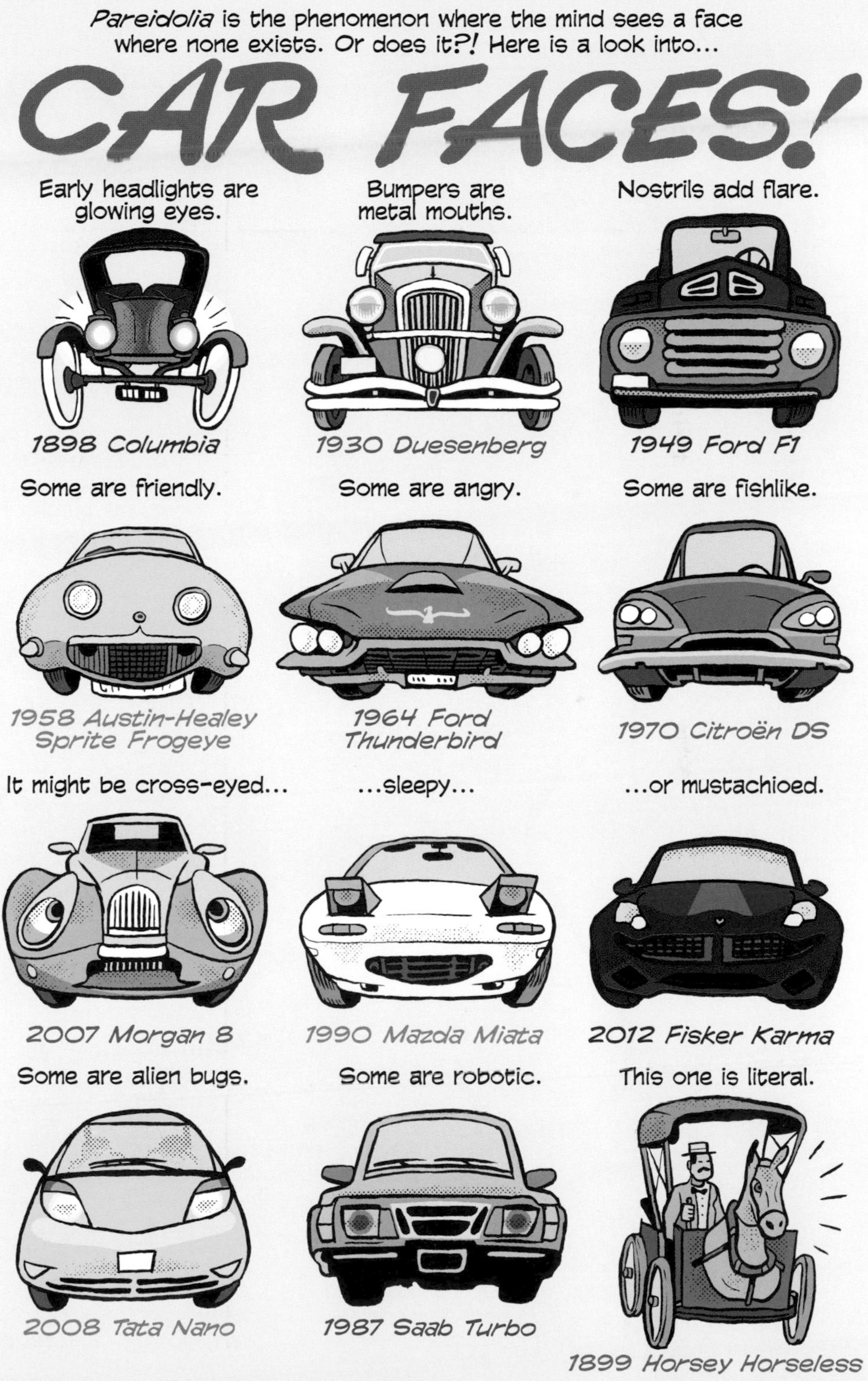
Pareidolia is the phenomenon where the mind sees a face where none exists. Or does it?! Here is a look into...
CAR FACES!
Early headlights are glowing eyes.
1898 Columbia
Bumpers are metal mouths.
1930 Duesenberg
Nostrils add flare.
1949 Ford F1
Some are friendly.
1958 Austin-Healey Sprite Frogeye
Some are angry.
1964 Ford Thunderbird
Some are fishlike.
1970 Citroën DS
It might be cross-eyed...
2007 Morgan 8
...sleepy...
1990 Mazda Miata
...or mustachioed.
2012 Fisker Karma
Some are alien bugs.
2008 Tata Nano
Some are robotic.
1987 Saab Turbo
This one is literal.
1899 Horsey Horseless

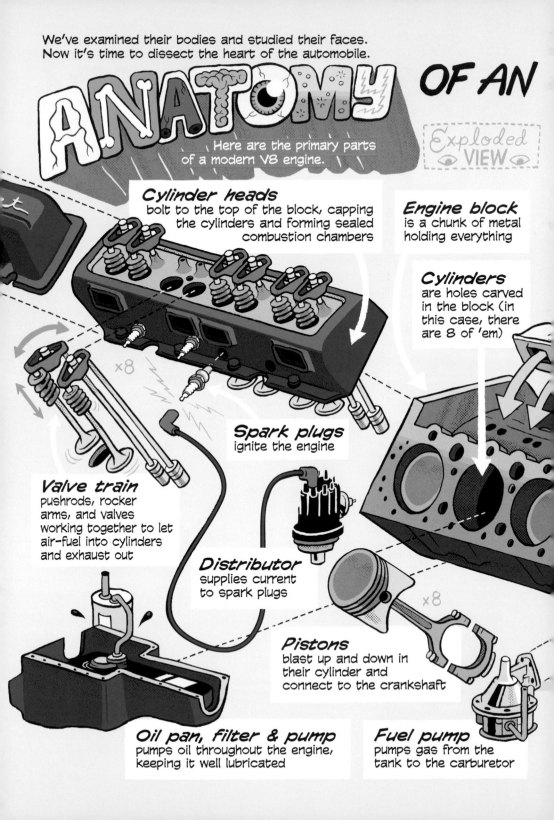

We've examined their bodies and studied their faces.
Now it's time to dissect the heart of the automobile.

ANATOMY OF AN

Here are the primary parts
of a modern V8 engine.

Cylinder heads
bolt to the top of the block, capping
the cylinders and forming sealed
combustion chambers

Engine block
is a chunk of metal
holding everything

Cylinders
are holes carved
in the block (in
this case, there
are 8 of 'em)

×8

Spark plugs
ignite the engine

Valve train
pushrods, rocker
arms, and valves
working together to let
air-fuel into cylinders
and exhaust out

Distributor
supplies current
to spark plugs

×8

Pistons
blast up and down in
their cylinder and
connect to the crankshaft

Oil pan, filter & pump
pumps oil throughout the engine,
keeping it well lubricated

Fuel pump
pumps gas from the
tank to the carburetor

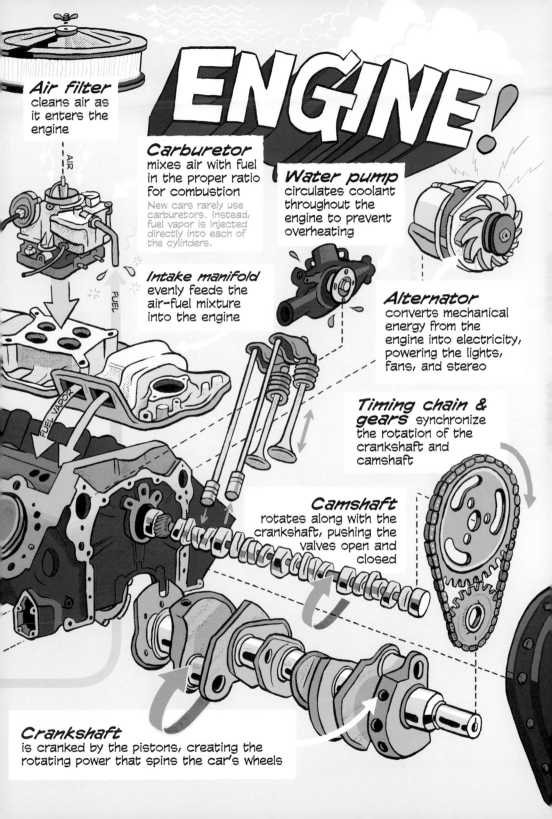

ENGINE!

Air filter cleans air as it enters the engine

AIR

Carburetor mixes air with fuel in the proper ratio for combustion
New cars rarely use carburetors. Instead, fuel vapor is injected directly into each of the cylinders.

FUEL

Intake manifold evenly feeds the air-fuel mixture into the engine

FUEL VAPOR

Water pump circulates coolant throughout the engine to prevent overheating

Alternator converts mechanical energy from the engine into electricity, powering the lights, fans, and stereo

Timing chain & gears synchronize the rotation of the crankshaft and camshaft

Camshaft rotates along with the crankshaft, pushing the valves open and closed

Crankshaft is cranked by the pistons, creating the rotating power that spins the car's wheels

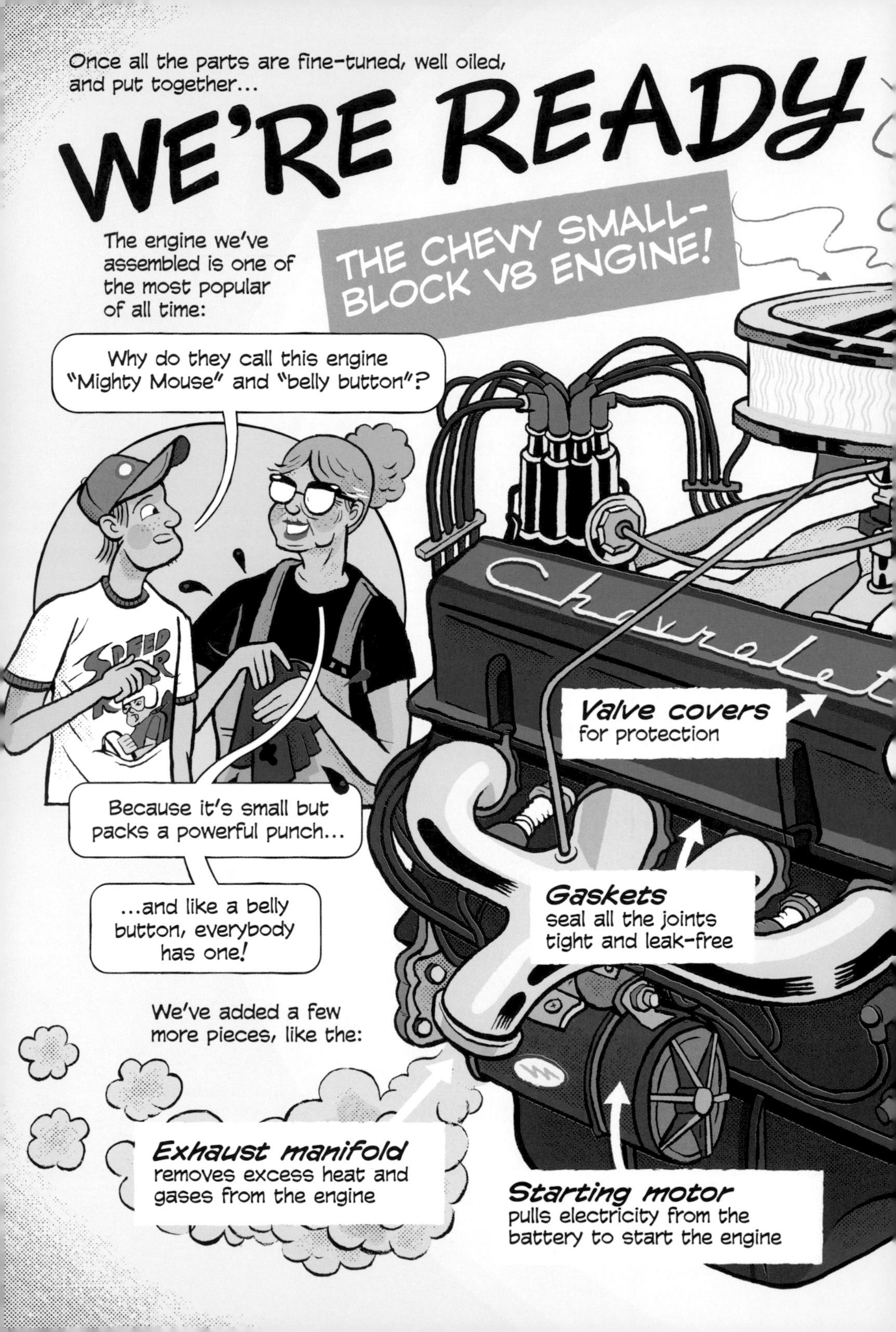
Once all the parts are fine-tuned, well oiled, and put together...
WE'RE READY
The engine we've assembled is one of the most popular of all time:
THE CHEVY SMALL-BLOCK V8 ENGINE!
Why do they call this engine "Mighty Mouse" and "belly button"?
Because it's small but packs a powerful punch...
...and like a belly button, everybody has one!
Chevrolet
Valve covers for protection
Gaskets seal all the joints tight and leak-free
We've added a few more pieces, like the:
Exhaust manifold removes excess heat and gases from the engine
Starting motor pulls electricity from the battery to start the engine

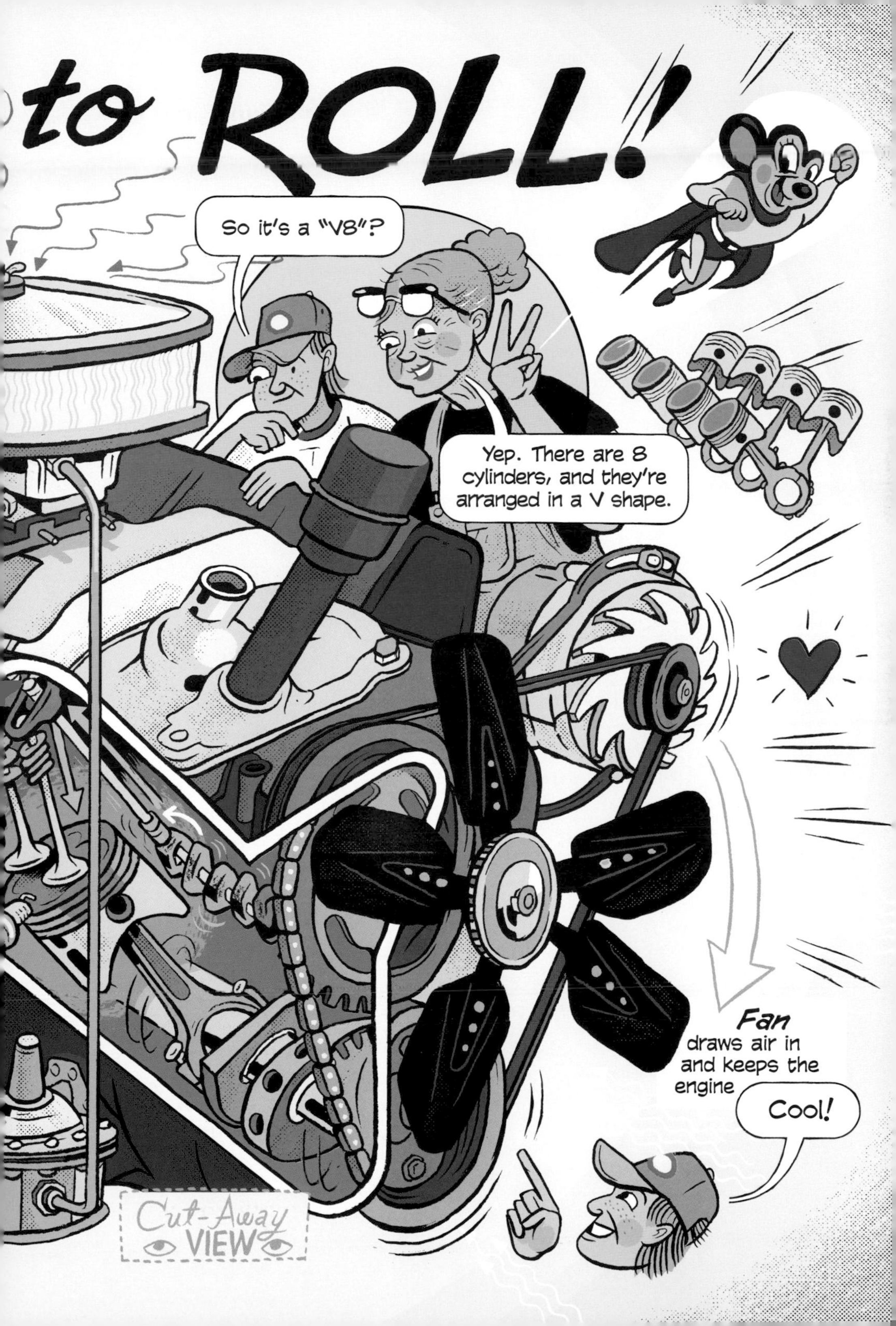

to ROLL!
So it's a "V8"?
Yep. There are 8 cylinders, and they're arranged in a V shape.
Fan draws air in and keeps the engine
Cool!
Cut-Away VIEW

STROKE 3: POWER

 Explosive Growth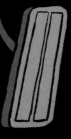

SUMMER 1967, OUTSIDE LOUISVILLE

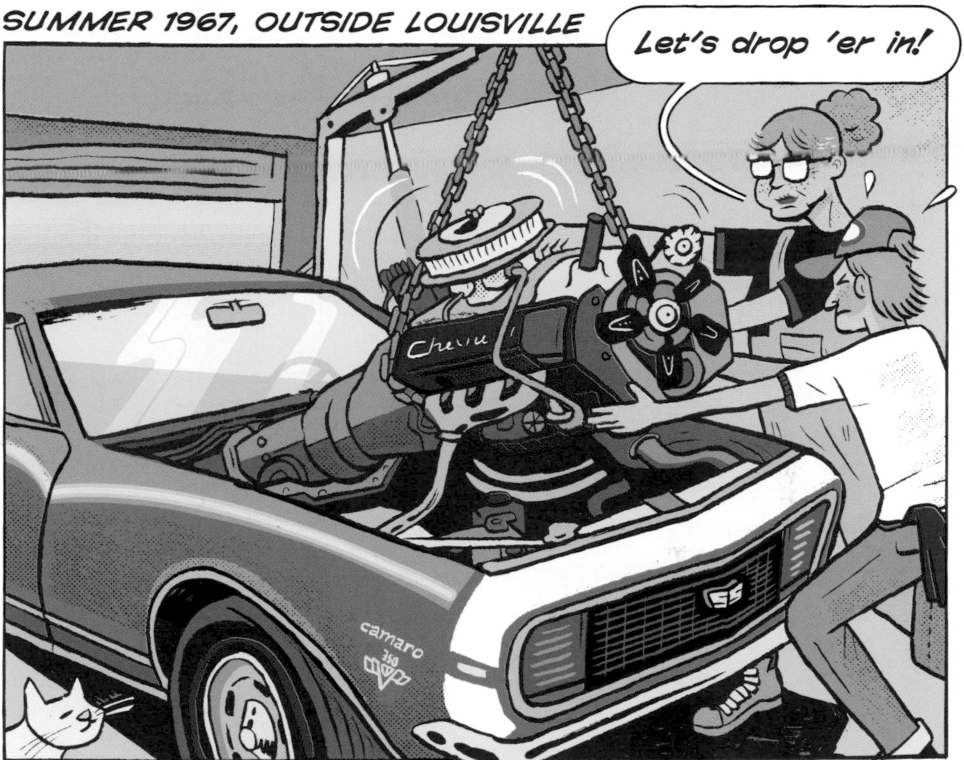
Let's drop 'er in!
Chevy
camaro
350
SS

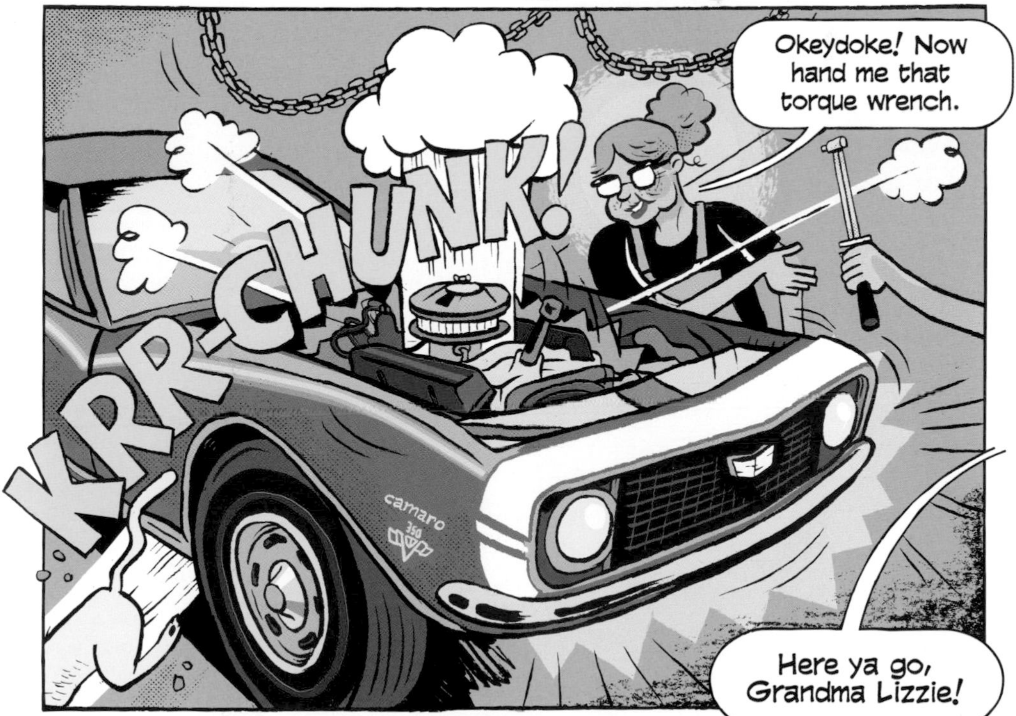
Okeydoke! Now hand me that torque wrench.
KRR-CHUNK!
camaro
350
Here ya go, Grandma Lizzie!

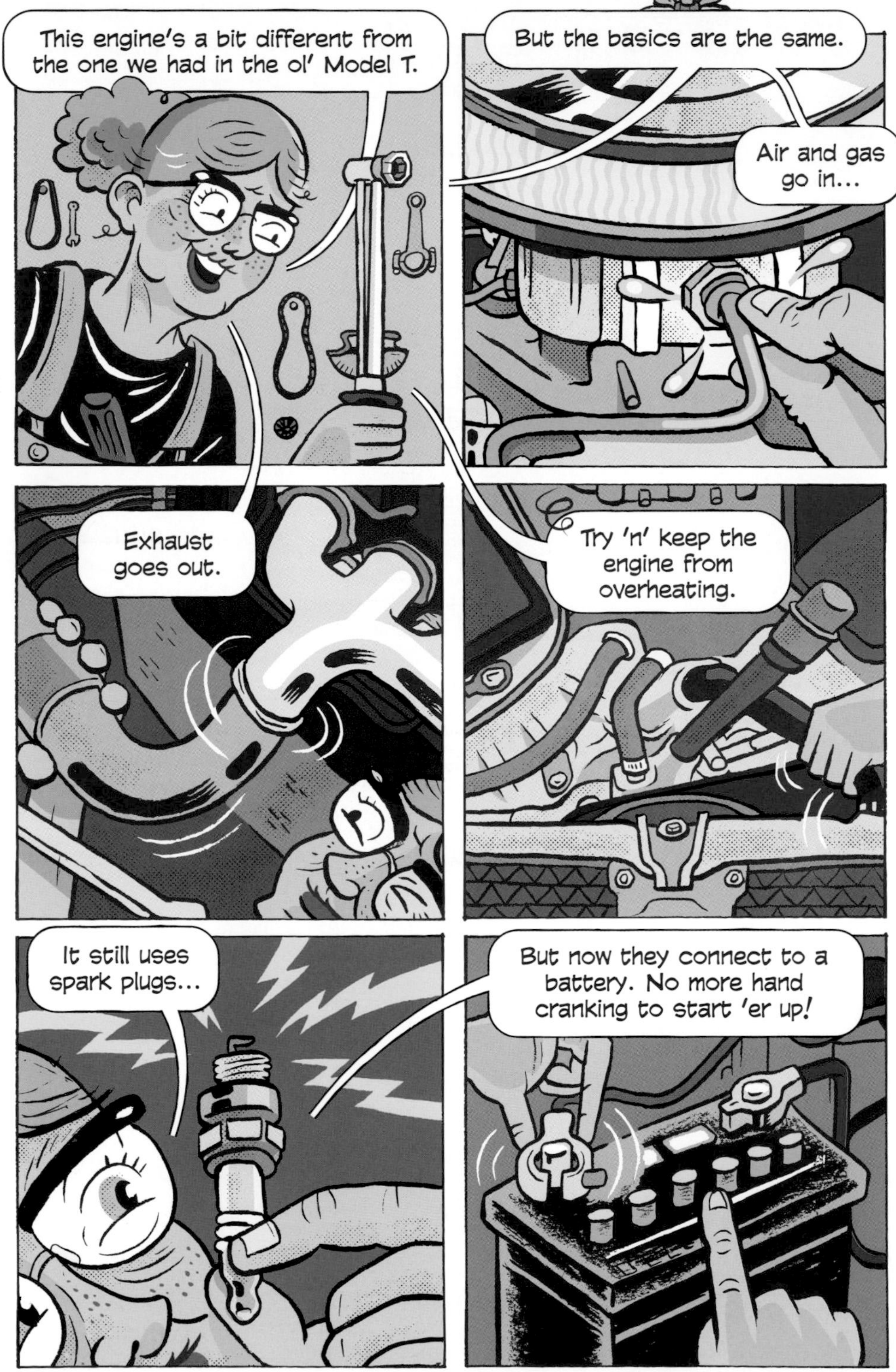
This engine's a bit different from the one we had in the ol' Model T.
But the basics are the same.
Air and gas go in...
Exhaust goes out.
Try 'n' keep the engine from overheating.
It still uses spark plugs...
But now they connect to a battery. No more hand cranking to start 'er up!

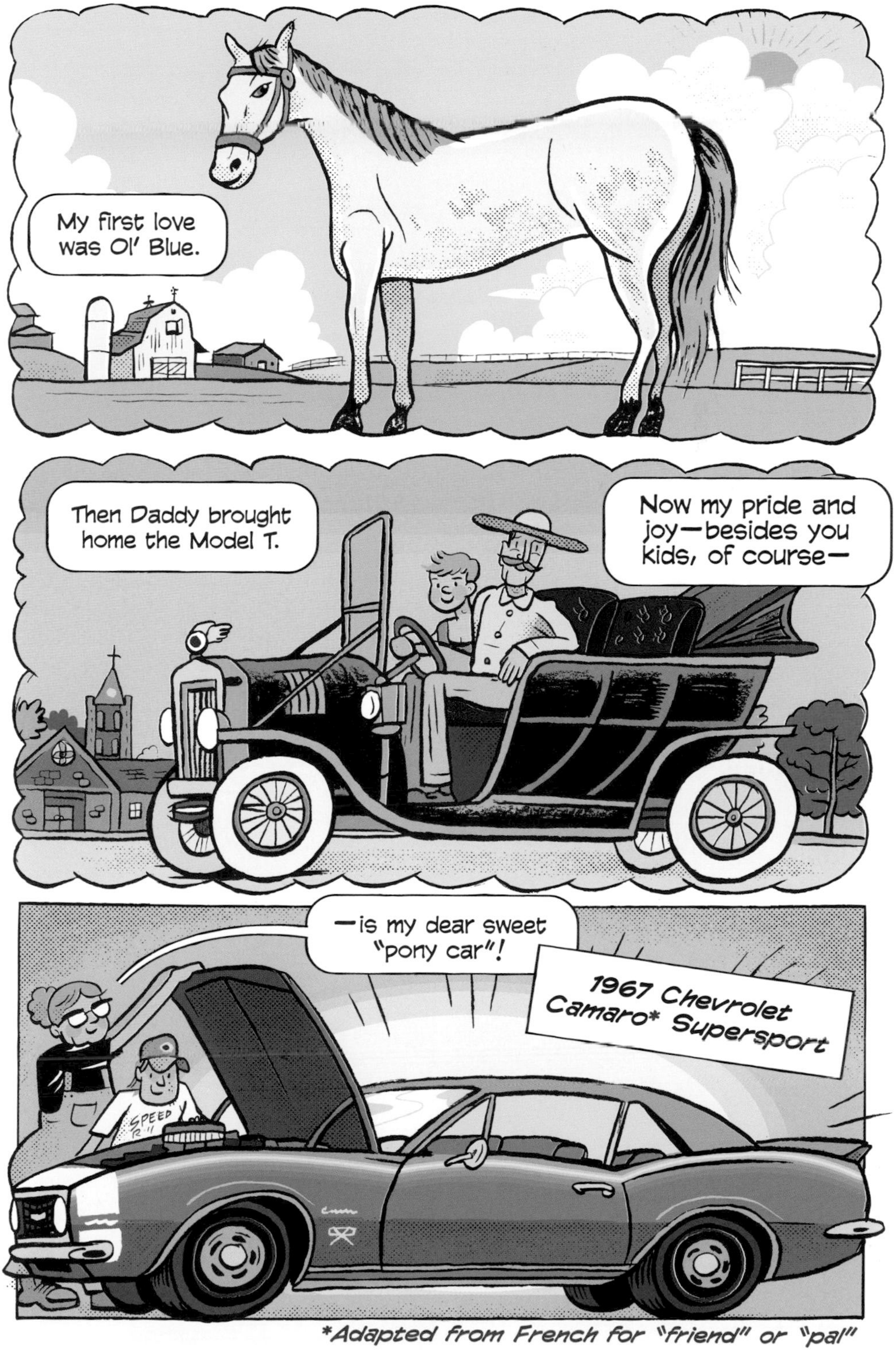
My first love was Ol' Blue.
Then Daddy brought home the Model T.
Now my pride and joy—besides you kids, of course—
—is my dear sweet "pony car"!
1967 Chevrolet Camaro* Supersport
SPEED

*Adapted from French for "friend" or "pal"

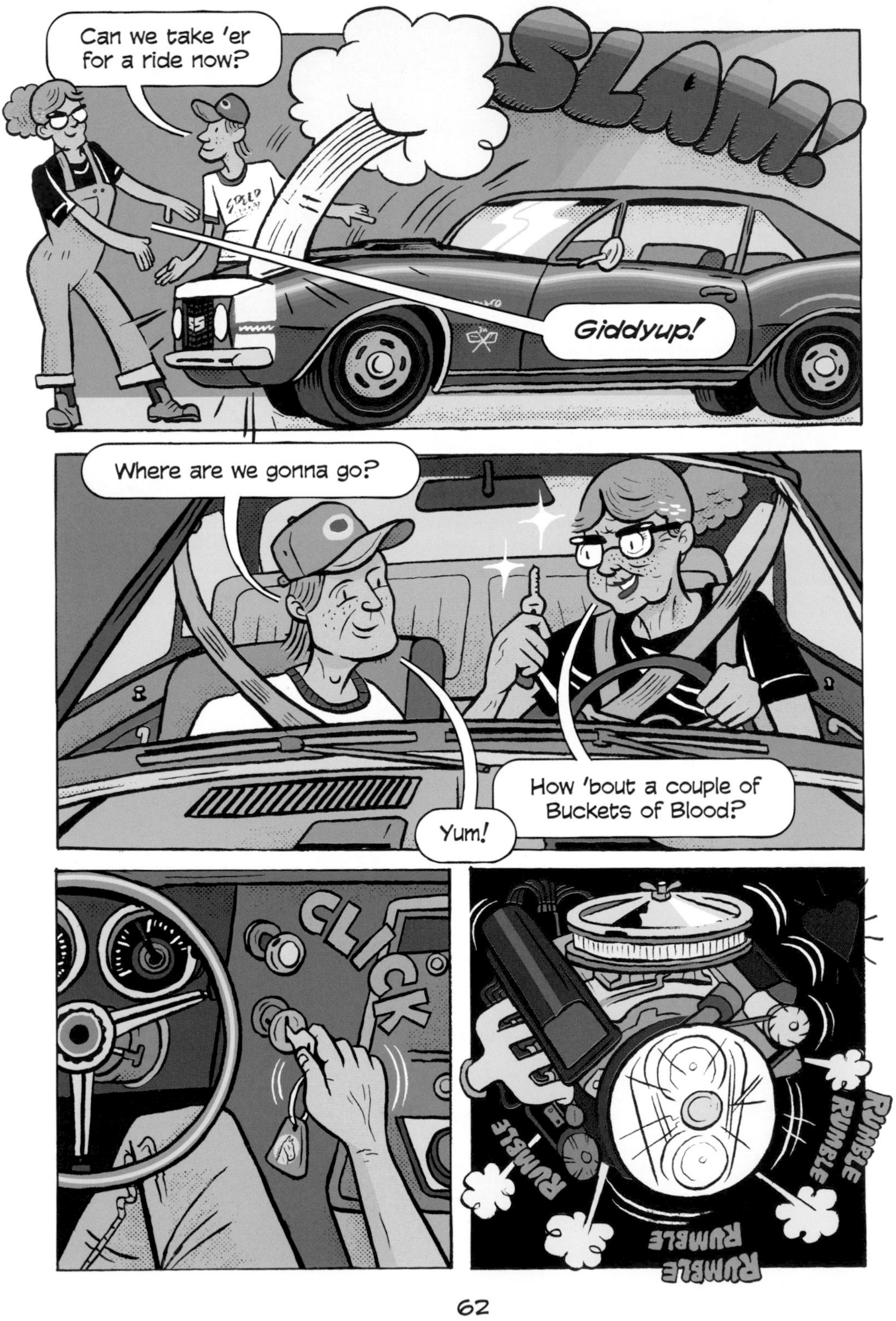
Can we take 'er for a ride now?
SLAM!
Giddyup!
Where are we gonna go?
How 'bout a couple of Buckets of Blood?
Yum!
CLICK
RUMBLE
RUMBLE RUMBLE
RUMBLE RUMBLE

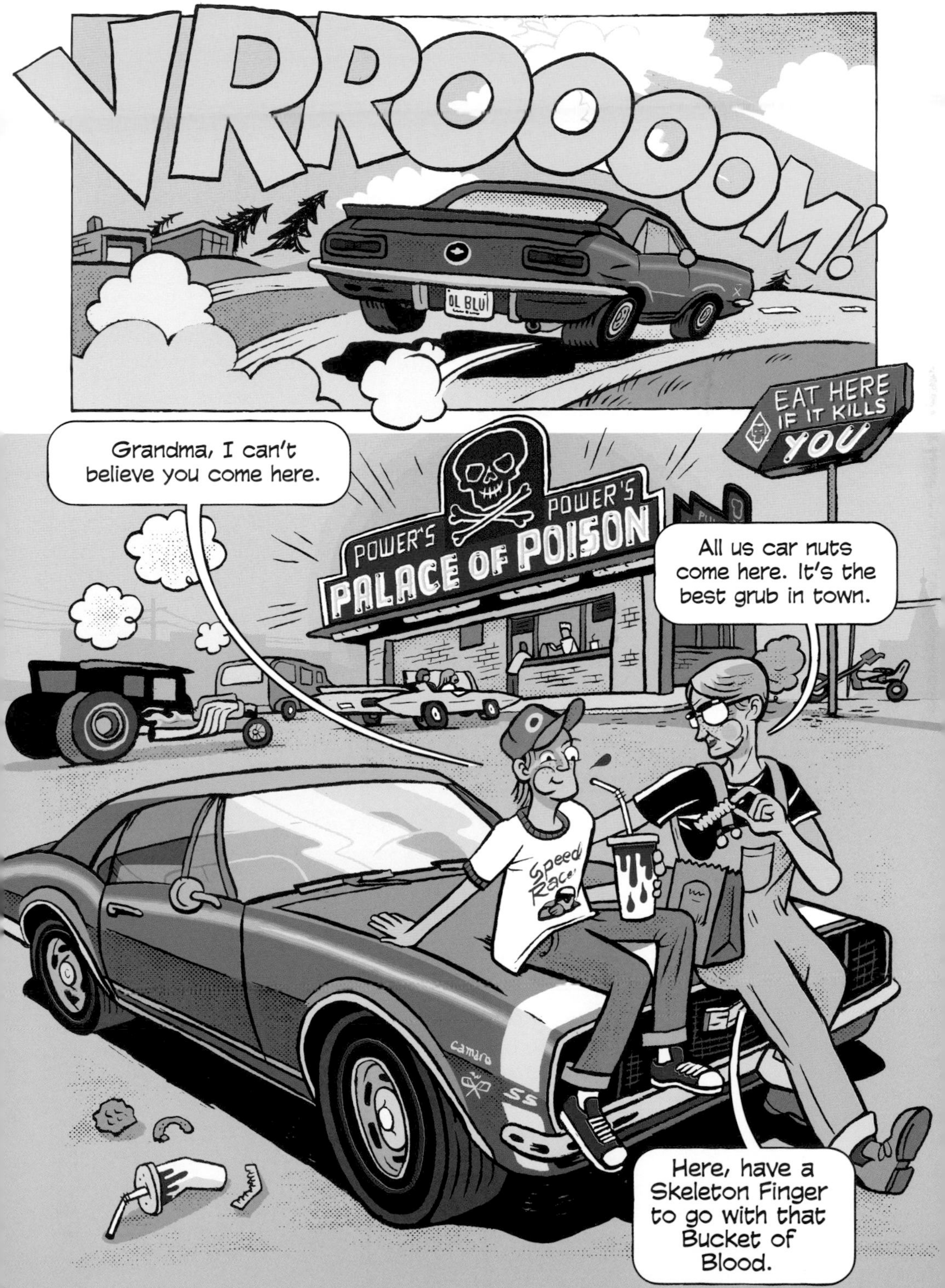
VRROOOOOM!
Grandma, I can't believe you come here.
EAT HERE IF IT KILLS YOU
POWER'S POWER'S
PALACE OF POISON
All us car nuts come here. It's the best grub in town.
Here, have a Skeleton Finger to go with that Bucket of Blood.

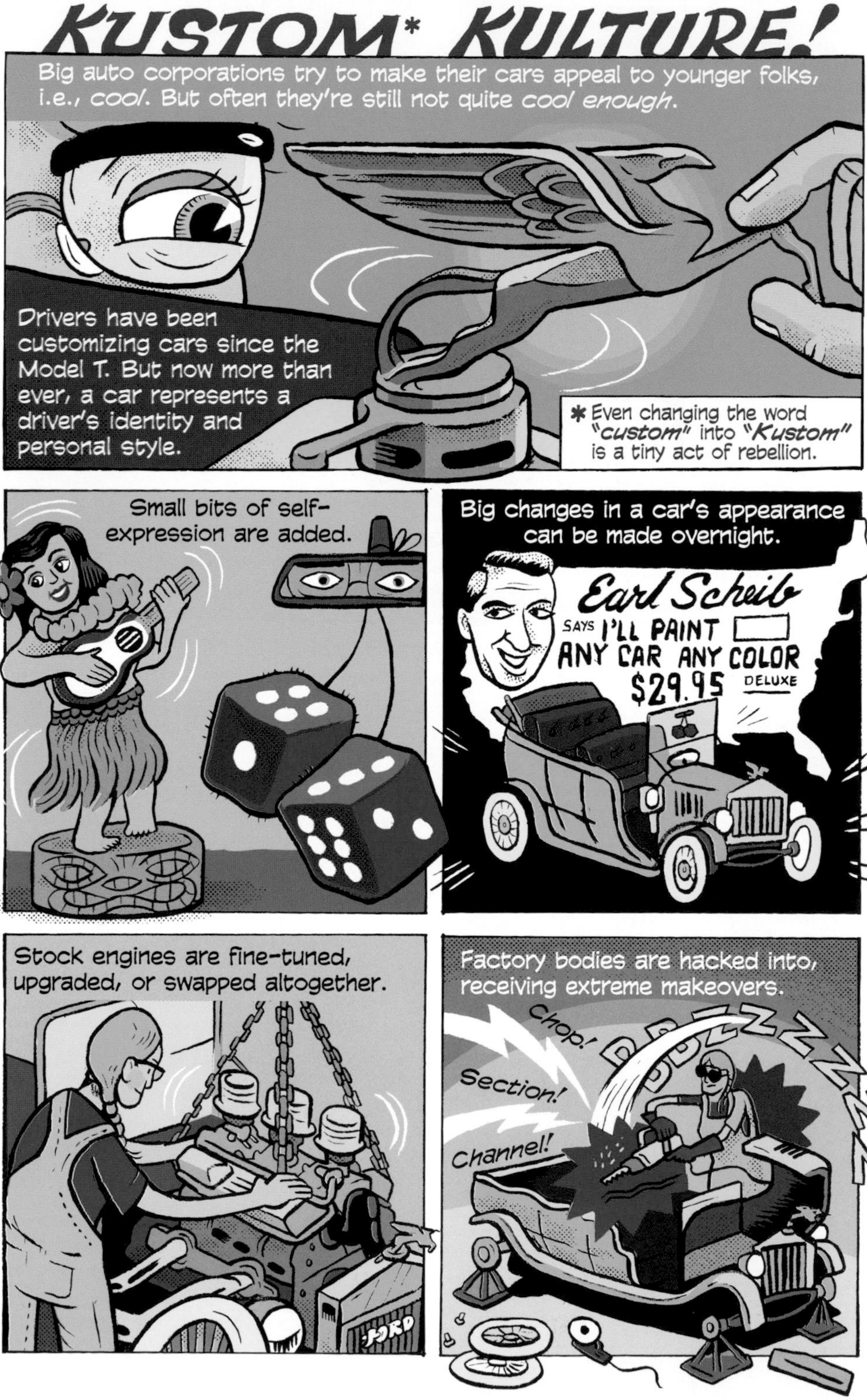
KUSTOM* KULTURE!
Big auto corporations try to make their cars appeal to younger folks, i.e., cool. But often they're still not quite cool enough.
Drivers have been customizing cars since the Model T. But now more than ever, a car represents a driver's identity and personal style.
* Even changing the word "custom" into "Kustom" is a tiny act of rebellion.
Small bits of self-expression are added.
Big changes in a car's appearance can be made overnight.
Earl Scheib
SAYS I'LL PAINT ANY CAR ANY COLOR $29.95 DELUXE
Stock engines are fine-tuned, upgraded, or swapped altogether.
FORD
Factory bodies are hacked into, receiving extreme makeovers.
Chop!
Section!
Channel!
BBBZZZZZZZZ

What used to be boring family transporters are transformed into fire-breathing Frankensteins of the freeway. They're known as:

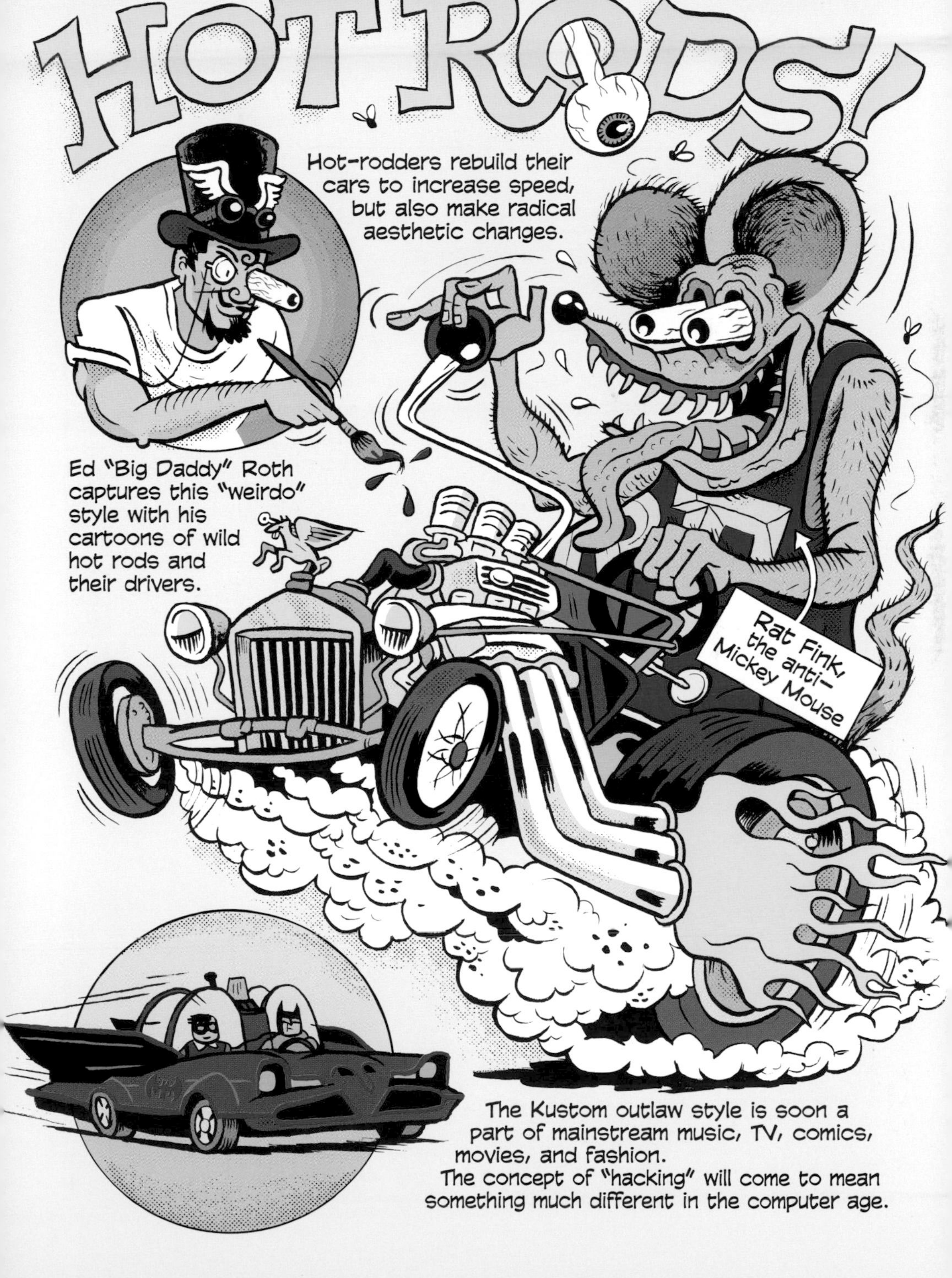
HOT RODS!
Hot-rodders rebuild their cars to increase speed, but also make radical aesthetic changes.
Ed "Big Daddy" Roth captures this "weirdo" style with his cartoons of wild hot rods and their drivers.
Rat Fink, the anti-Mickey Mouse
The Kustom outlaw style is soon a part of mainstream music, TV, comics, movies, and fashion.
The concept of "hacking" will come to mean something much different in the computer age.

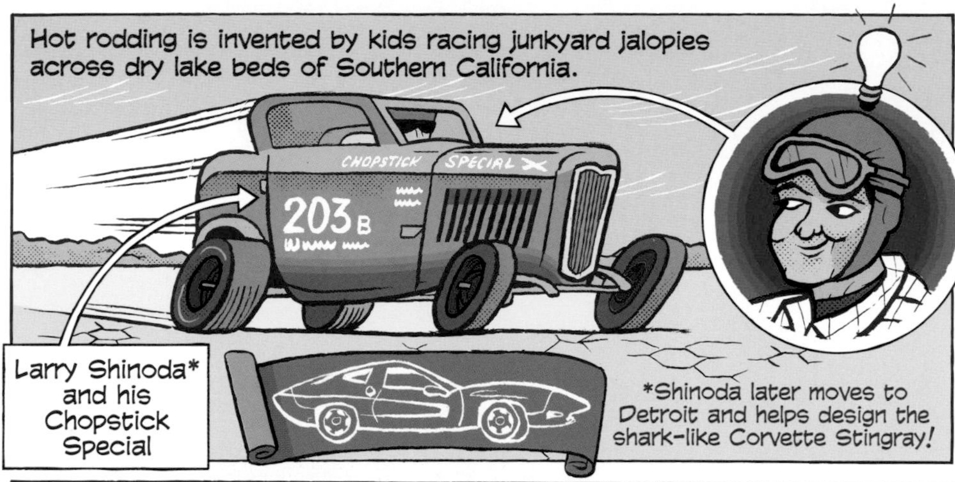
Hot rodding is invented by kids racing junkyard jalopies across dry lake beds of Southern California.
CHOPSTICK SPECIAL
203B
Larry Shinoda* and his Chopstick Special
*Shinoda later moves to Detroit and helps design the shark-like Corvette Stingray!

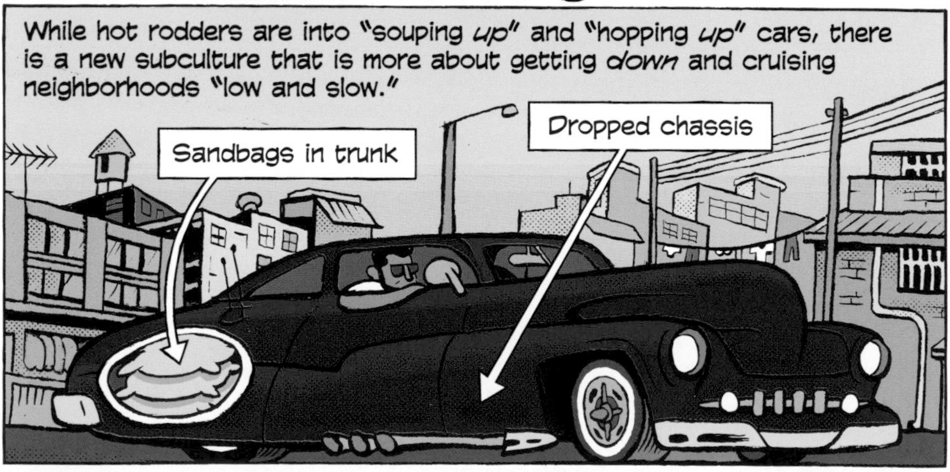
While hot rodders are into "souping *up*" and "hopping *up*" cars, there is a new subculture that is more about getting *down* and cruising neighborhoods "low and slow."
Sandbags in trunk
Dropped chassis

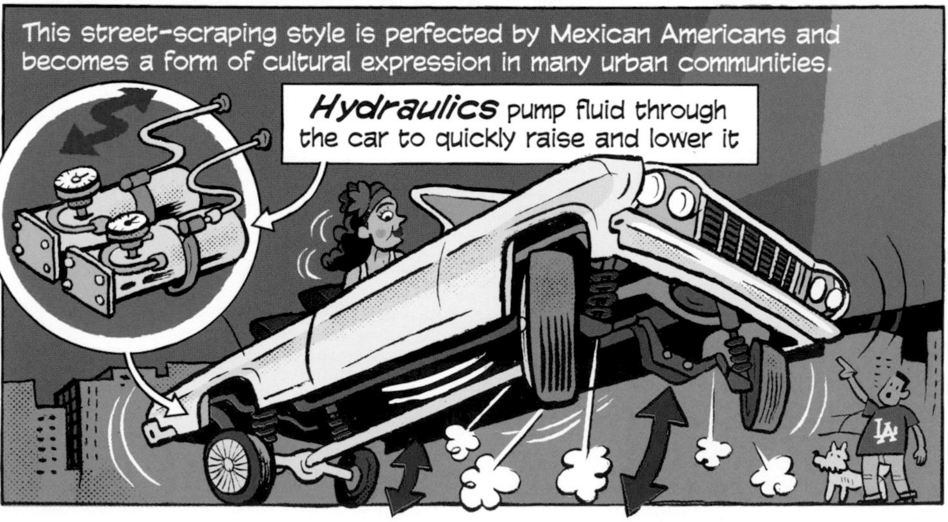
This street-scraping style is perfected by Mexican Americans and becomes a form of cultural expression in many urban communities.
Hydraulics pump fluid through the car to quickly raise and lower it
LA

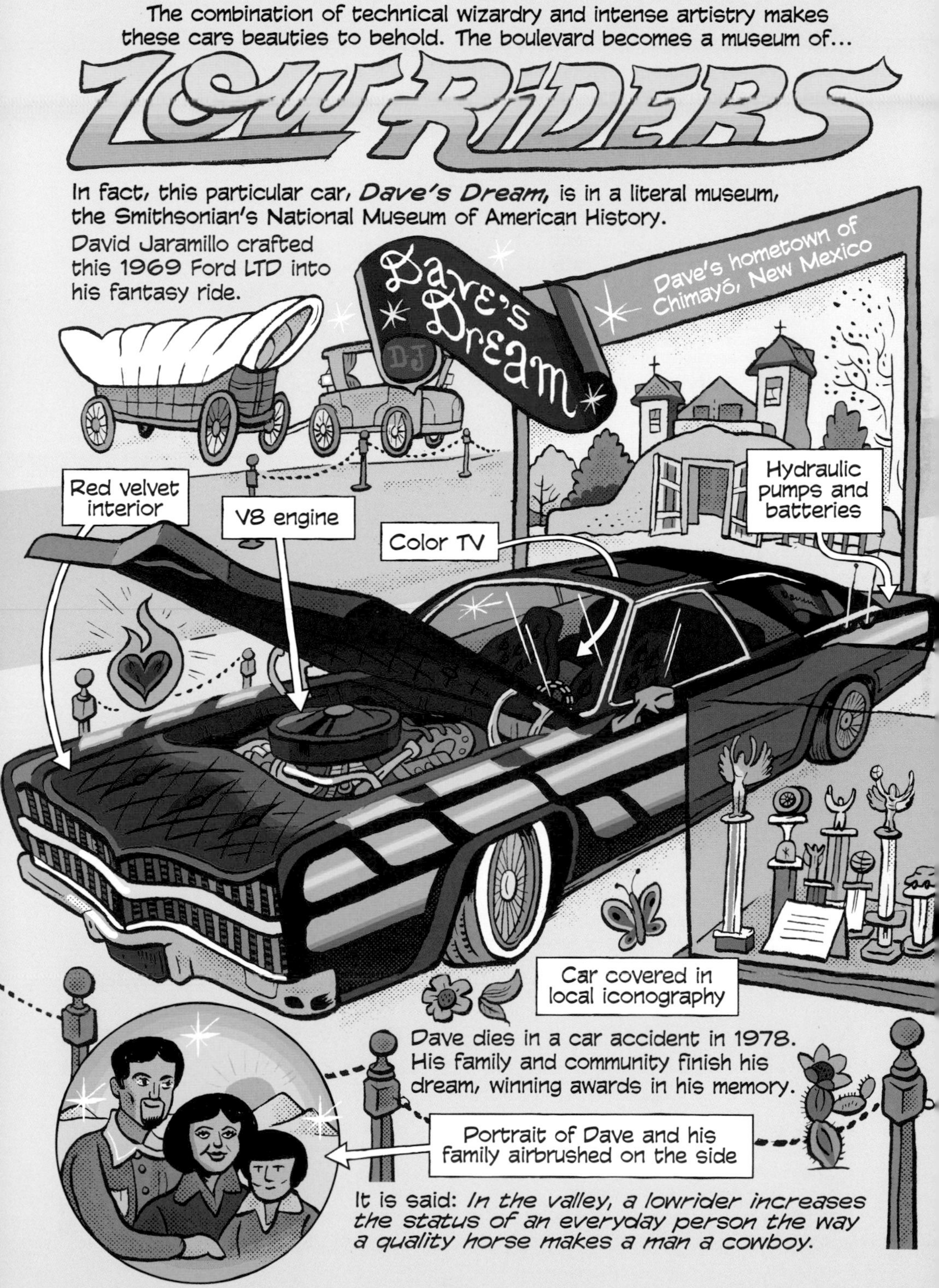
The combination of technical wizardry and intense artistry makes these cars beauties to behold. The boulevard becomes a museum of...
LOWRIDERS
In fact, this particular car, *Dave's Dream,* is in a literal museum, the Smithsonian's National Museum of American History.
David Jaramillo crafted this 1969 Ford LTD into his fantasy ride.
Dave's Dream
DJ
Dave's hometown of Chimayó, New Mexico
Red velvet interior
V8 engine
Color TV
Hydraulic pumps and batteries
Car covered in local iconography
Dave dies in a car accident in 1978. His family and community finish his dream, winning awards in his memory.
Portrait of Dave and his family airbrushed on the side
It is said: *In the valley, a lowrider increases the status of an everyday person the way a quality horse makes a man a cowboy.*

ENGINE TYPES

We've looked closely at the V8, but there are an endless variety of engine configurations. Here are some of them.

INTERNAL COMBUSTION

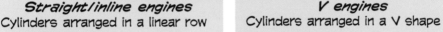

Straight/inline engines

Cylinders arranged in a linear row

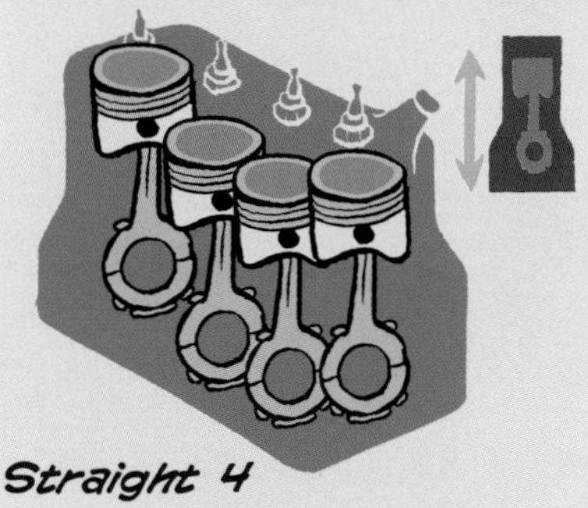

Straight 4

V engines

Cylinders arranged in a V shape

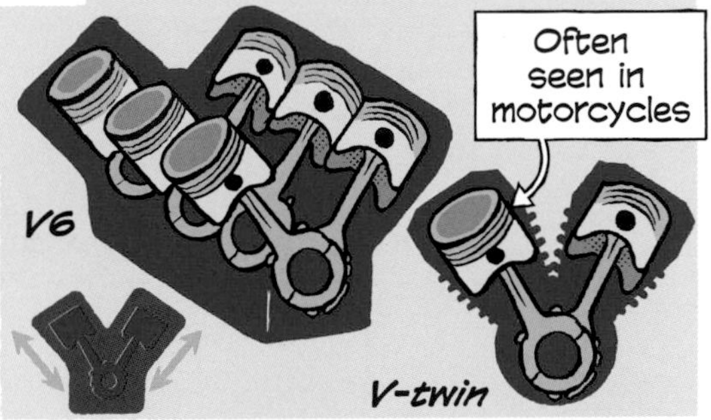

Often seen in motorcycles
V6
V-twin

Slant engines

Cylinders arranged in straight line but tilted to one side

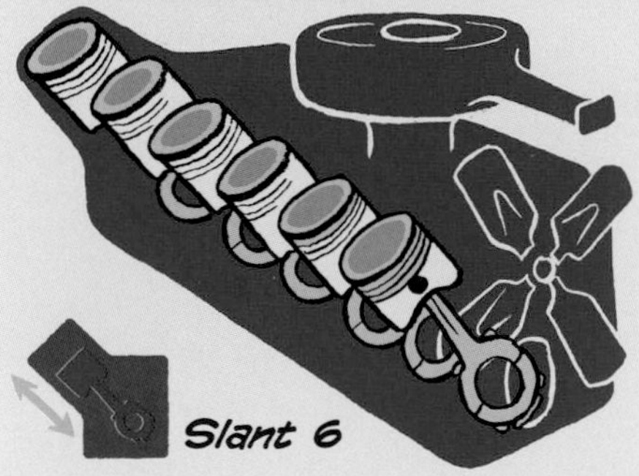

Slant 6

Flat engines aka *the Boxer*

Cylinders horizontally opposed

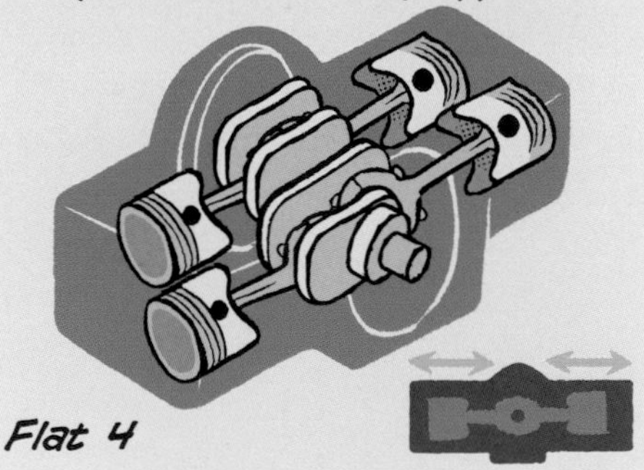

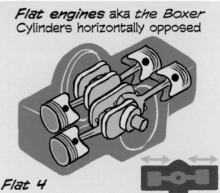

Flat 4

Rotary engines

Cylinders arranged radially and spin around a central stationary crankshaft

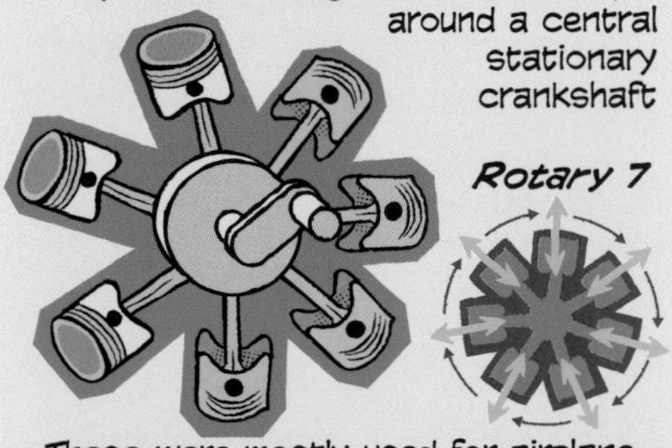

Rotary 7

These were mostly used for airplane and helicopter propellers.

Things start to get out of control with ***W engines***

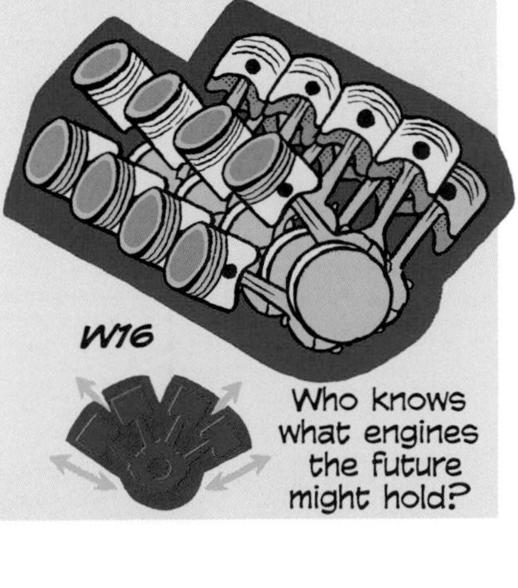

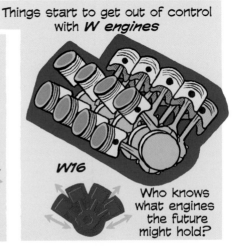

W16

Who knows what engines the future might hold?

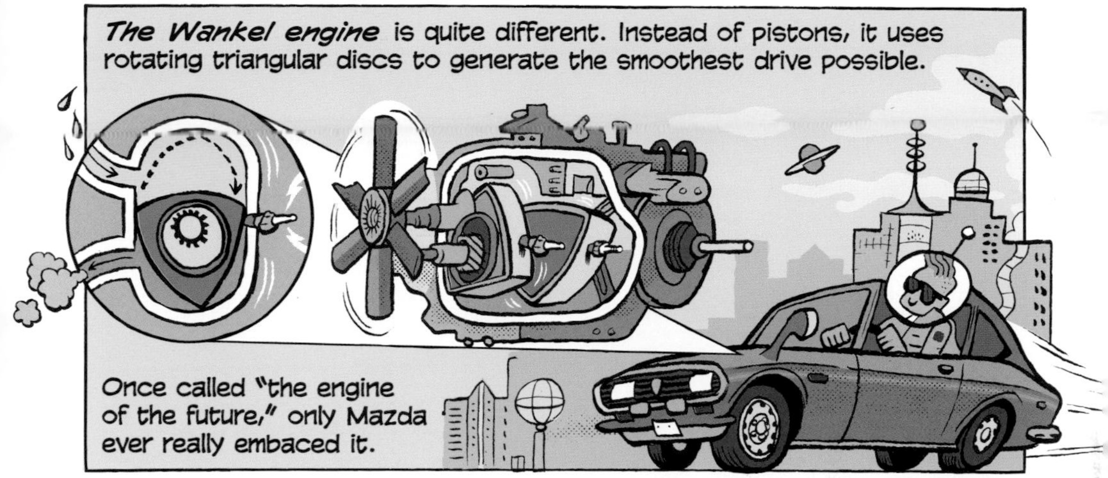

The Wankel engine is quite different. Instead of pistons, it uses rotating triangular discs to generate the smoothest drive possible.
Once called "the engine of the future," only Mazda ever really embaced it.

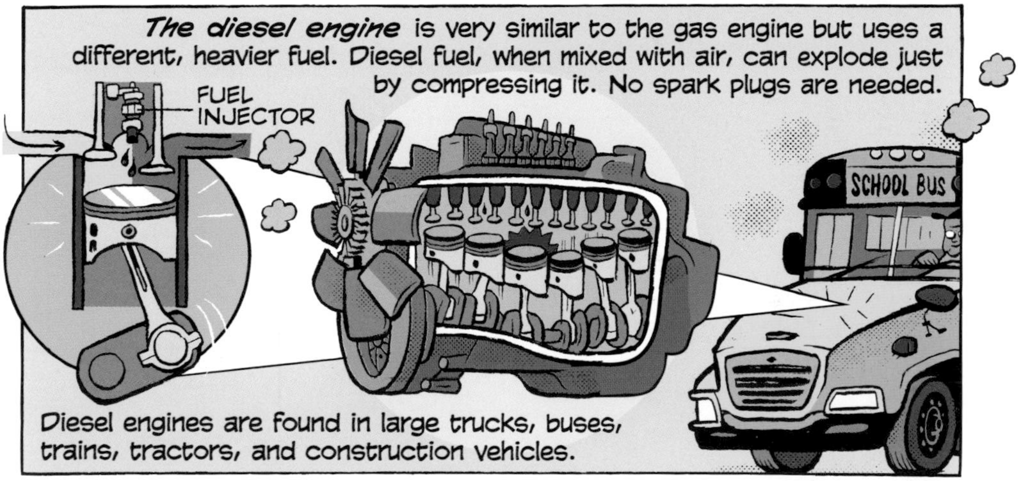

The diesel engine is very similar to the gas engine but uses a different, heavier fuel. Diesel fuel, when mixed with air, can explode just by compressing it. No spark plugs are needed.
FUEL INJECTOR
SCHOOL BUS
Diesel engines are found in large trucks, buses, trains, tractors, and construction vehicles.

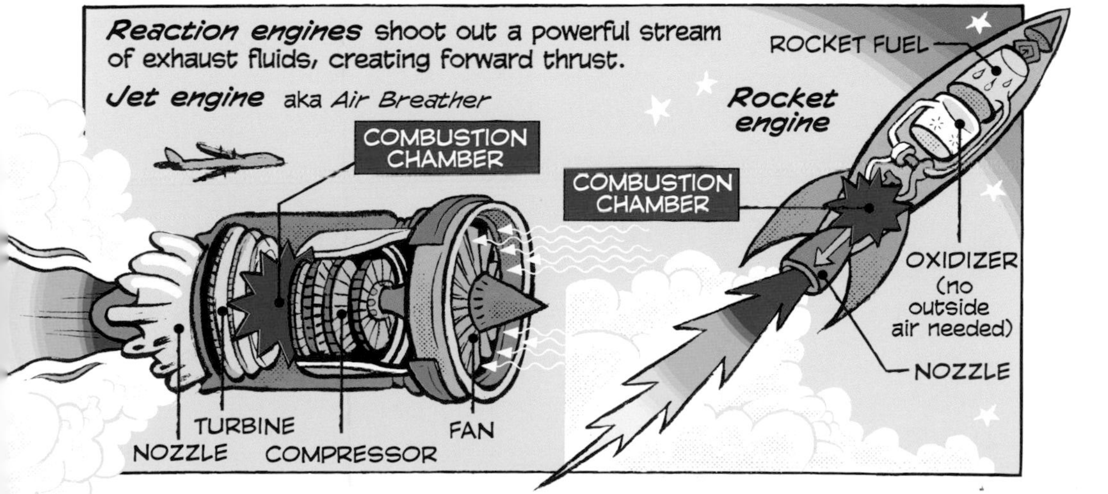

Reaction engines shoot out a powerful stream of exhaust fluids, creating forward thrust.
Jet engine aka Air Breather
COMBUSTION CHAMBER
TURBINE
NOZZLE
COMPRESSOR
FAN
Rocket engine
ROCKET FUEL
COMBUSTION CHAMBER
OXIDIZER (no outside air needed)
NOZZLE

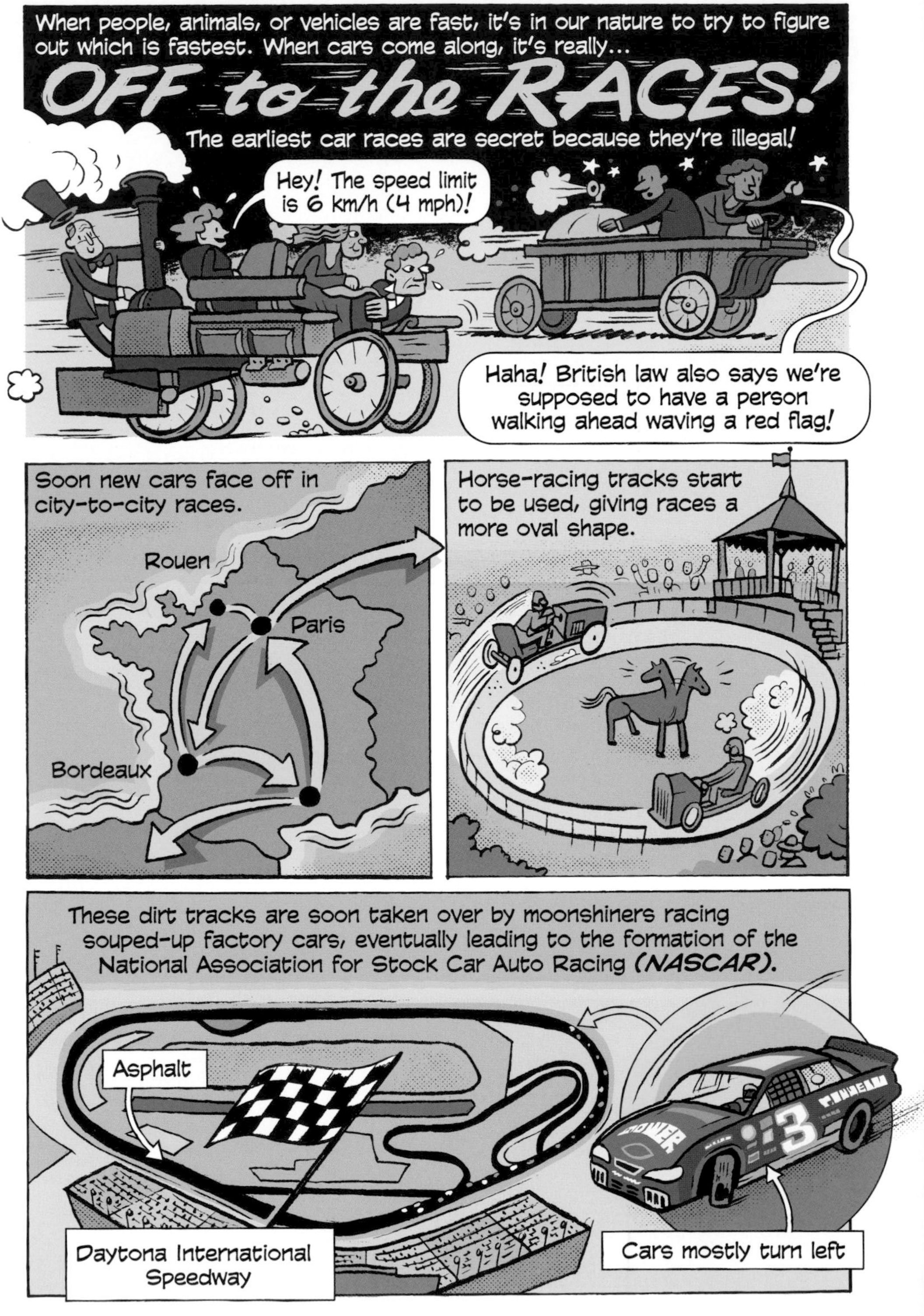

When people, animals, or vehicles are fast, it's in our nature to try to figure out which is fastest. When cars come along, it's really...
OFF to the RACES!
The earliest car races are secret because they're illegal!
Hey! The speed limit is 6 km/h (4 mph)!
Haha! British law also says we're supposed to have a person walking ahead waving a red flag!
Soon new cars face off in city-to-city races.
Rouen
Paris
Bordeaux
Horse-racing tracks start to be used, giving races a more oval shape.
These dirt tracks are soon taken over by moonshiners racing souped-up factory cars, eventually leading to the formation of the National Association for Stock Car Auto Racing (NASCAR).
Asphalt
3
Daytona International Speedway
Cars mostly turn left

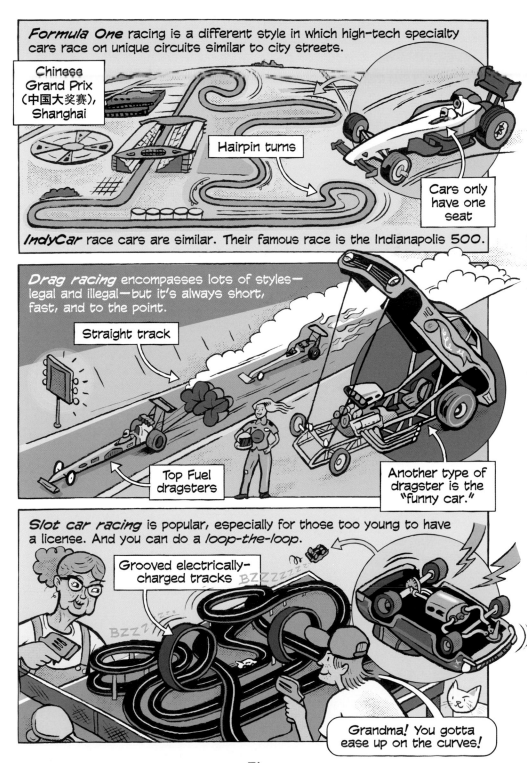

Formula One racing is a different style in which high-tech specialty cars race on unique circuits similar to city streets.

Chinese Grand Prix （中国大奖赛）, Shanghai

Hairpin turns

Cars only have one seat

IndyCar race cars are similar. Their famous race is the Indianapolis 500.

Drag racing encompasses lots of styles—legal and illegal—but it's always short, fast, and to the point.

Straight track

Top Fuel dragsters

Another type of dragster is the "funny car."

Slot car racing is popular, especially for those too young to have a license. And you can do a _loop-the-loop_.

Grooved electrically-charged tracks

BZZZZZZZ

BZZZ

Grandma! You gotta ease up on the curves!

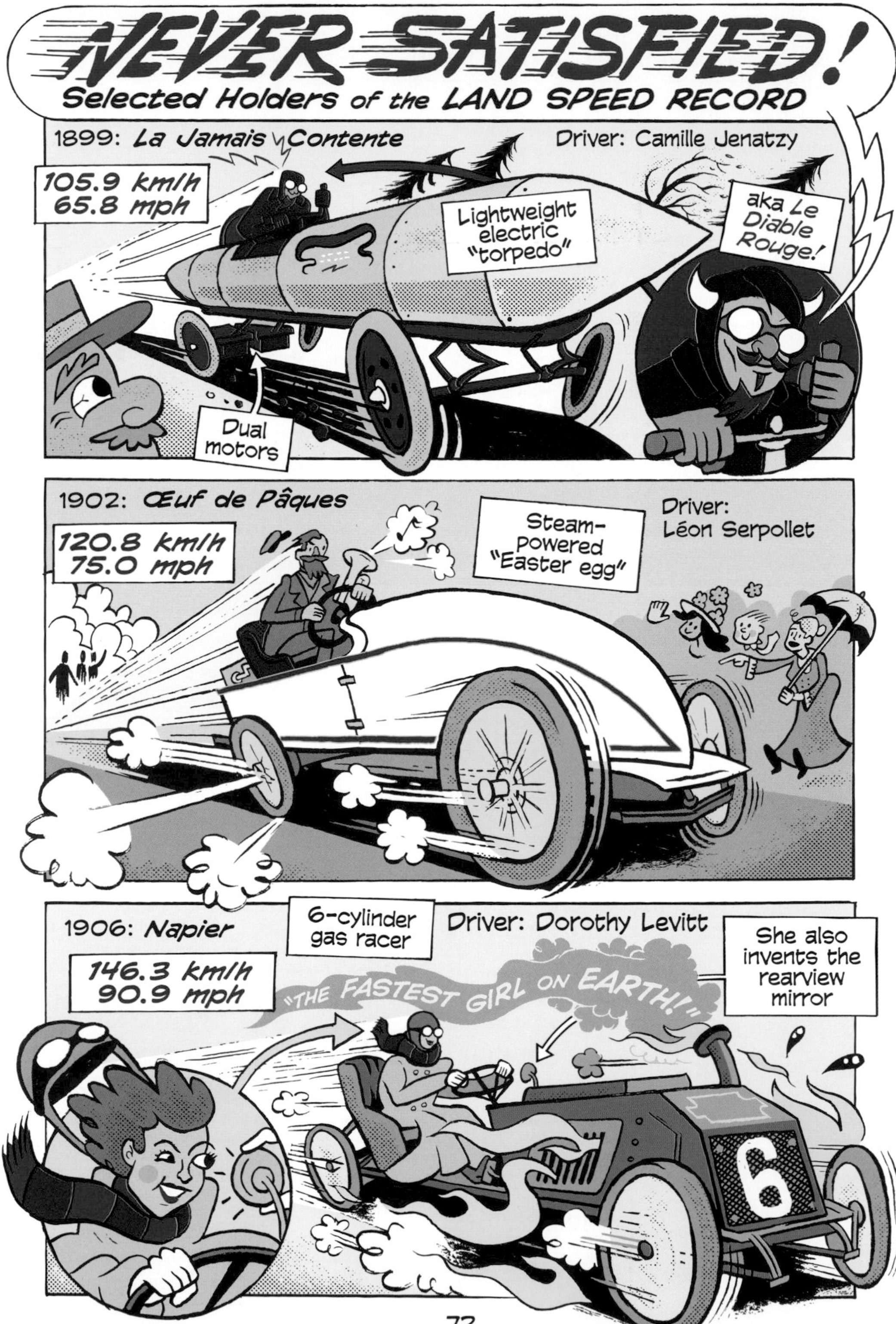

NEVER SATISFIED!
Selected Holders of the LAND SPEED RECORD
1899: La Jamais Contente
Driver: Camille Jenatzy
105.9 km/h
65.8 mph
Lightweight electric "torpedo"
aka Le Diable Rouge!
Dual motors
1902: Œuf de Pâques
Driver: Léon Serpollet
120.8 km/h
75.0 mph
Steam-powered "Easter egg"
1906: Napier
6-cylinder gas racer
Driver: Dorothy Levitt
146.3 km/h
90.9 mph
She also invents the rearview mirror
"THE FASTEST GIRL ON EARTH!"
6

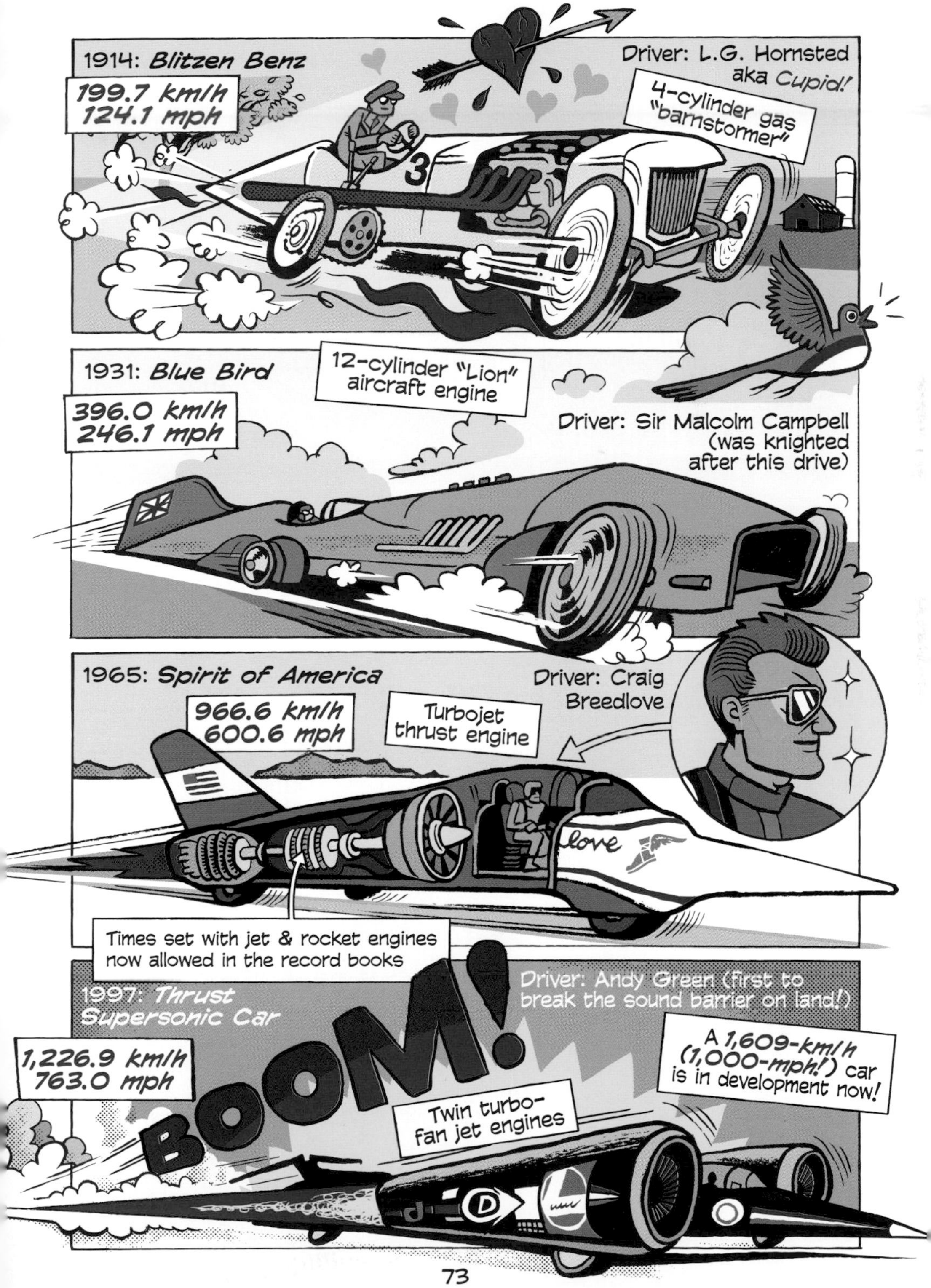

1914: Blitzen Benz
199.7 km/h
124.1 mph
Driver: L.G. Hornsted
aka Cupid!
4-cylinder gas "barnstormer"
1931: Blue Bird
12-cylinder "Lion" aircraft engine
396.0 km/h
246.1 mph
Driver: Sir Malcolm Campbell (was knighted after this drive)
1965: Spirit of America
966.6 km/h
600.6 mph
Turbojet thrust engine
Driver: Craig Breedlove
Times set with jet & rocket engines now allowed in the record books
1997: Thrust Supersonic Car
Driver: Andy Green (first to break the sound barrier on land!)
1,226.9 km/h
763.0 mph
BOOM!
Twin turbo-fan jet engines
A 1,609-km/h (1,000-mph!) car is in development now!

You remember ***Oruktor Amphibolos*** *(see page 17)*, but there have been many attempts to build the ultimate land/water vehicle.

AMPHIBIOUS CARS!

1931: ***Land-boat***
(or sea-auto)

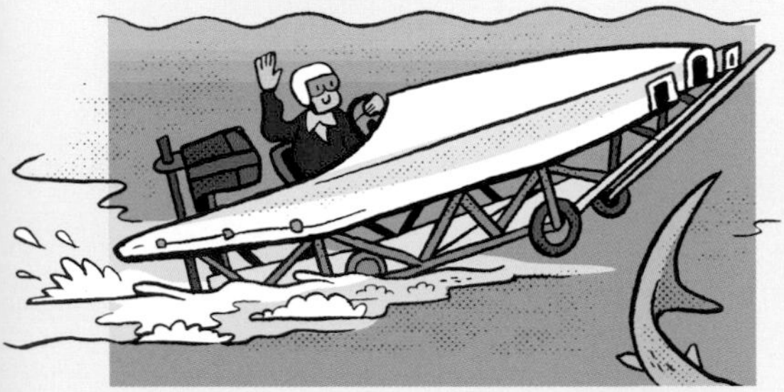

1942: ***VW Schwimmwagen***

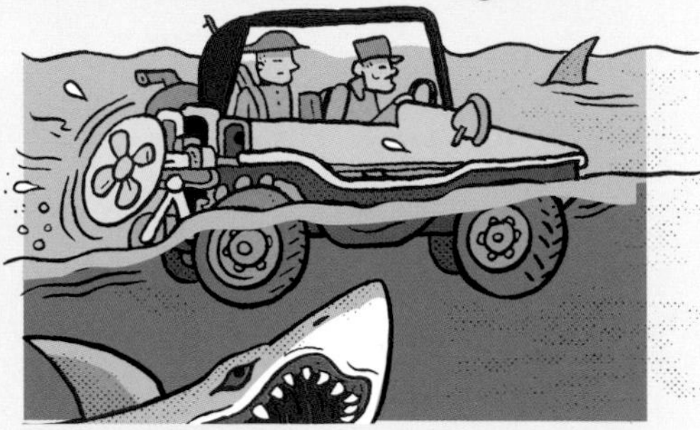

1961: ***Amphicar***

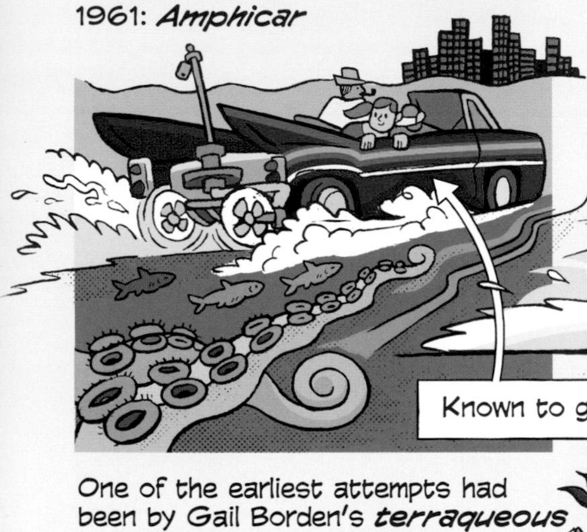
Known to get very rusty

2016: ***WaterCar Panther***

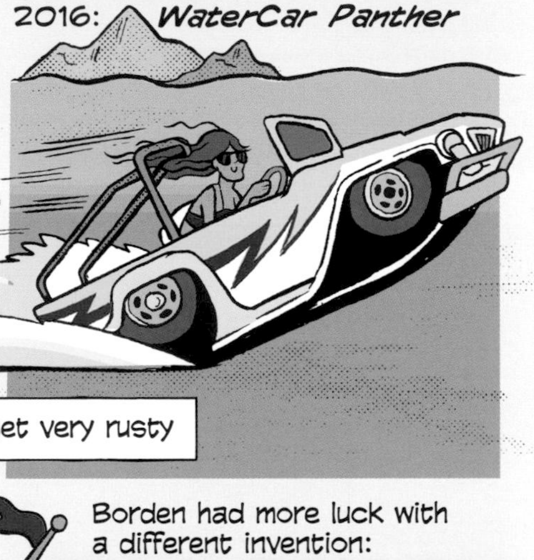

One of the earliest attempts had been by Gail Borden's ***terraqueous sail wagon*** in the 1840s.

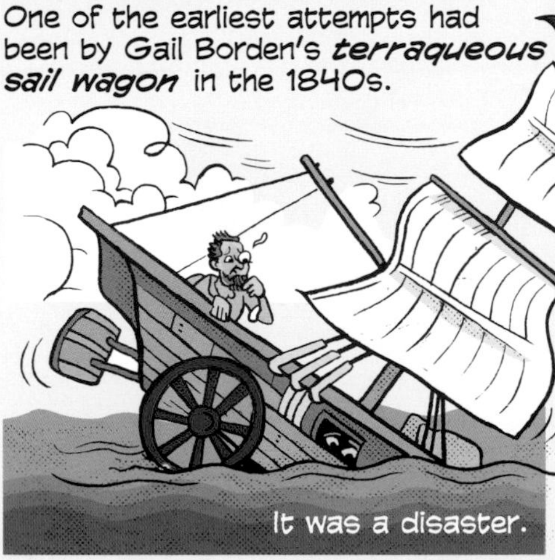
It was a disaster.

Borden had more luck with a different invention:

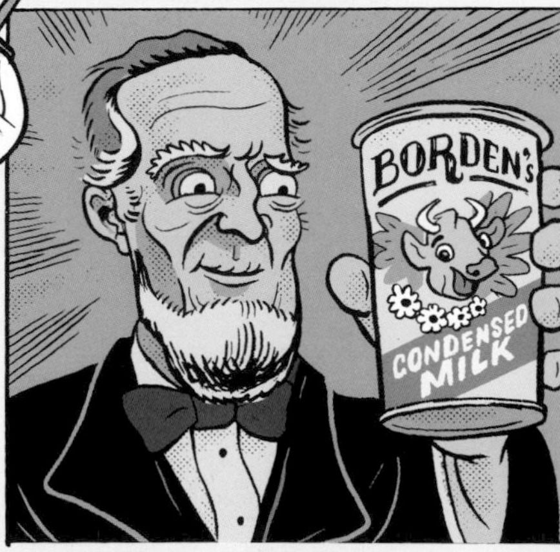
BORDEN's
CONDENSED MILK

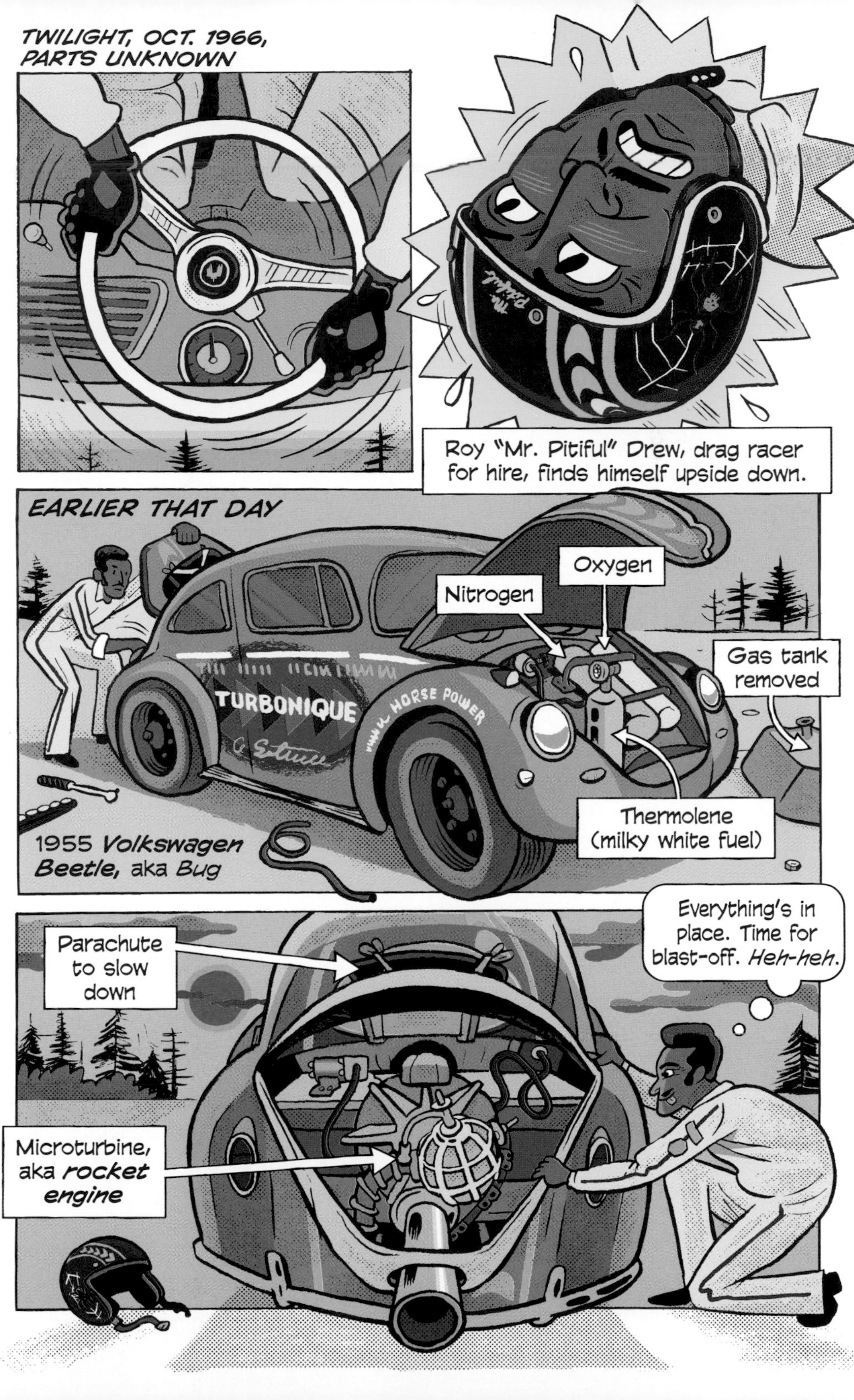
TWILIGHT, OCT. 1966, PARTS UNKNOWN
Roy "Mr. Pitiful" Drew, drag racer for hire, finds himself upside down.
EARLIER THAT DAY
Oxygen
Nitrogen
Gas tank removed
TURBONIQUE
HORSE POWER
Thermolene (milky white fuel)
1955 *Volkswagen Beetle*, aka *Bug*
Everything's in place. Time for blast-off. *Heh-heh*.
Parachute to slow down
Microturbine, aka ***rocket engine***

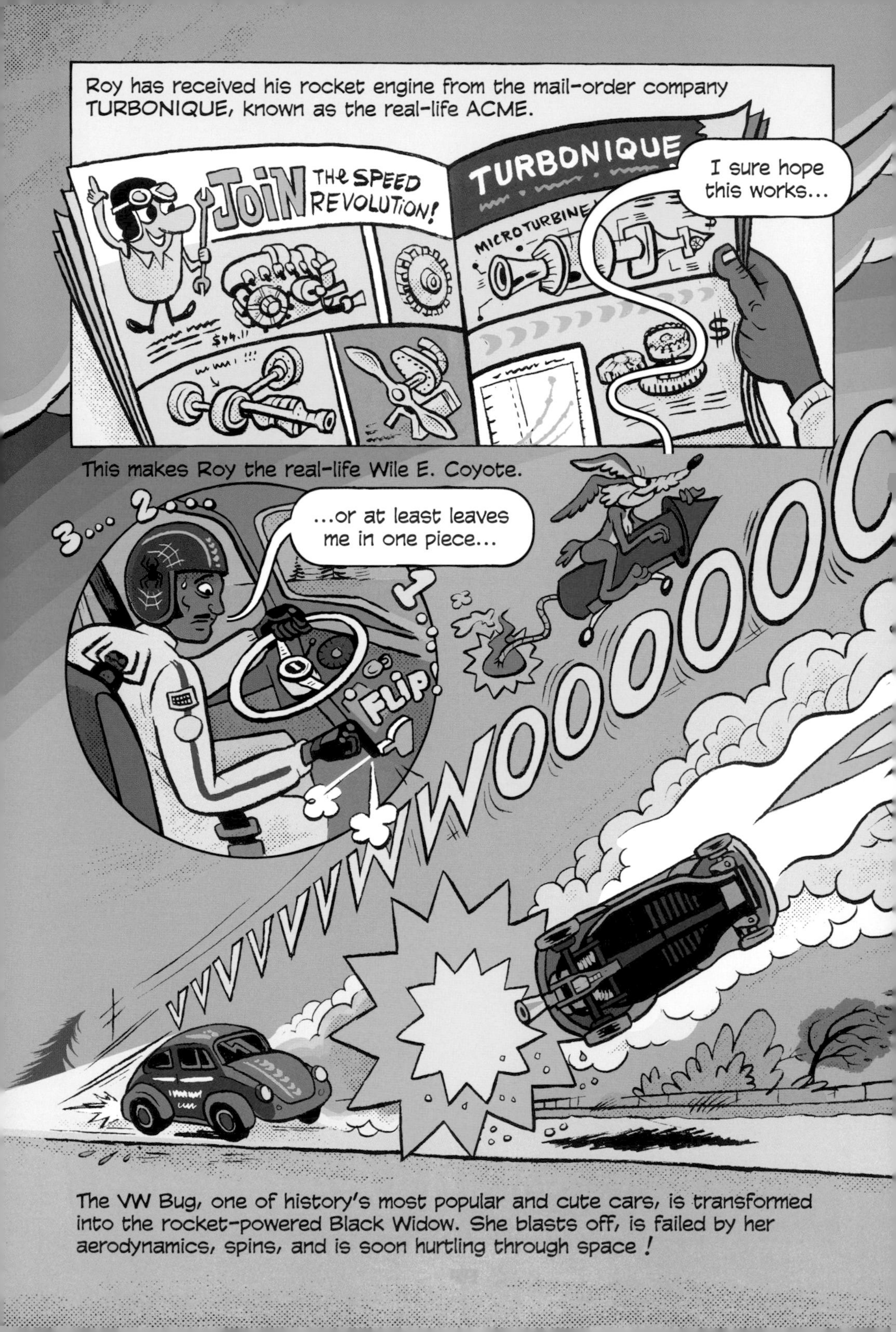

Roy has received his rocket engine from the mail-order company TURBONIQUE, known as the real-life ACME.
JOIN THE SPEED REVOLUTION!
TURBONIQUE
MICROTURBINE
I sure hope this works...
This makes Roy the real-life Wile E. Coyote.
3... 2... 1
...or at least leaves me in one piece...
FLIP!
VVVVVVVVWOOOOOOOO
The VW Bug, one of history's most popular and cute cars, is transformed into the rocket-powered Black Widow. She blasts off, is failed by her aerodynamics, spins, and is soon hurtling through space!

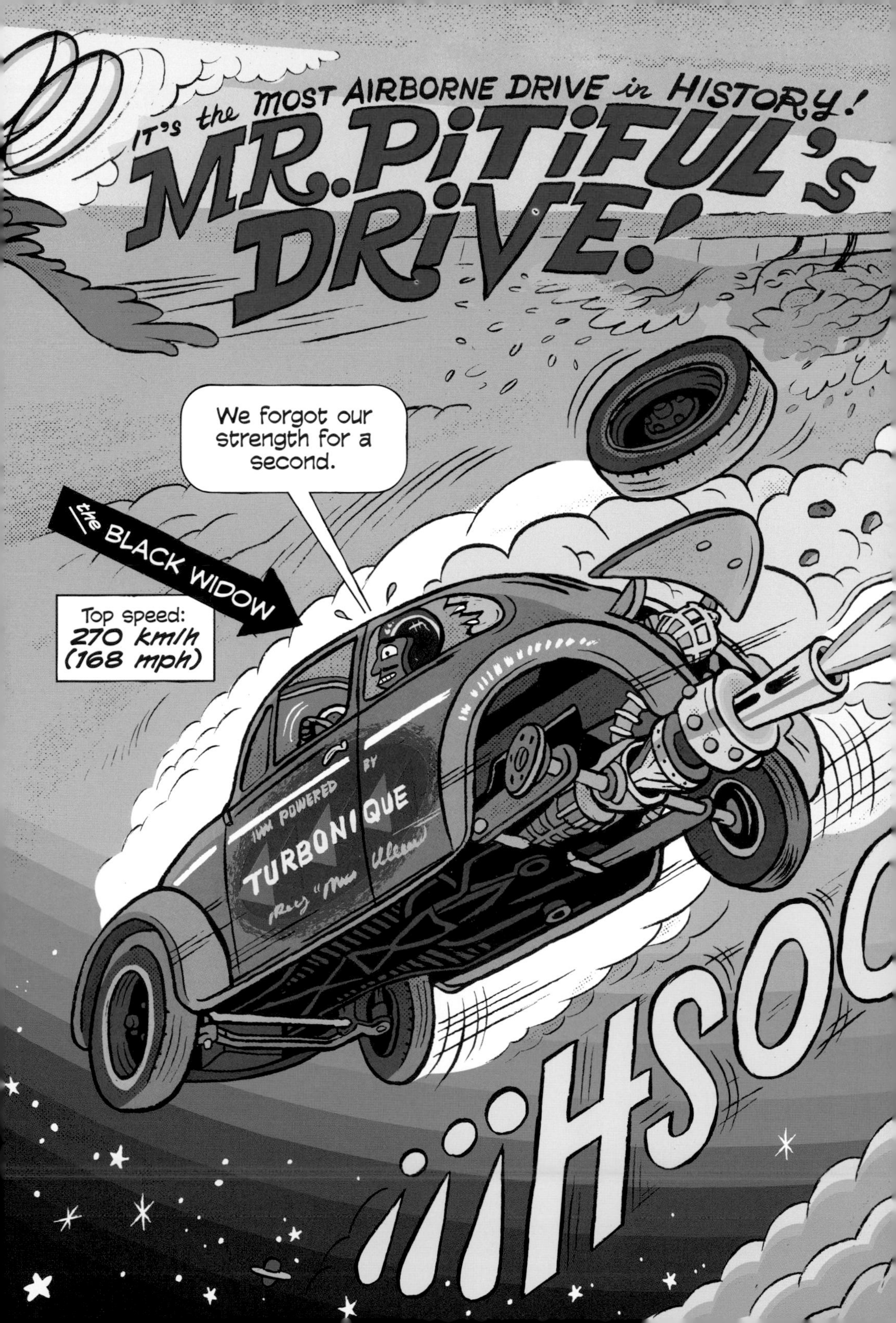
IT'S the MOST AIRBORNE DRIVE in HISTORY!
MR. PITIFUL'S DRIVE!
We forgot our strength for a second.
the BLACK WIDOW
Top speed: 270 km/h (168 mph)
TURBONIQUE
POWERED BY
...OOSH!!!

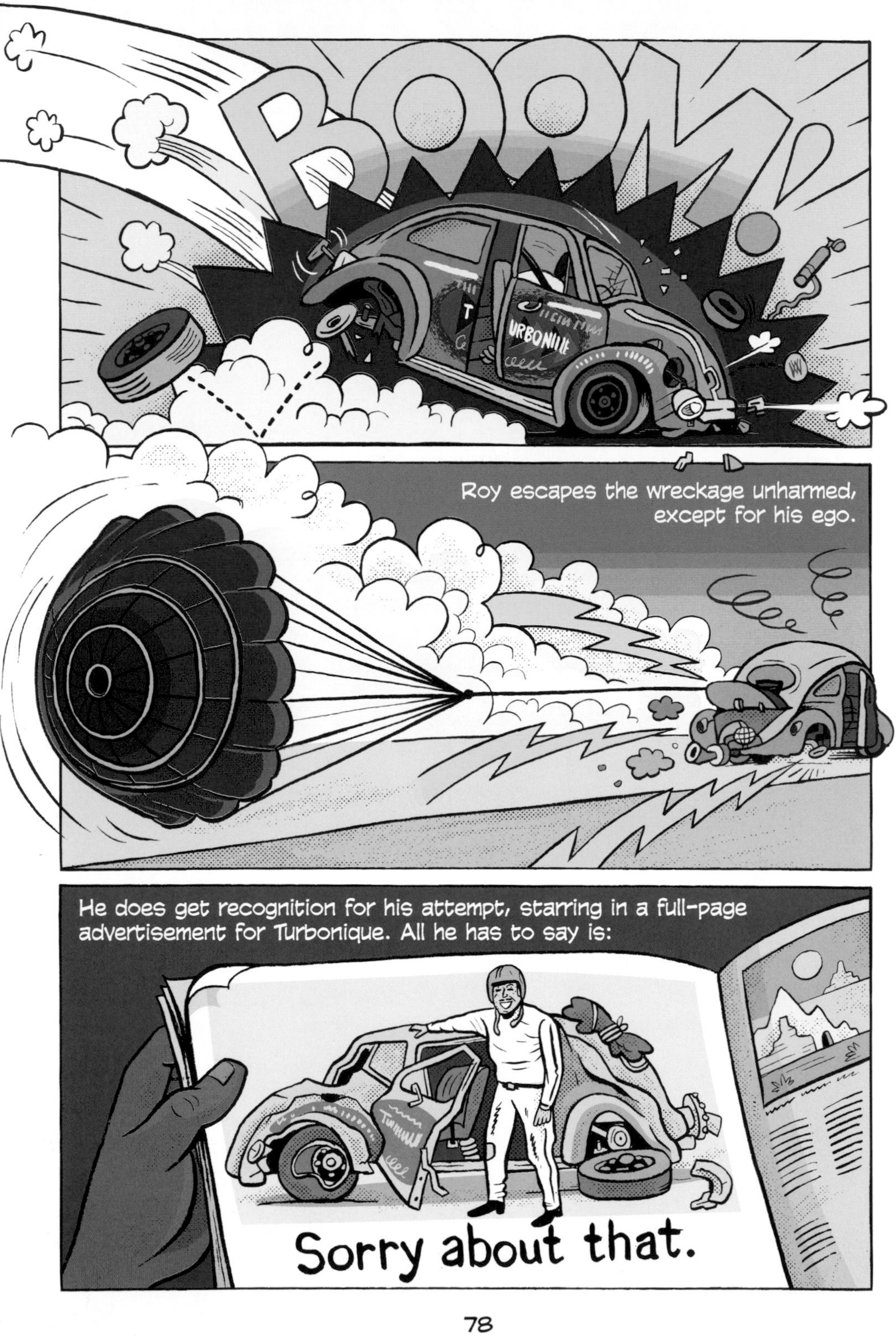
BOOM!
URBONIQUE
Roy escapes the wreckage unharmed, except for his ego.
He does get recognition for his attempt, starring in a full-page advertisement for Turbonique. All he has to say is:
Sorry about that.

Just as the human body is organized into systems that work together, so is the automobile. Let's peel off its steel skin and take a look.

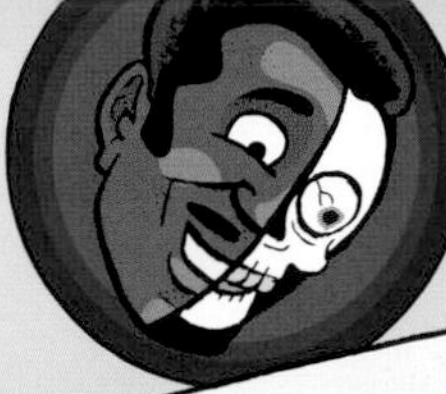

The SYSTEMS of the CAR

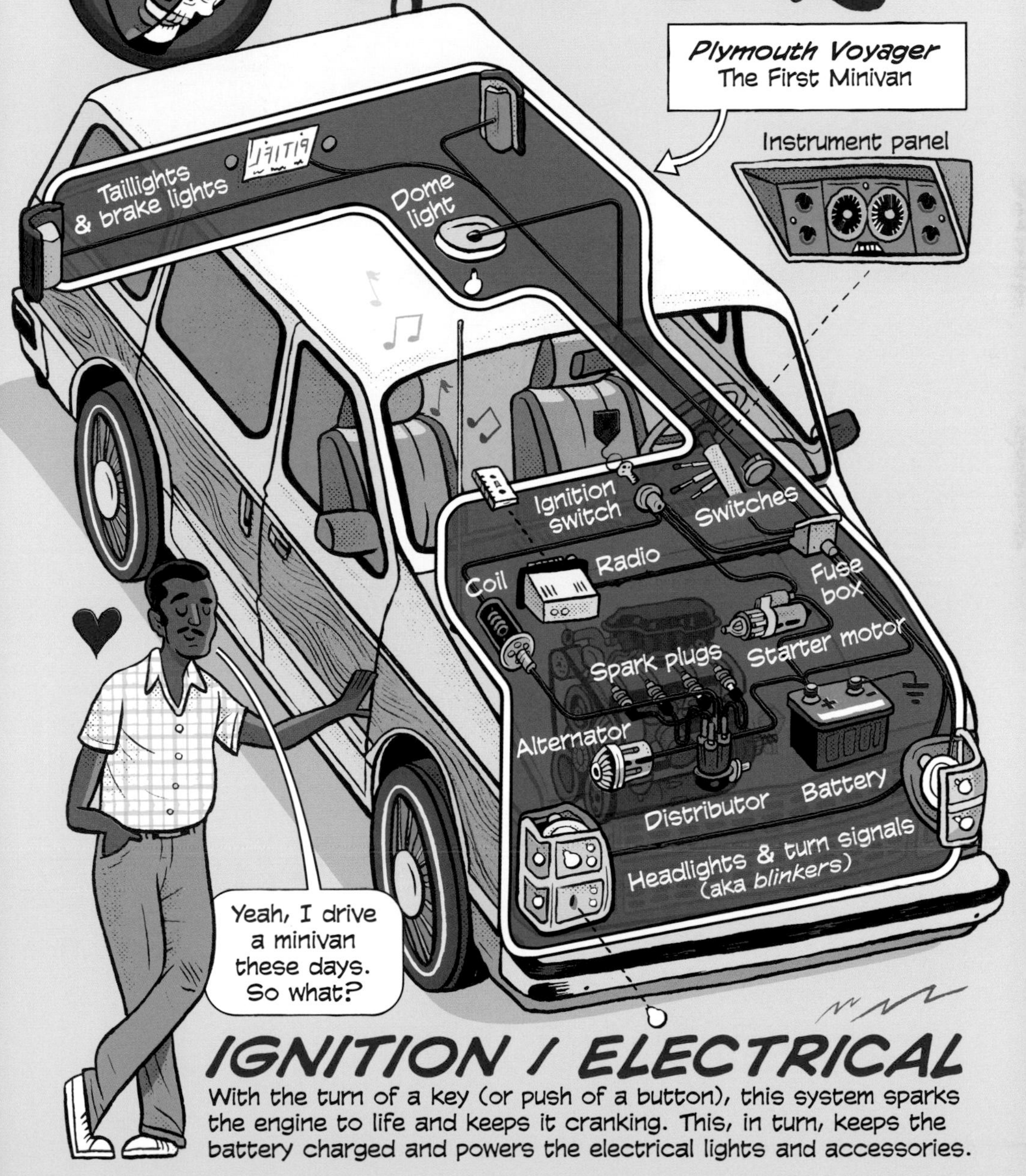

Plymouth Voyager
The First Minivan
Instrument panel
Taillights & brake lights
Dome light
Ignition switch
Switches
Radio
Coil
Fuse box
Starter motor
Spark plugs
Alternator
Distributor
Battery
Headlights & turn signals (aka *blinkers*)
Yeah, I drive a minivan these days. So what?

IGNITION / ELECTRICAL

With the turn of a key (or push of a button), this system sparks the engine to life and keeps it cranking. This, in turn, keeps the battery charged and powers the electrical lights and accessories.

There are a few typical ways cars are laid out:

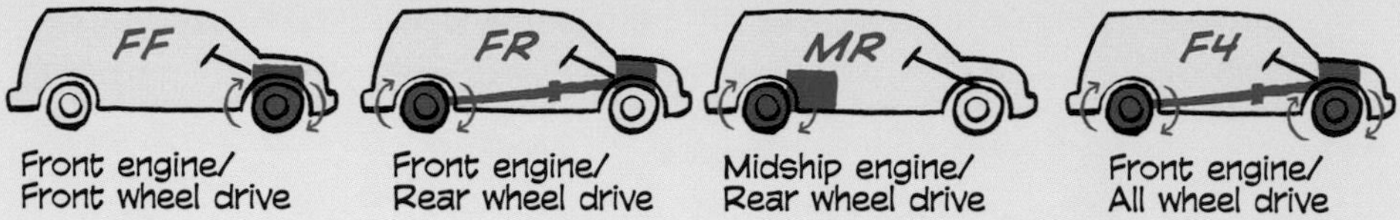

FF
FR
MR
F4
Front engine/ Front wheel drive
Front engine/ Rear wheel drive
Midship engine/ Rear wheel drive
Front engine/ All wheel drive

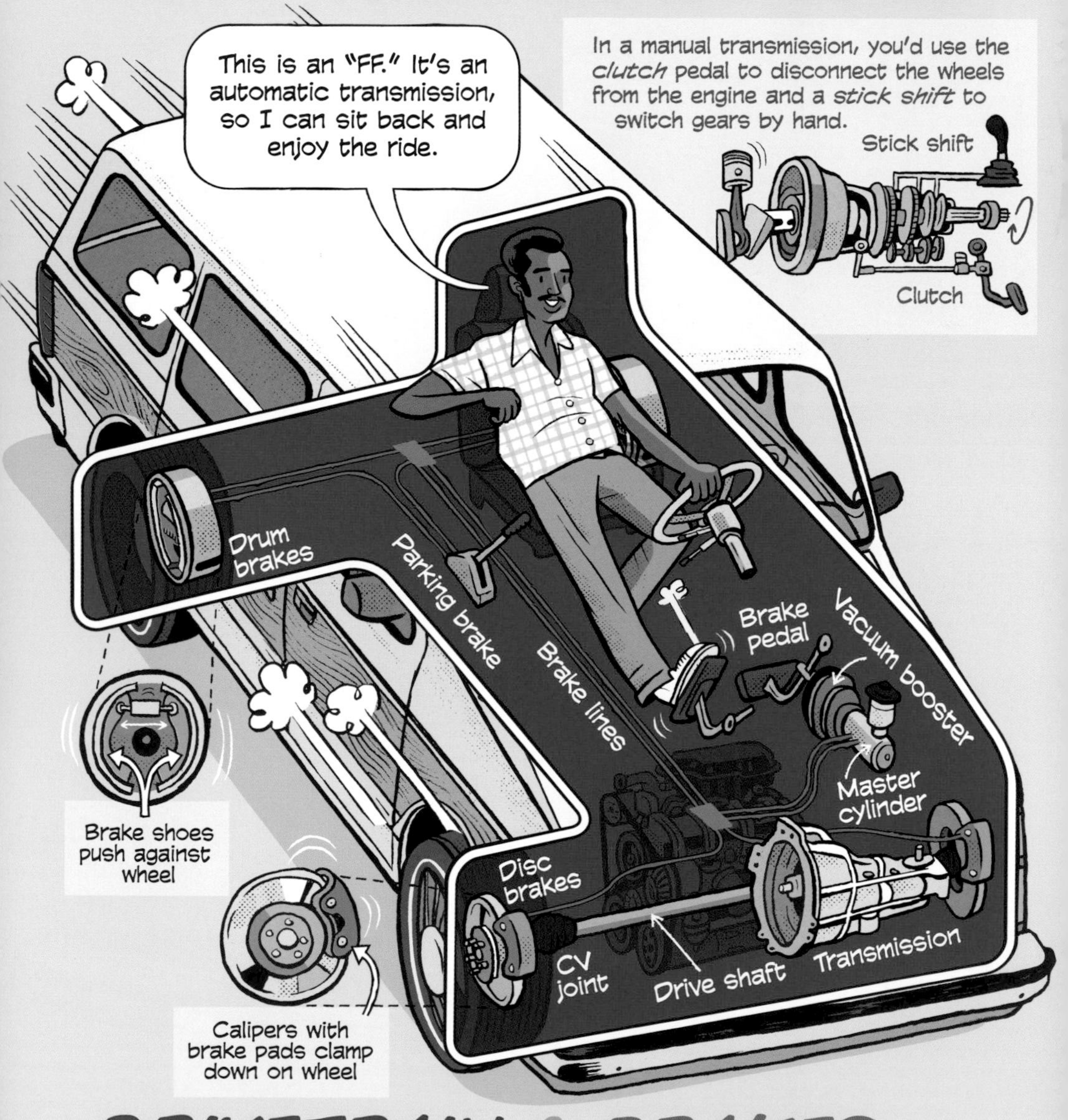

This is an "FF." It's an automatic transmission, so I can sit back and enjoy the ride.
In a manual transmission, you'd use the *clutch* pedal to disconnect the wheels from the engine and a *stick shift* to switch gears by hand.
Stick shift
Clutch
Drum brakes
Parking brake
Brake lines
Brake pedal
Vacuum booster
Master cylinder
Disc brakes
CV joint
Drive shaft
Transmission
Brake shoes push against wheel
Calipers with brake pads clamp down on wheel

DRIVETRAIN & BRAKES

The drivetrain, which includes the transmission and axles, takes power from the engine and transmits it to the wheels. A series of gears controls how fast the wheels turn. Brakes try to stop them from turning.

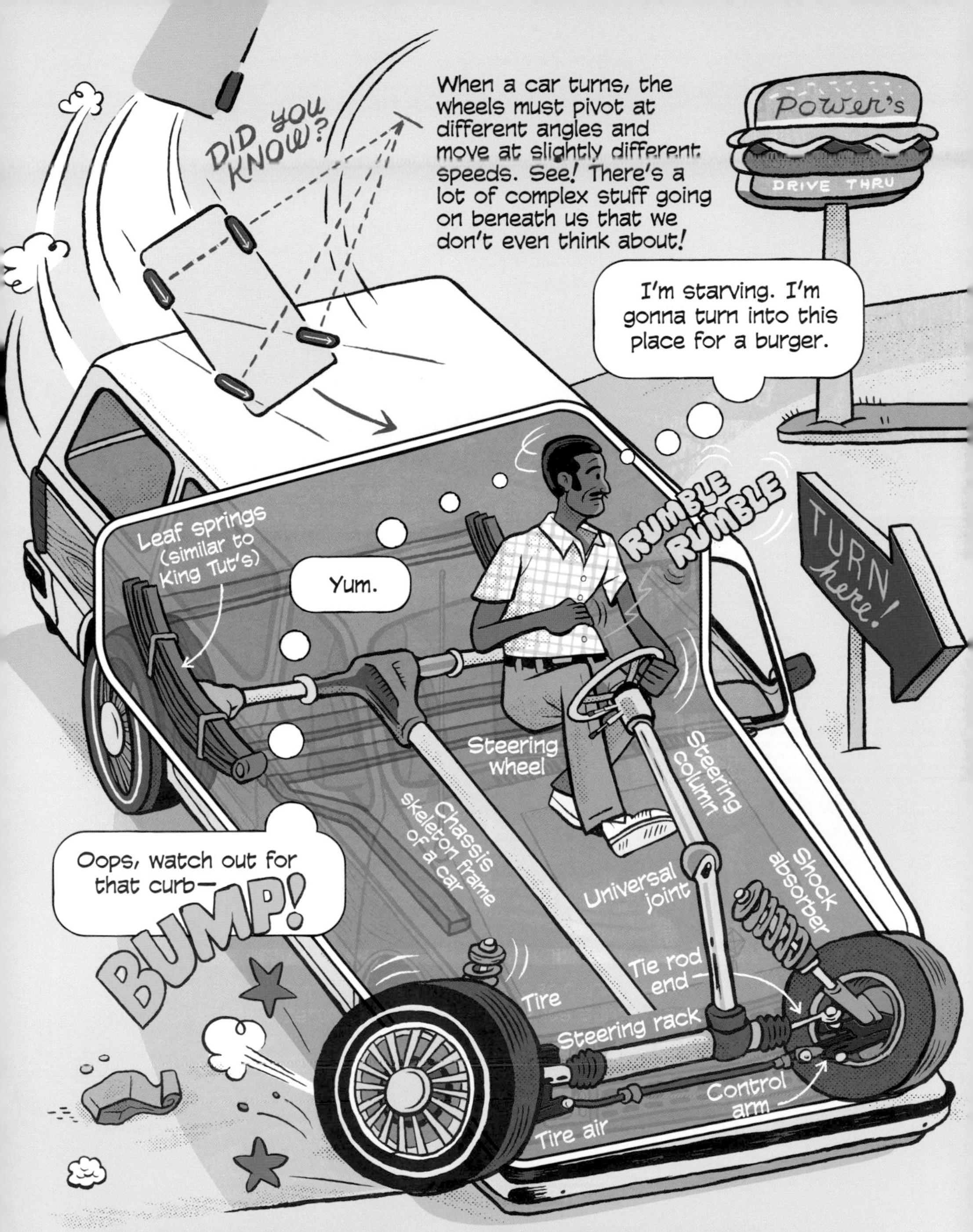
DID YOU KNOW?
When a car turns, the wheels must pivot at different angles and move at slightly different speeds. See! There's a lot of complex stuff going on beneath us that we don't even think about!
POWER'S
DRIVE THRU
I'm starving. I'm gonna turn into this place for a burger.
Yum.
RUMBLE RUMBLE
TURN here!
Leaf springs (similar to King Tut's)
Steering wheel
Steering column
Chassis skeleton frame of a car
Oops, watch out for that curb—
BUMP!
Universal joint
Shock absorber
Tie rod end
Tire
Steering rack
Control arm
Tire air

STEERING / SUSPENSION

The steering system will get you exactly where you want to go, and your suspension makes the ride as smooth as possible. There are different types, including luxury air suspensions, but these are the tried 'n' true basics.

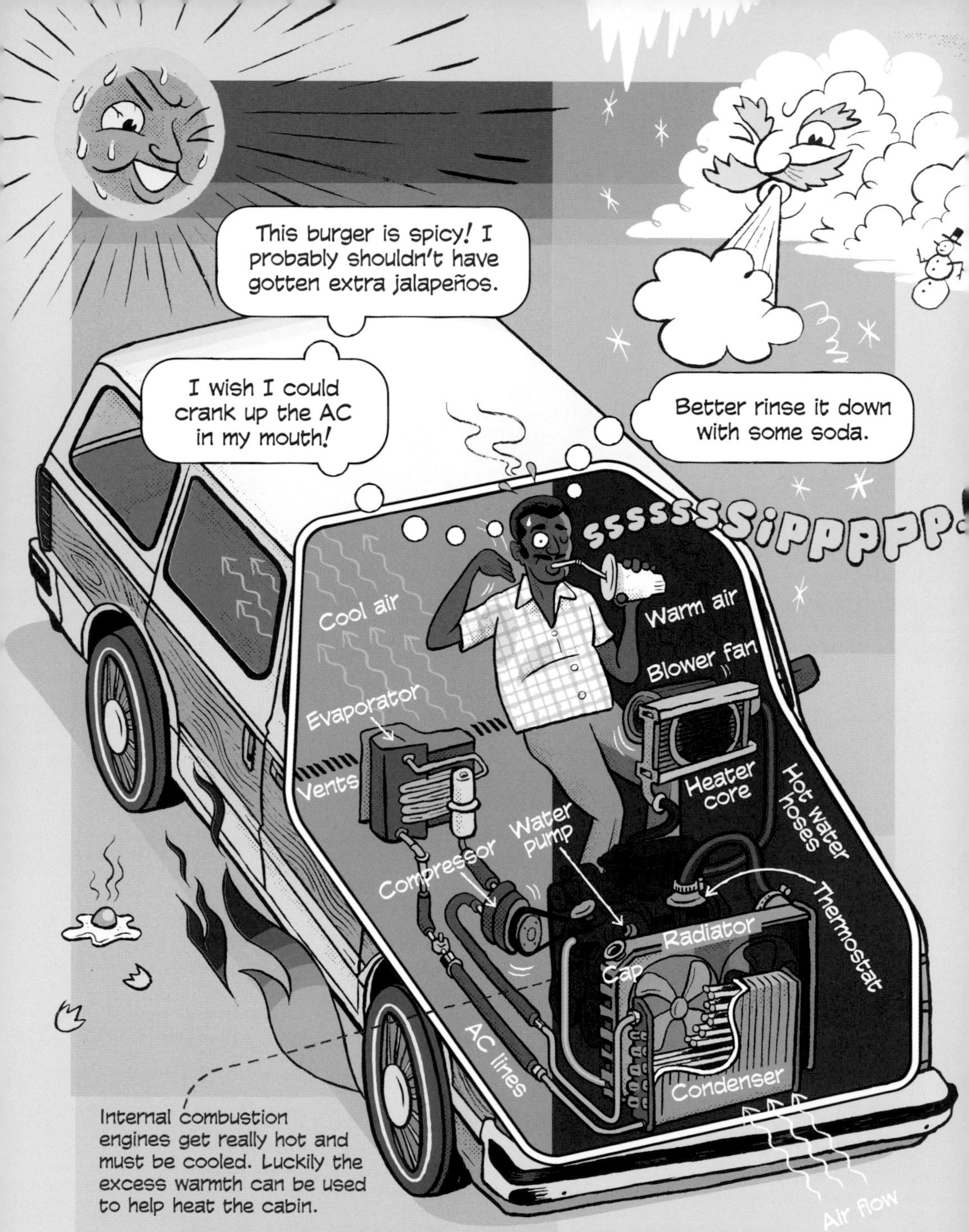
This burger is spicy! I probably shouldn't have gotten extra jalapeños.
I wish I could crank up the AC in my mouth!
Better rinse it down with some soda.
SSSSSSSiPPPPPP
Cool air
Warm air
Blower fan
Evaporator
Vents
Heater core
Hot water hoses
Water pump
Compressor
Thermostat
Radiator
Cap
AC lines
Condenser
Air flow
Internal combustion engines get really hot and must be cooled. Luckily the excess warmth can be used to help heat the cabin.

COOLING & HEATING

Even if the weather is brutal, you want your car to feel nice inside. The air conditioner and heating system pipe fluids around, which change the temperature and eventually become icy blasts or warm gusts of air blown into the cabin.

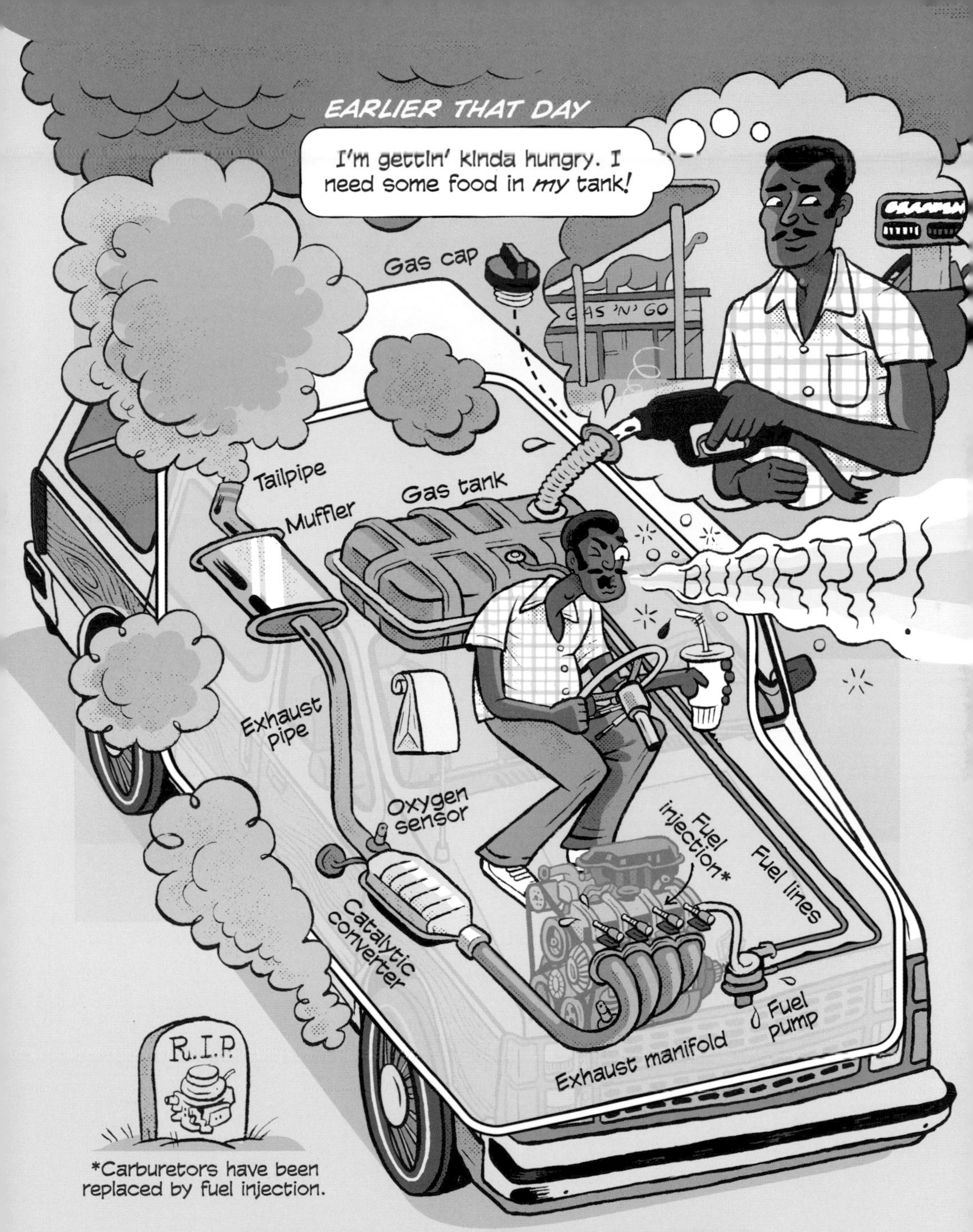
EARLIER THAT DAY
I'm gettin' kinda hungry. I need some food in *my* tank!
GAS 'N' GO
Gas cap
Tailpipe
Gas tank
Muffler
BURRRP!
Exhaust pipe
Oxygen sensor
Fuel injection*
Fuel lines
Catalytic converter
Fuel pump
Exhaust manifold
R.I.P.
*Carburetors have been replaced by fuel injection.

FUEL & EXHAUST

A car is like a human body: Fuel goes in and waste comes out. Energy is created, but much of it goes up in smoke. There have been improvements to make gas-burning engines less harmful and wasteful, but it's exhausting.

STROKE 4: EXHAUST

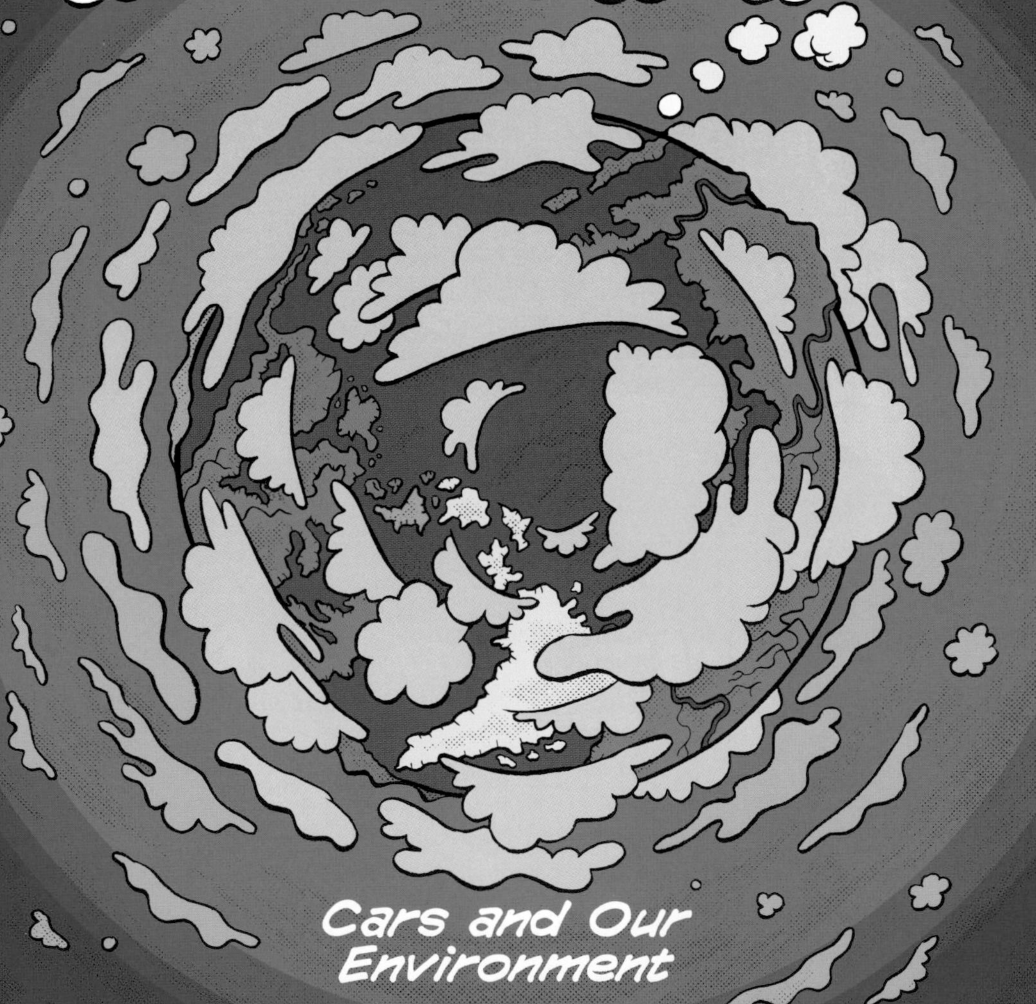

Cars and Our Environment

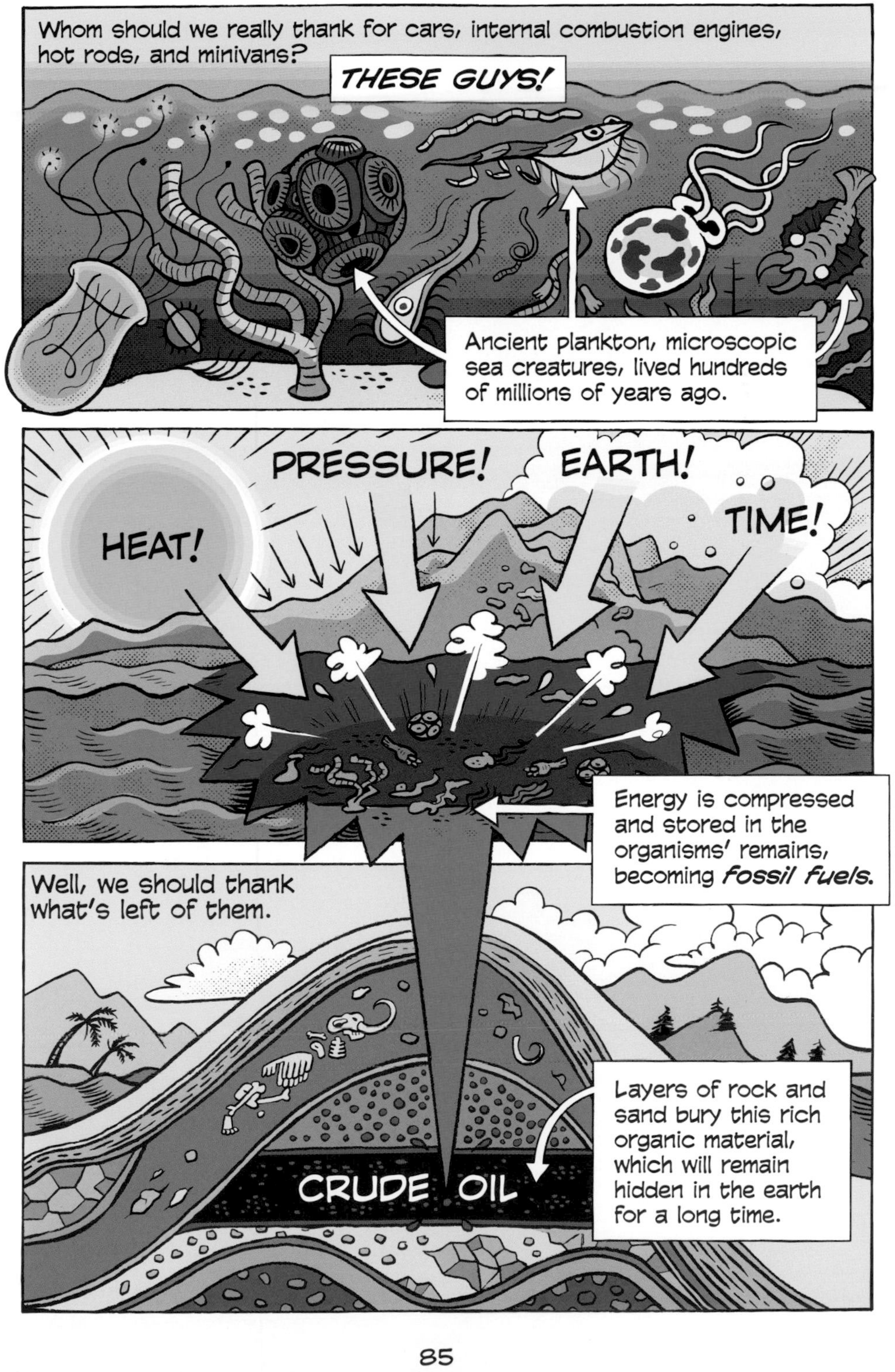
Whom should we really thank for cars, internal combustion engines, hot rods, and minivans?
THESE GUYS!
Ancient plankton, microscopic sea creatures, lived hundreds of millions of years ago.
PRESSURE!
EARTH!
HEAT!
TIME!
Energy is compressed and stored in the organisms' remains, becoming *fossil fuels*.
Well, we should thank what's left of them.
Layers of rock and sand bury this rich organic material, which will remain hidden in the earth for a long time.
CRUDE OIL

Crude oil was originally discovered by ancient peoples at natural seepages.

Known as *bitumen*, this sticky black stuff was immediately useful.

GLORP!

Mesopotamians used it to build boats, buildings, and roads.

Egyptians used it to embalm their mummies.

By the early 1800s, oil becomes less crude...

Kerosene

...replacing whale blubber as the main source of lamp oil.

Whew!

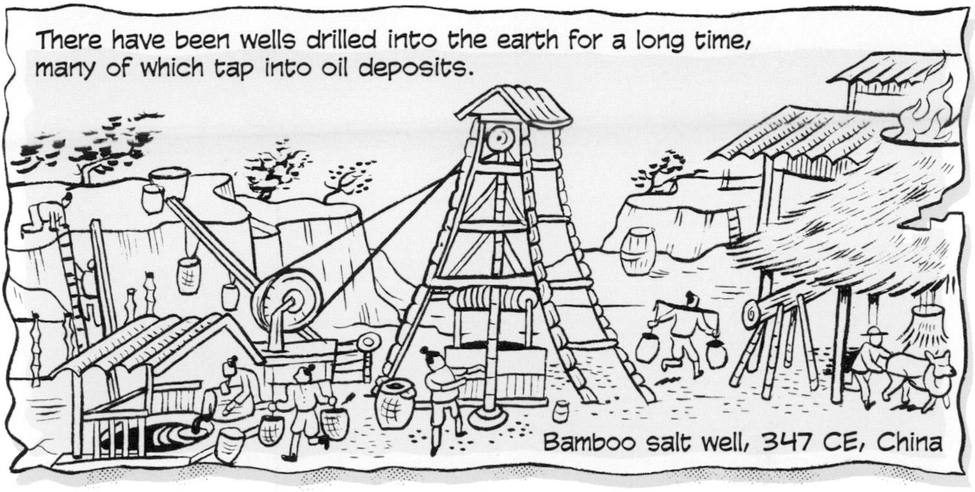
There have been wells drilled into the earth for a long time, many of which tap into oil deposits.
Bamboo salt well, 347 CE, China

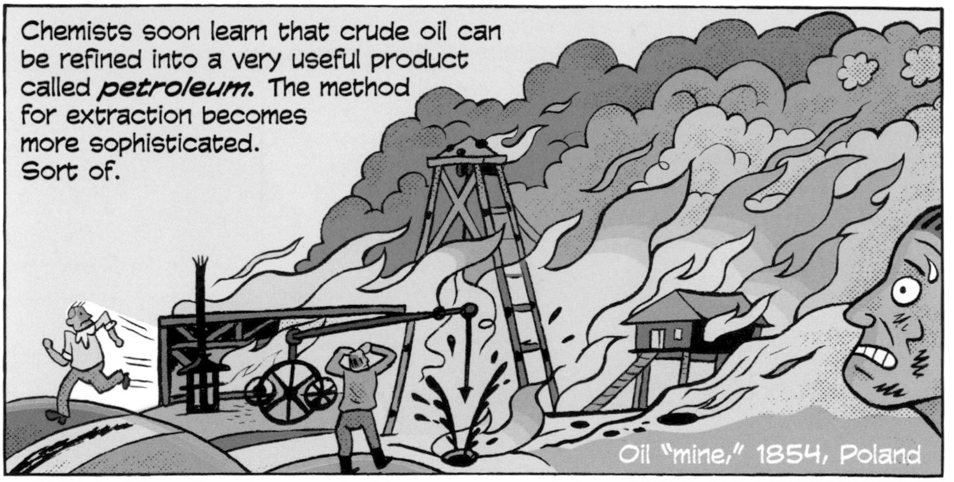
Chemists soon learn that crude oil can be refined into a very useful product called *petroleum.* The method for extraction becomes more sophisticated. Sort of.
Oil "mine," 1854, Poland

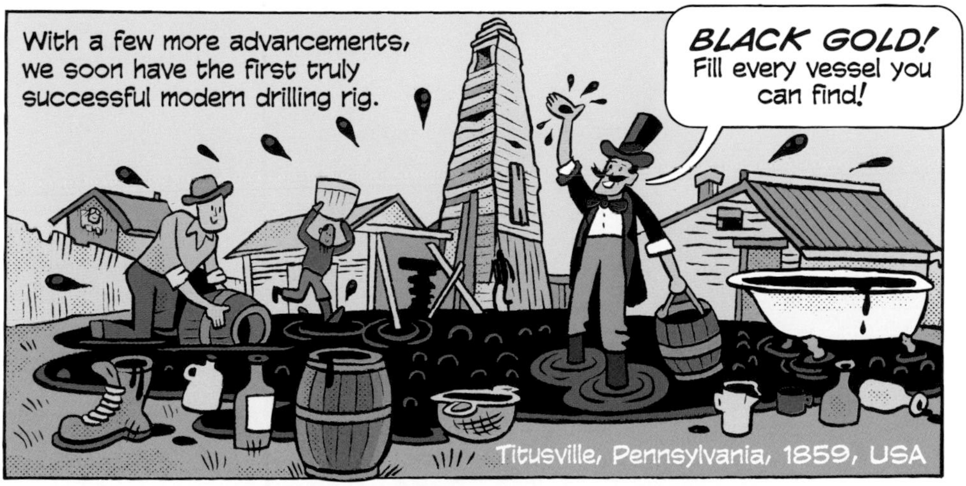
With a few more advancements, we soon have the first truly successful modern drilling rig.
BLACK GOLD! Fill every vessel you can find!
Titusville, Pennsylvania, 1859, USA

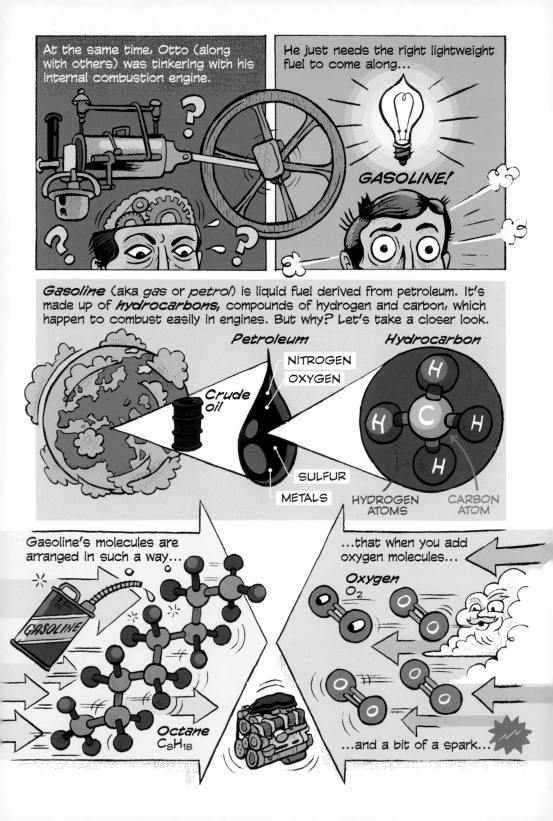

At the same time, Otto (along with others) was tinkering with his internal combustion engine.

He just needs the right lightweight fuel to come along...

GASOLINE!

Gasoline (aka gas or petrol) is liquid fuel derived from petroleum. It's made up of *hydrocarbons,* compounds of hydrogen and carbon, which happen to combust easily in engines. But why? Let's take a closer look.

Petroleum

Hydrocarbon

Crude oil

NITROGEN
OXYGEN

SULFUR
METALS

H
H   C   H
H

HYDROGEN ATOMS

CARBON ATOM

Gasoline's molecules are arranged in such a way...

GASOLINE

Octane
C_8H_{18}

...that when you add oxygen molecules...

Oxygen
O_2

...and a bit of a spark...

COMBUSTION!

The molecules recombine. Heat and light are released.

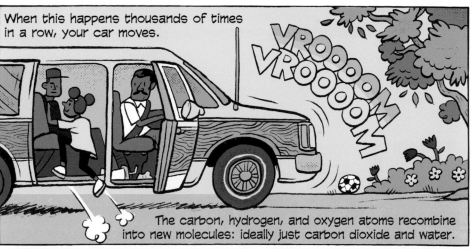

When this happens thousands of times in a row, your car moves.

VROOOOM VROOOOM

The carbon, hydrogen, and oxygen atoms recombine into new molecules: ideally just carbon dioxide and water.

But engines are inefficient, combustion is often incomplete, and the result is less-than-ideal exhaust:

Smog

Ozone (O_3)

Carbon monoxide (CO)

Soot

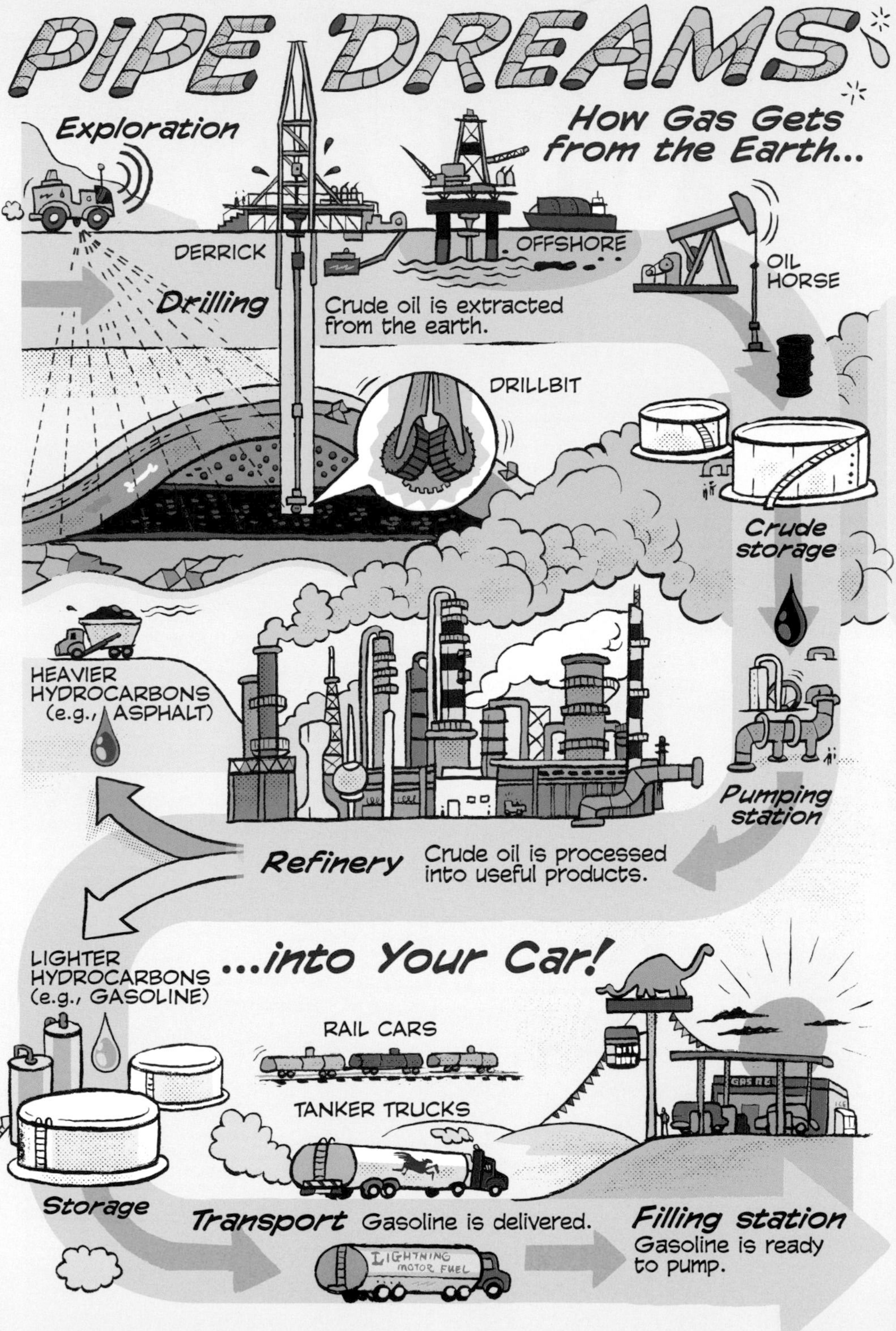
PIPE DREAMS
How Gas Gets from the Earth...
Exploration
DERRICK
OFFSHORE
OIL HORSE
Drilling
Crude oil is extracted from the earth.
DRILLBIT
Crude storage
HEAVIER HYDROCARBONS (e.g., ASPHALT)
Pumping station
Refinery
Crude oil is processed into useful products.
LIGHTER HYDROCARBONS (e.g., GASOLINE)
...into Your Car!
RAIL CARS
TANKER TRUCKS
GAS
Storage
Transport
Gasoline is delivered.
Filling station
Gasoline is ready to pump.
LIGHTNING MOTOR FUEL

GAS STATIONS Past & Present

1888: Bertha Benz's pit stop at a village pharmacy makes it history's first "gas station."

Apotheke

1890s: Motorists usually fill up at roadside hardware stores or blacksmith shops.

BLACKSMITH

1900s: Bowser's "Self-Measuring Gasoline Storage Pump" becomes widely adopted.

GLUG GLUG

1913: The first purpose-built drive-in gas station opens in Pittsburgh.

GOOD GULF GASOLINE

Now: Here's how a typical modern gas station works:

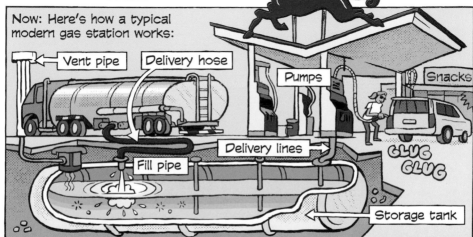

Vent pipe

Delivery hose

Pumps

Snacks

Delivery lines

Fill pipe

CLUG CLUG

Storage tank

KEEP ON

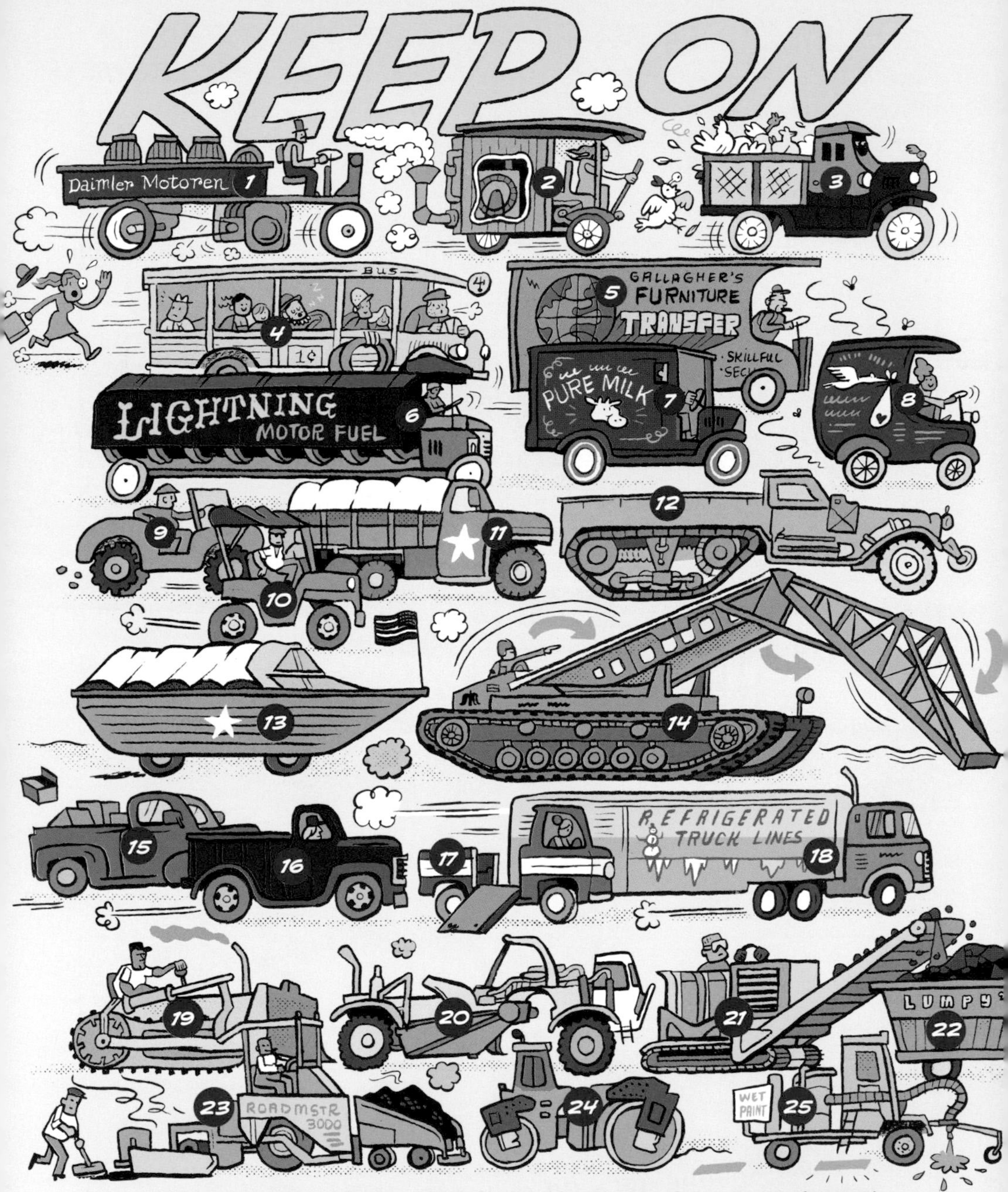
Daimler Motoren
BUS
1¢
GALLAGHER'S FURNITURE TRANSFER
SKILLFUL
LIGHTNING MOTOR FUEL
PURE MILK
REFRIGERATED TRUCK LINES
ROADMSTR 3000
WET PAINT
LUMPY

1 Earliest gas-powered truck (1896) *2* Czech NW First Truck (1899) *3* Model T retrofitted with hauling box (1913) *4* Chevy omnibus (1926) *5* GMC electric moving truck *6* Oil truck *7* Milk truck *8* Laundry truck *9* WWII Ford Pygmy *10* Jeep *11* Army truck *12* Soviet half-track *13* DUKW amphibious vehicle (aka *Duck*) *14* *Brückenleger* (bridgelayer) *15* Dodge Power Wagon, first civilian 4x4 *16* First Ford F-series truck *17* Corvair rampside *18* "Thermo King" refrigerated Mack 18-wheeler *19* Bulldozer *20* Tractor-scraper *21* Rock crusher *22* Dump truck *23* Asphalt mixer, spreader, and paver *24* Steamroller *25* Sign-painting truck

TRUCKIN'!

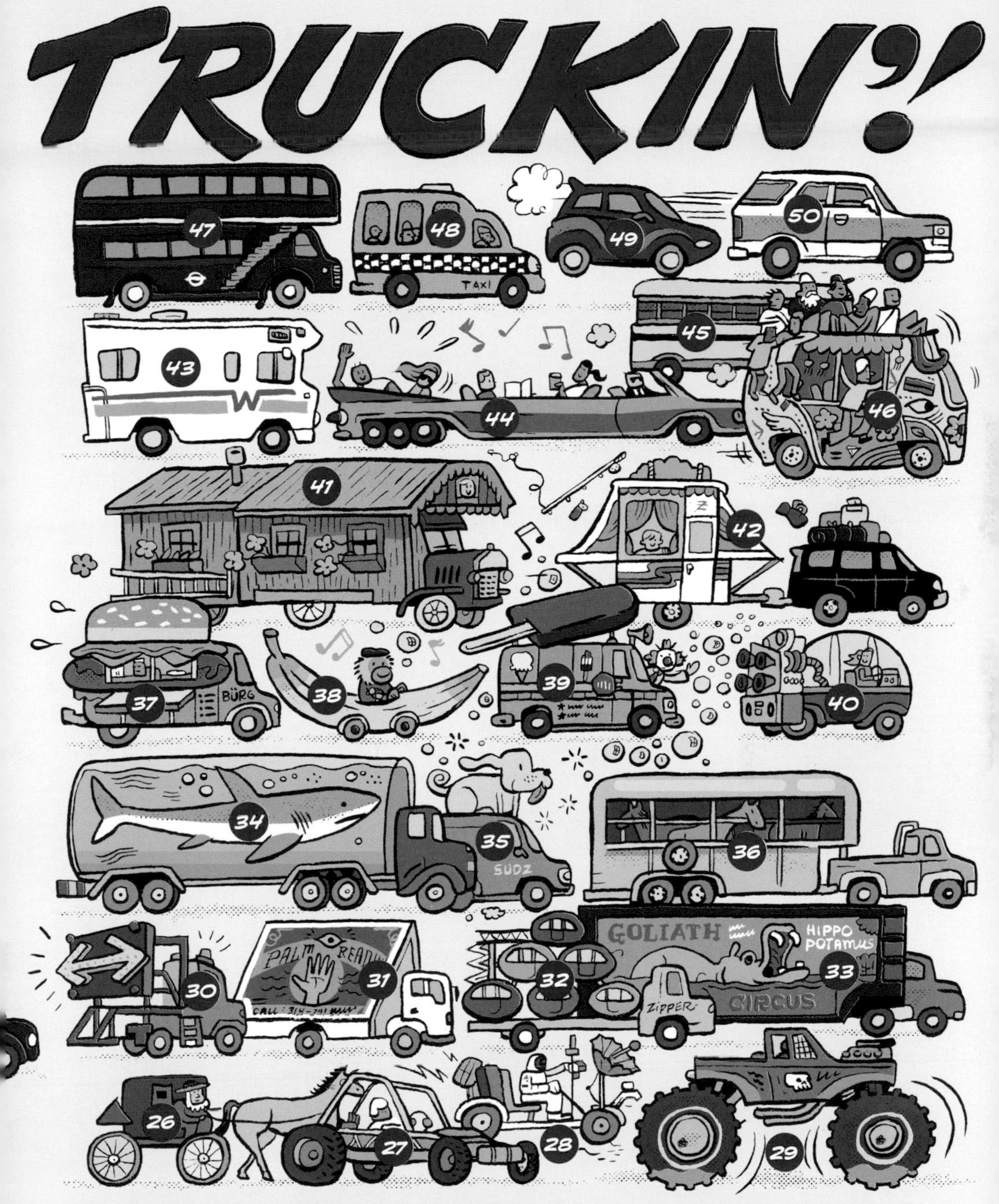

TAXI
BÜRG
SUDZ
GOLIATH
HIPPO POTAMUS
CIRCUS
ZIPPER

26 Horse and buggy **27** Dune buggy **28** Moon buggy (electric) **29** Monster truck
30 Blinking arrow **31** Moving billboard **32** Carnival carrier **33** Circus truck
34 Aquarium truck **35** Mobile pet-grooming vehicle **36** Horse trailer
37 Food truck **38** Bananamobile **39** Ice cream truck **40** Bubble bus
41 Model T cottage-on-wheels (early mobile home) **42** Pop-up camper
43 Winnebago motorhome **44** Limousine **45** Schoolbus **46** Pakistani bus
47 Double-decker bus **48** Shuttle-bus taxi **49** Crossover vehicle **50** SUV

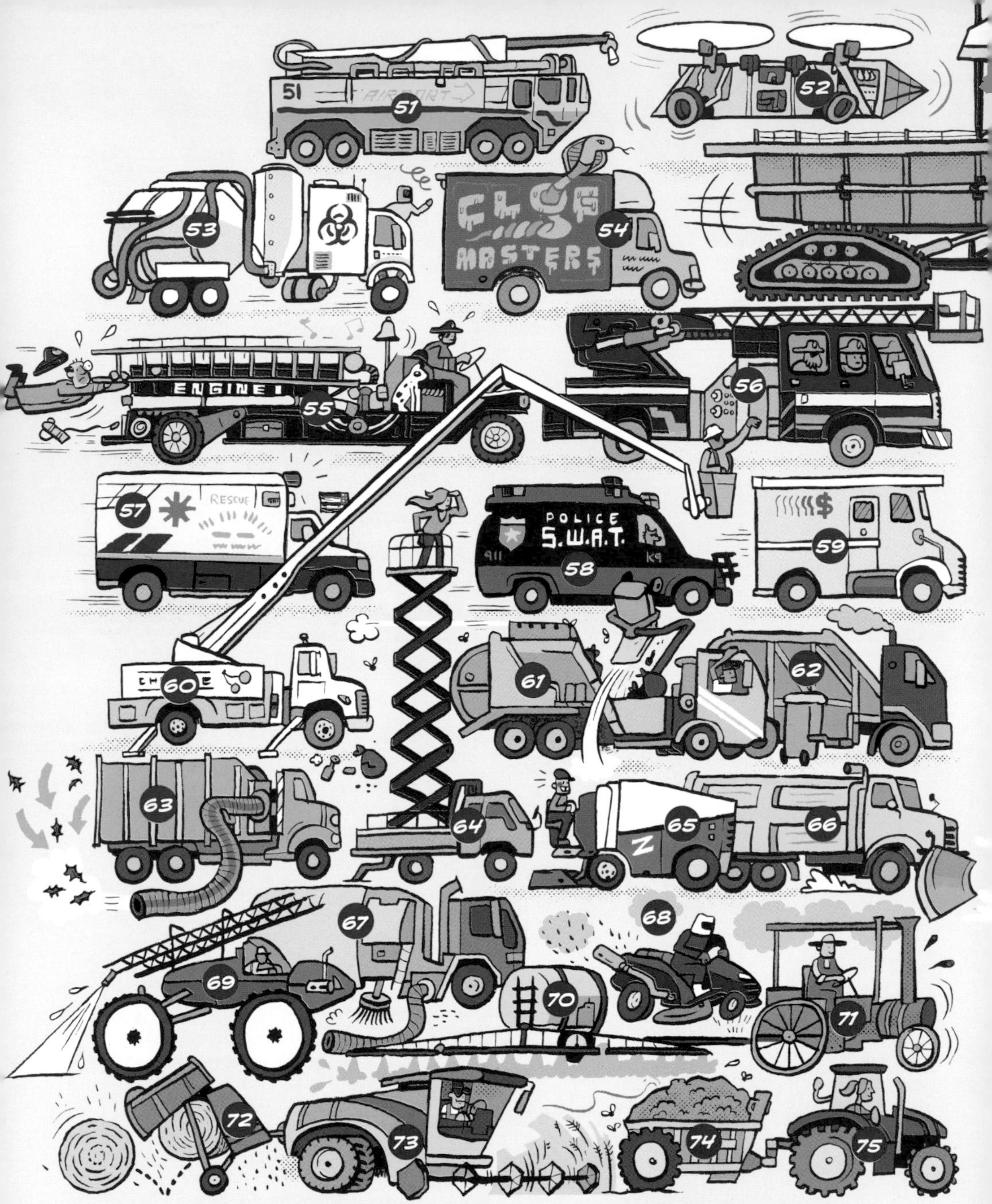
51
AIRPORT
CLOG MASTERS
ENGINE 1
RESCUE
POLICE
S.W.A.T.
911
K9

51 Airport emergency vehicle *52* Black Knight helicopter-truck hybrid
53 Hazardous waste disposal truck *54* Plumbing service truck
55 First horseless fire engine (1905) *56* Tower ladder firetruck
57 Ambulance *58* Police SWAT van *59* Armored cash transport
60 Bucket truck (aka *cherry picker*) *61* Garbage truck *62* Recycling truck
63 Leaf vacuum truck *64* Scissor lift *65* Ice resurfacer *66* Snowplow
67 Street sweeper *68* Mean mower (world's fastest lawn mower, 186 km/h, 116mph)
69 Irrigation truck *70* Fertilizer sprayer *71* Antique steam tractor
72 Hay baler *73* Combine harvester *74* Manure spreader *75* Tractor

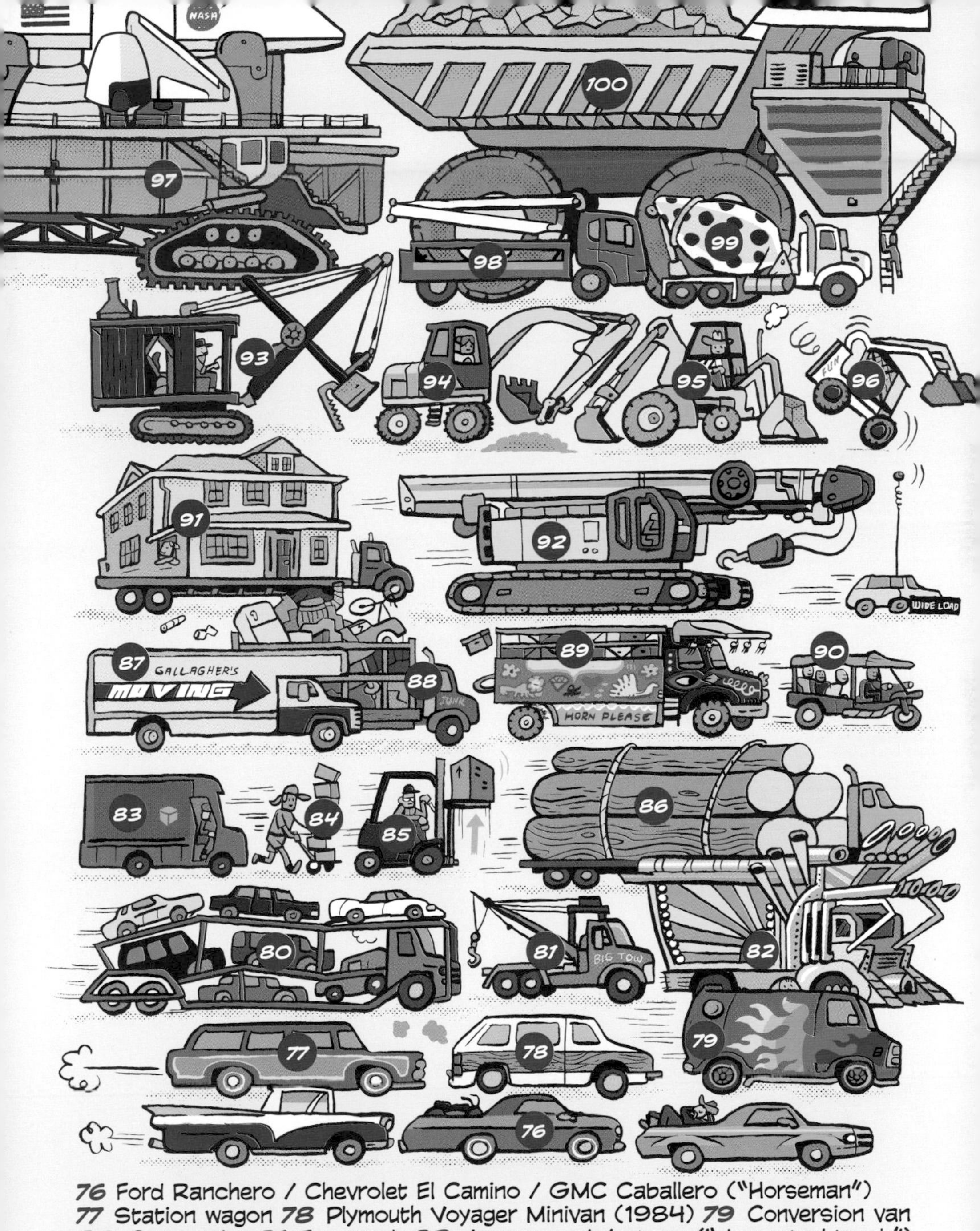
NASA
100
97
98
99
93
94
95
FUN
96
91
92
WIDE LOAD
87
GALLAGHER'S
MOVING
88
JUNK
89
HORN PLEASE
90
83
84
85
86
80
81
BIG TOW
82
77
78
79
76

76 Ford Ranchero / Chevrolet El Camino / GMC Caballero ("Horseman")
77 Station wagon *78* Plymouth Voyager Minivan (1984) *79* Conversion van
80 Car carrier *81* Tow truck *82* Japanese *dekotora* ("decorated truck")
83 Delivery van *84* Hand truck *85* Forklift *86* Logging truck
87 Moving truck *88* Junk truck *89* Indian cargo truck *90* Tuk-tuk
91 House mover *92* Crawler crane with oversized-load escort vehicle
93 Steam shovel *94* Modern excavator *95* Backhoe *96* Skid steer
97 NASA crawler transport *98* Concrete boom pump *99* Concrete mixer
100 BelAZ 75710 ultra-class dump truck (world's largest truck size)

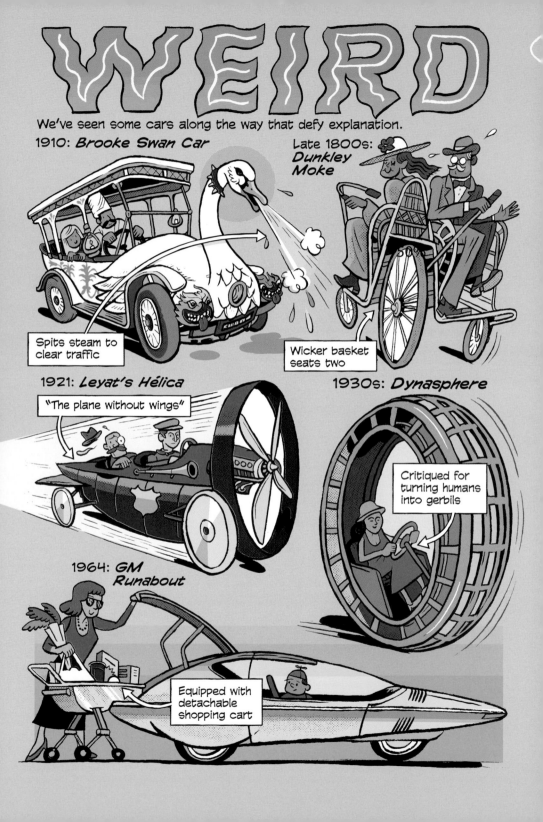

WEIRD

We've seen some cars along the way that defy explanation.

1910: *Brooke Swan Car*

Spits steam to clear traffic

Late 1800s: *Dunkley Moke*

Wicker basket seats two

1921: *Leyat's Hélica*

"The plane without wings"

1930s: *Dynasphere*

Critiqued for turning humans into gerbils

1964: *GM Runabout*

Equipped with detachable shopping cart

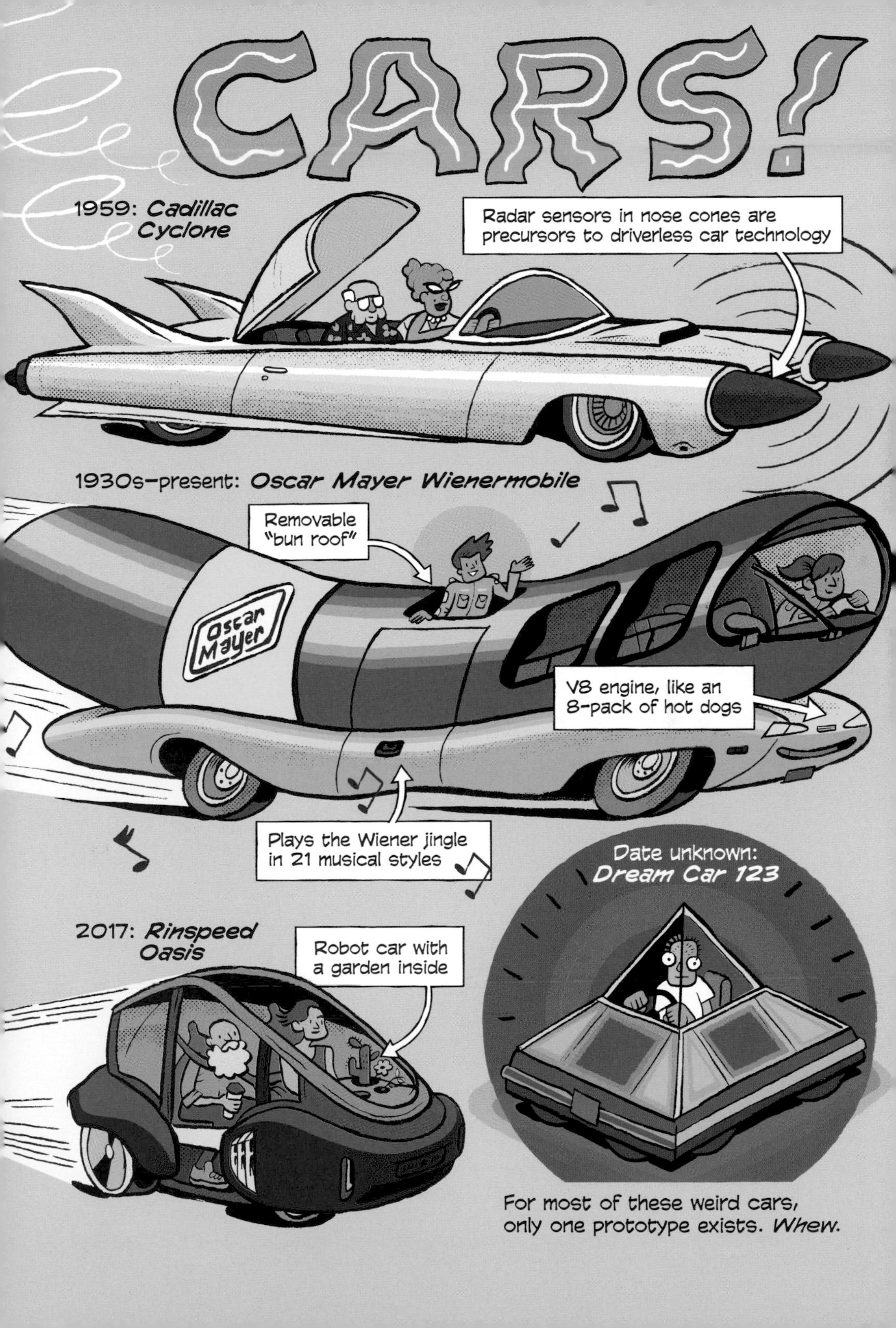
CARS!
1959: Cadillac Cyclone
Radar sensors in nose cones are precursors to driverless car technology
1930s–present: Oscar Mayer Wienermobile
Removable "bun roof"
Oscar Mayer
V8 engine, like an 8-pack of hot dogs
Plays the Wiener jingle in 21 musical styles
Date unknown: Dream Car 123
2017: Rinspeed Oasis
Robot car with a garden inside
For most of these weird cars, only one prototype exists. Whew.

EXTREME

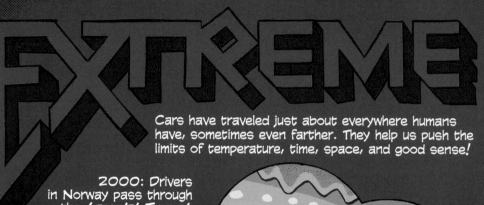

Cars have traveled just about everywhere humans have, sometimes even farther. They help us push the limits of temperature, time, space, and good sense!

2000: Drivers in Norway pass through the ***Lærdal Tunnel***. At 24.5 km (15.2 miles), it is the world's longest.

2010: Daredevil motorcyclist ***Mustafa Danger*** crosses a tightope 130 meters high!

2009: The robotic ***Benthic Rover*** crawls along the bottom of the ocean 4 km (2.5 miles) deep.

1958: ***Sir Edmund Hillary*** and his crew are the first to drive motorized vehicles to the South Pole.

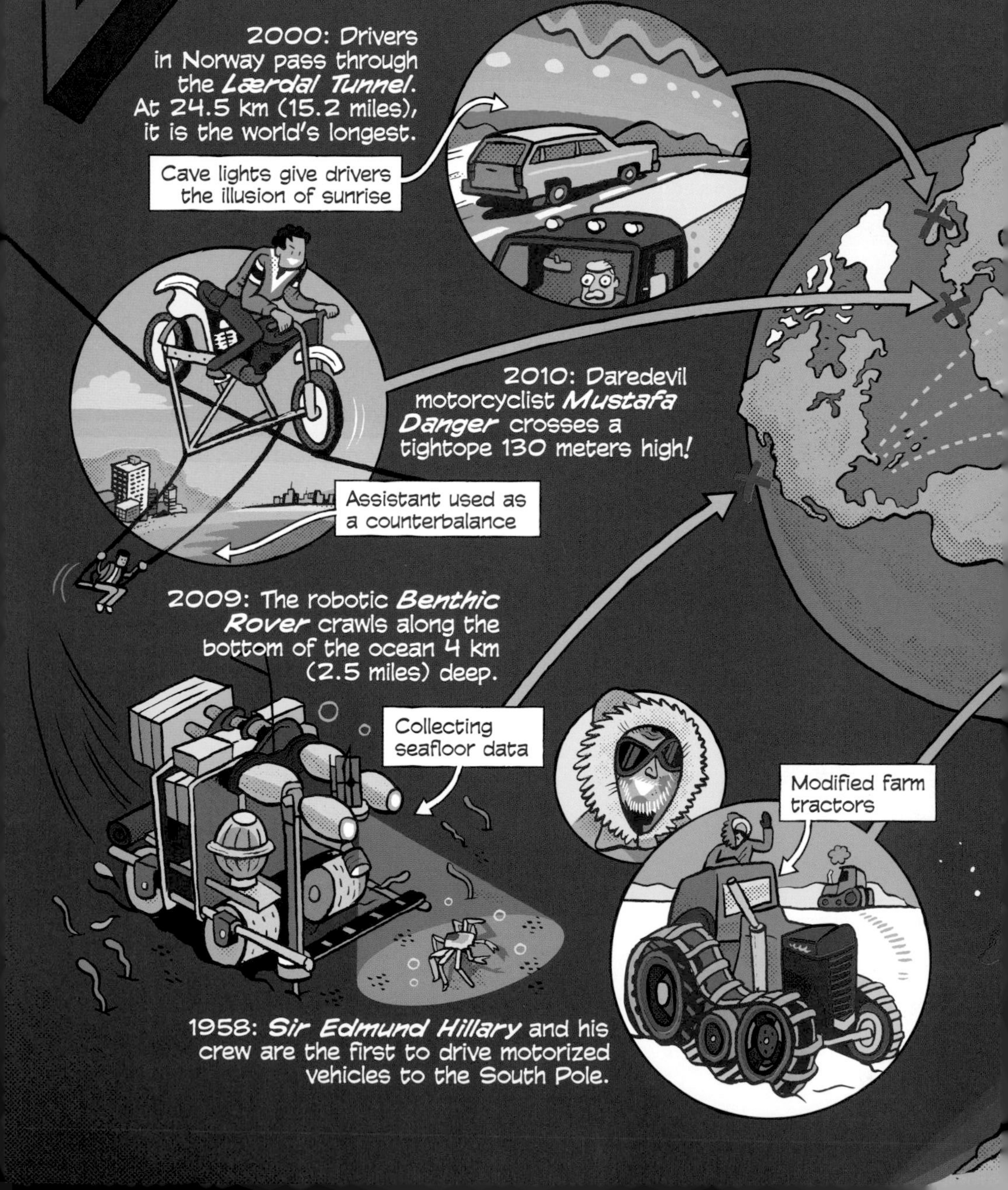
Cave lights give drivers the illusion of sunrise
Assistant used as a counterbalance
Collecting seafloor data
Modified farm tractors

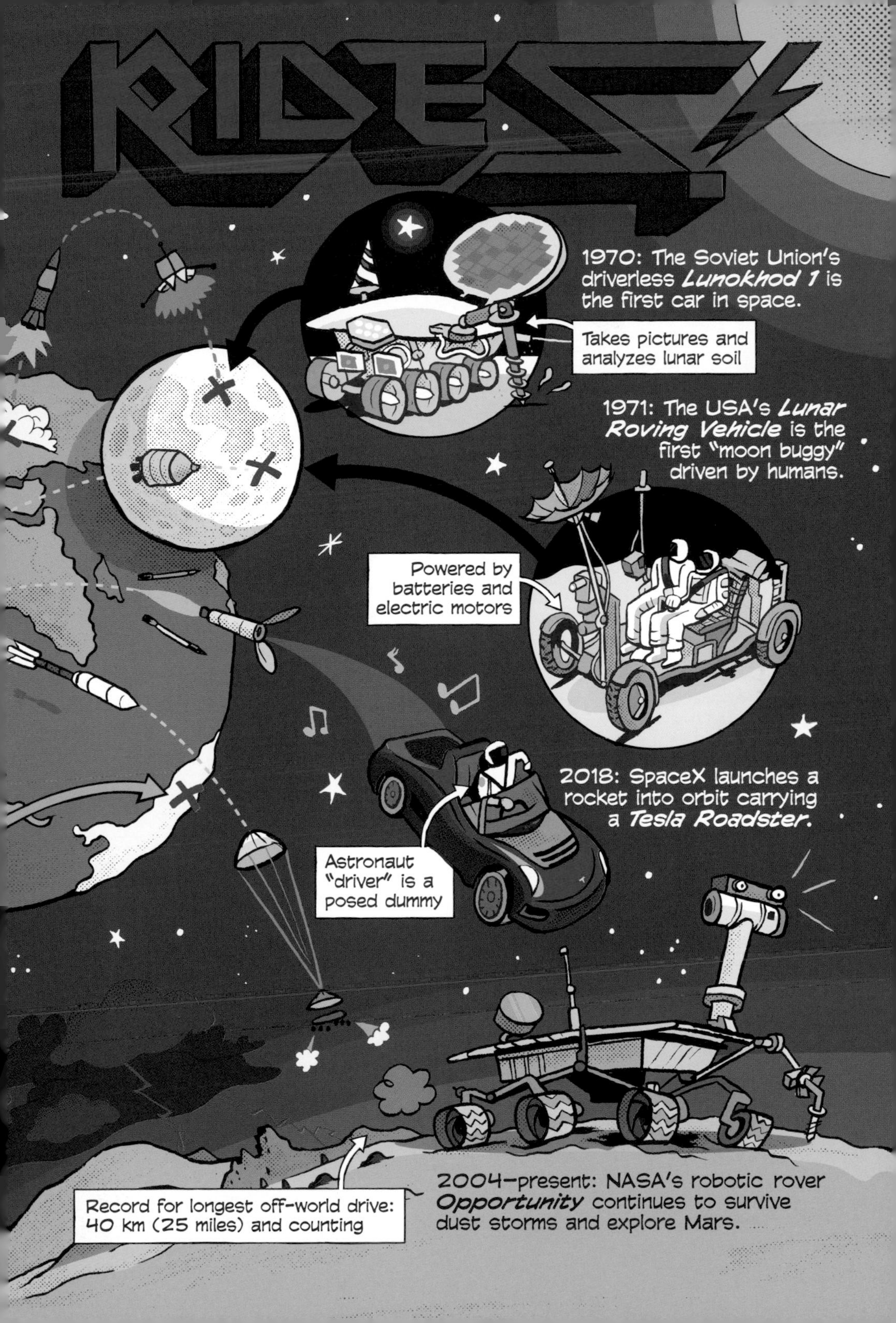
RIDES!
1970: The Soviet Union's driverless *Lunokhod 1* is the first car in space.
Takes pictures and analyzes lunar soil
1971: The USA's *Lunar Roving Vehicle* is the first "moon buggy" driven by humans.
Powered by batteries and electric motors
2018: SpaceX launches a rocket into orbit carrying a *Tesla Roadster*.
Astronaut "driver" is a posed dummy
2004–present: NASA's robotic rover *Opportunity* continues to survive dust storms and explore Mars.
Record for longest off-world drive: 40 km (25 miles) and counting

TIMELINE of AUTOMOTIVE SAFETY

Accidents, from minor fender benders to catastrophic crashes, are a fact of today's car-filled streets. Advancements over the years have tried to reduce their frequency or at least their impact.

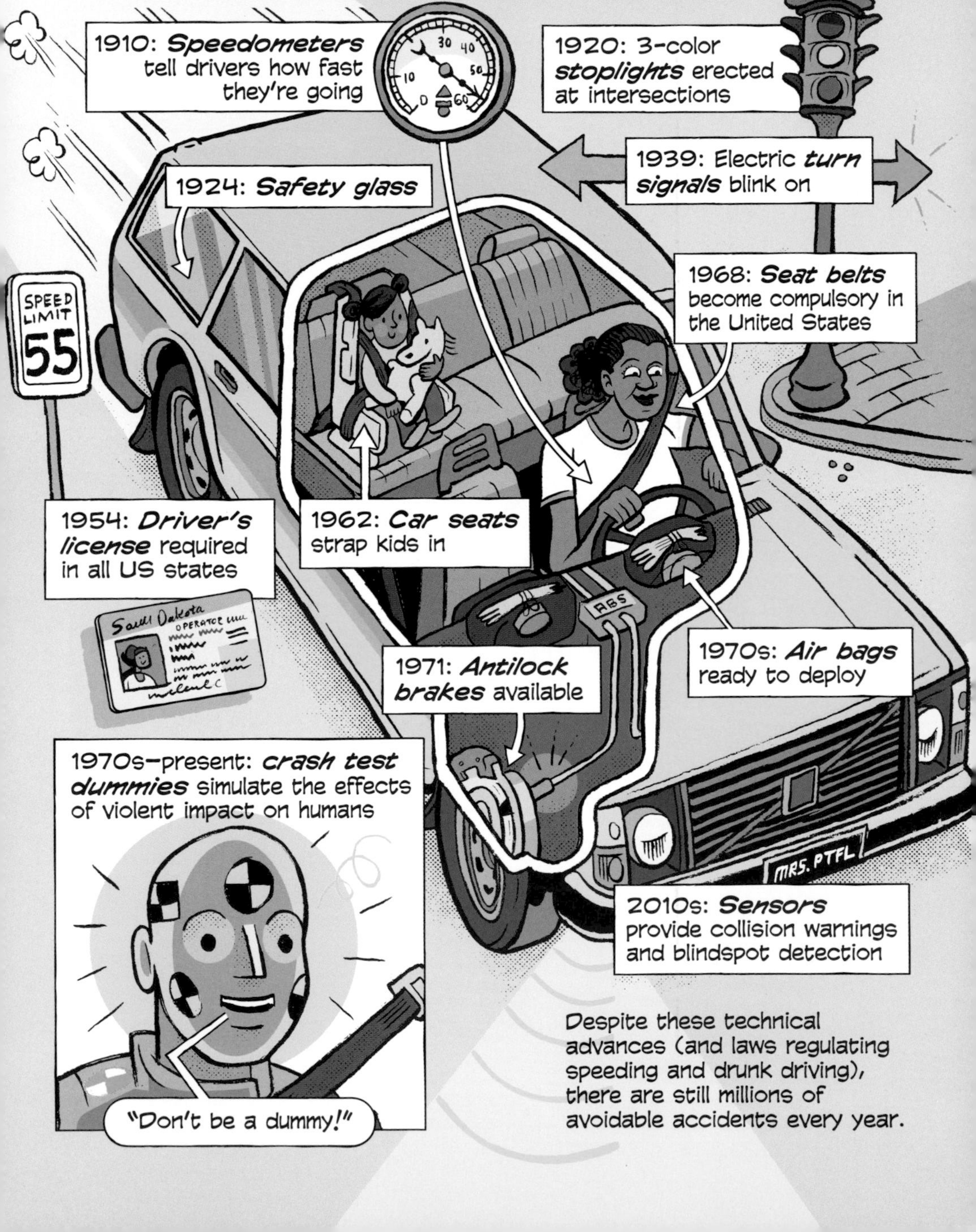
1910: *Speedometers* tell drivers how fast they're going
1920: 3-color *stoplights* erected at intersections
1924: *Safety glass*
1939: Electric *turn signals* blink on
1968: *Seat belts* become compulsory in the United States
SPEED LIMIT 55
1954: *Driver's license* required in all US states
1962: *Car seats* strap kids in
ABS
1971: *Antilock brakes* available
1970s: *Air bags* ready to deploy
1970s–present: *crash test dummies* simulate the effects of violent impact on humans
"Don't be a dummy!"
MRS. PTFL
2010s: *Sensors* provide collision warnings and blindspot detection
Despite these technical advances (and laws regulating speeding and drunk driving), there are still millions of avoidable accidents every year.

SCIENCE of SPEED!

We've covered combustion, but there is a lot more science-y stuff you could study to better understand your two-ton hunk of metal.

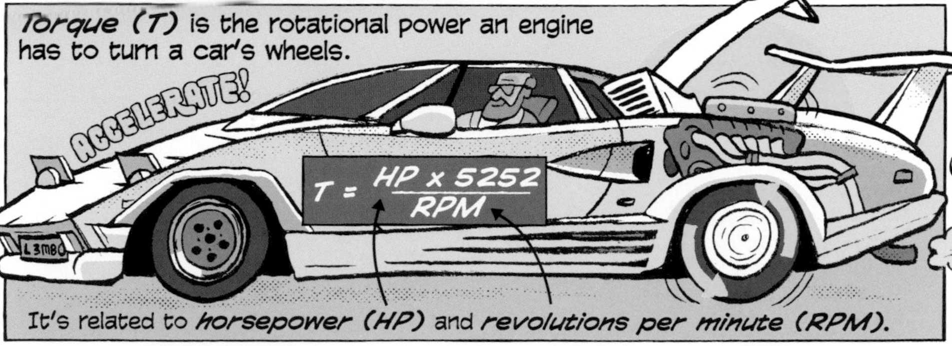

Torque (T) is the rotational power an engine has to turn a car's wheels.
ACCELERATE!
T = HP x 5252 / RPM
L3MBO
It's related to *horsepower (HP)* and *revolutions per minute (RPM)*.

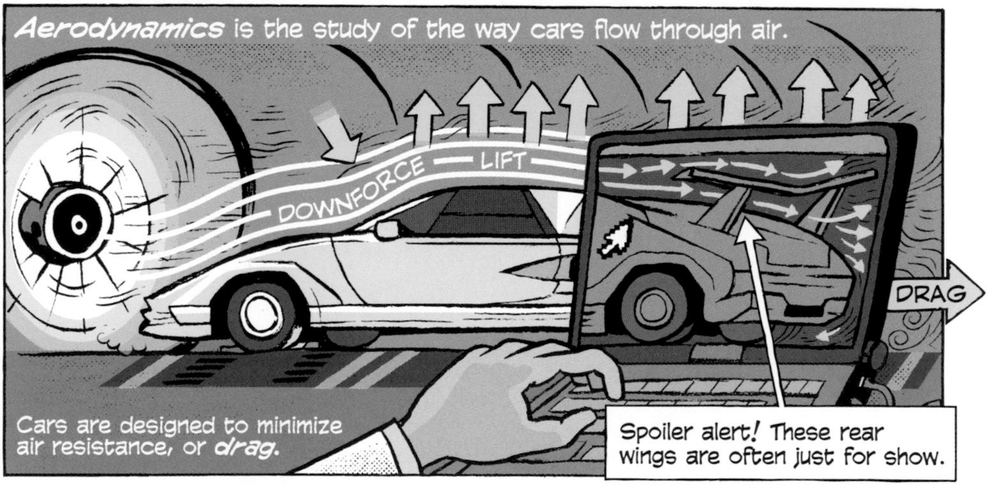

Aerodynamics is the study of the way cars flow through air.
DOWNFORCE
LIFT
DRAG
Cars are designed to minimize air resistance, or *drag*.
Spoiler alert! These rear wings are often just for show.

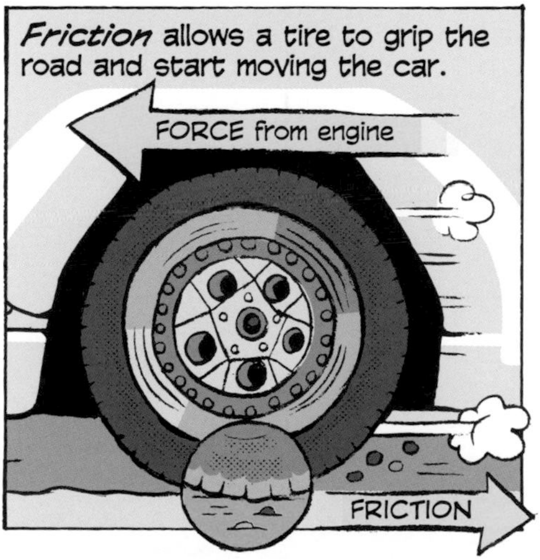

Friction allows a tire to grip the road and start moving the car.
FORCE from engine
FRICTION

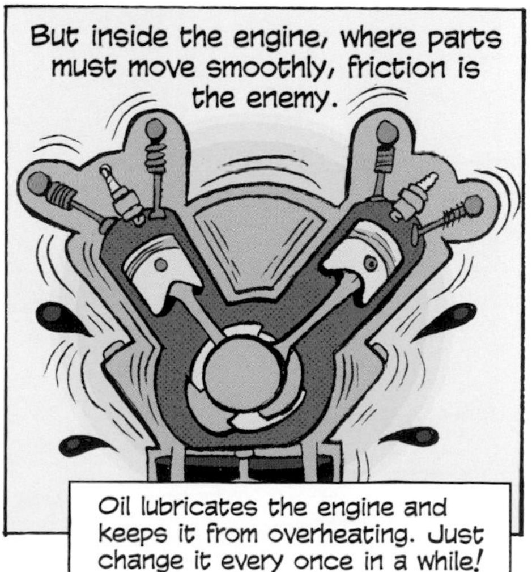

But inside the engine, where parts must move smoothly, friction is the enemy.
Oil lubricates the engine and keeps it from overheating. Just change it every once in a while!

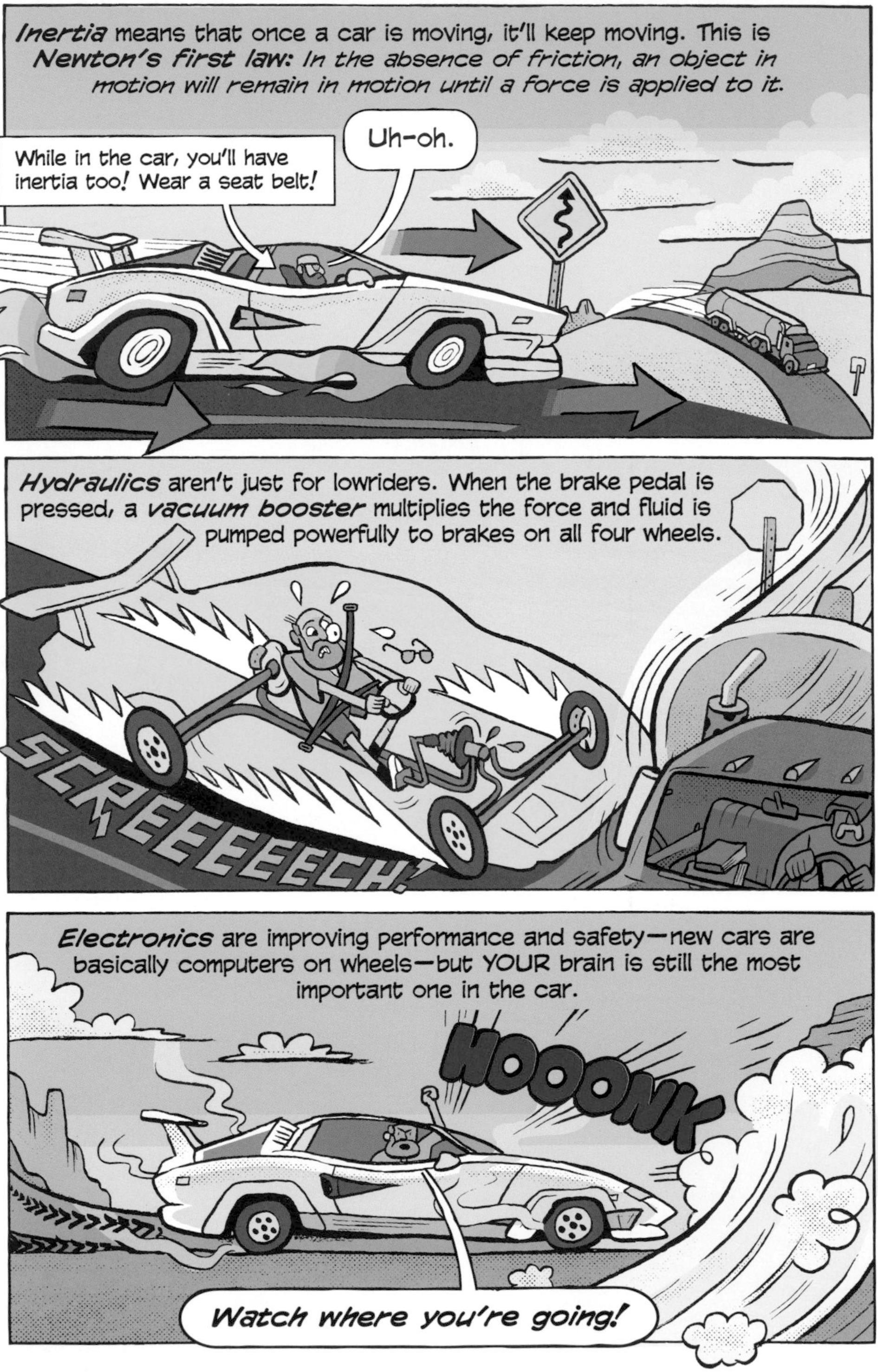

Inertia means that once a car is moving, it'll keep moving. This is ***Newton's first law:*** *In the absence of friction, an object in motion will remain in motion until a force is applied to it.*
While in the car, you'll have inertia too! Wear a seat belt!
Uh-oh.
Hydraulics aren't just for lowriders. When the brake pedal is pressed, a ***vacuum booster*** multiplies the force and fluid is pumped powerfully to brakes on all four wheels.
SCREEEEEEECH!
Electronics are improving performance and safety—new cars are basically computers on wheels—but YOUR brain is still the most important one in the car.
HOOONK
Watch where you're going!

HONK! — IF YOU WANT TO LEARN THE HISTORY OF CAR HORNS!

Around the turn of the century, the clip-clop of horses' hooves is replaced by a new "music" of the streets. Have a listen.

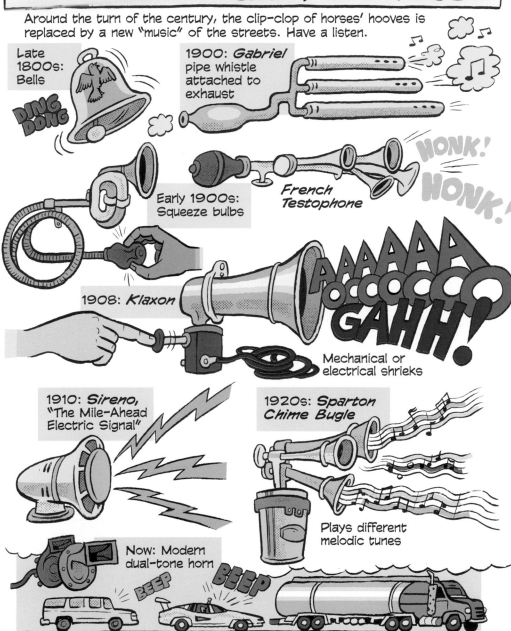

Late 1800s: Bells

DING DONG

1900: *Gabriel* pipe whistle attached to exhaust

Early 1900s: Squeeze bulbs

French Testophone

HONK! HONK!

1908: *Klaxon*

AAAAAA OOOOO GAHH!

Mechanical or electrical shrieks

1910: *Sireno, "The Mile-Ahead Electric Signal"*

1920s: *Sparton Chime Bugle*

Plays different melodic tunes

Now: Modern dual-tone horn

BEEP BEEP

As cars become more soundproof, horns must keep getting louder. Help reduce noise pollution by using your horn only in an emergency!

It's unthinkable now, but there was a time when you couldn't hear music, news, ball games, or podcasts in your car. Tune in to a...

SHORT HISTORY OF the CAR RADIO

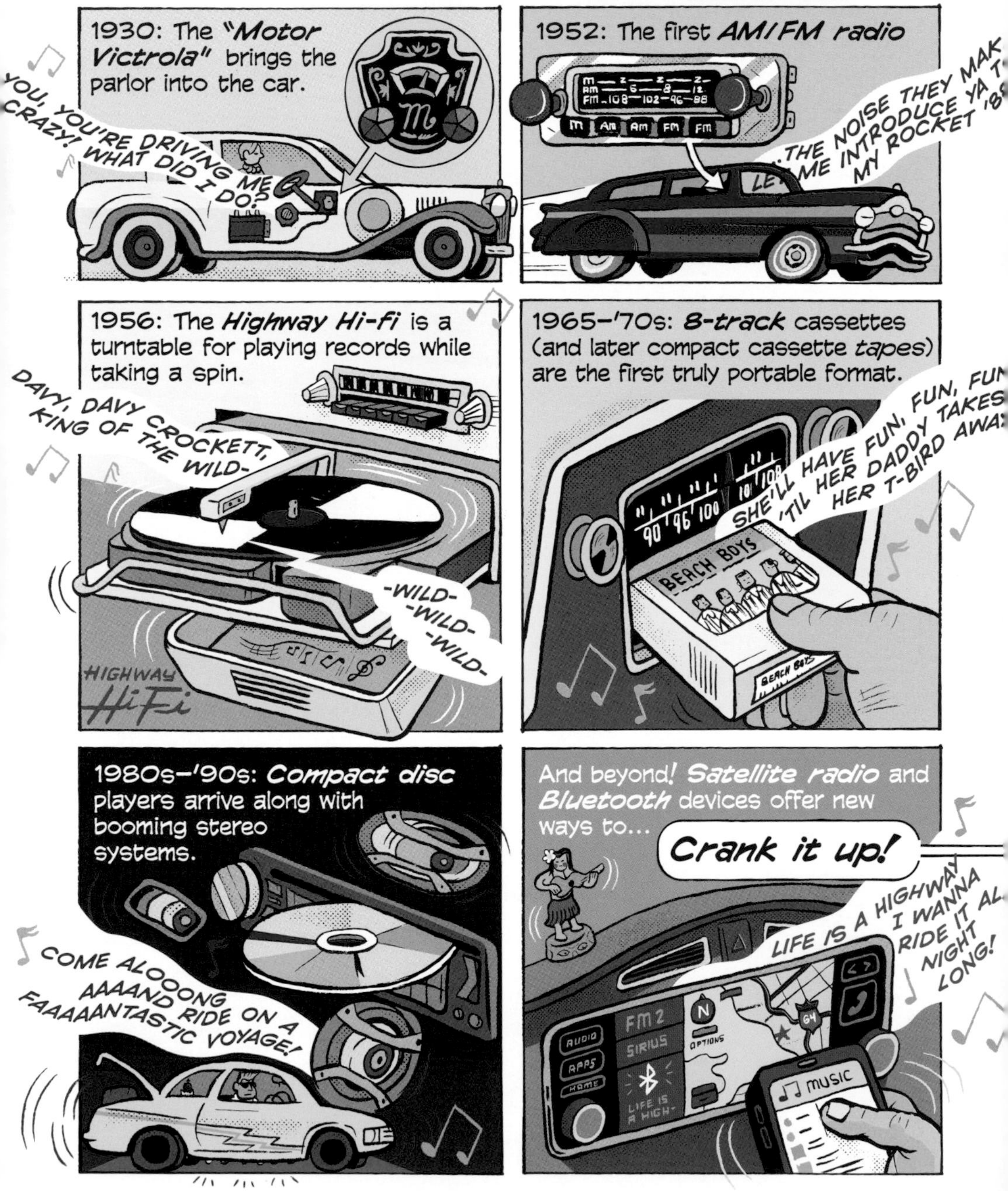

1930: The *"Motor Victrola"* brings the parlor into the car.
YOU, YOU'RE DRIVING ME CRAZY! WHAT DID I DO?
1952: The first *AM/FM radio*
...THE NOISE THEY MAK
LET ME INTRODUCE YA T
MY ROCKET '8
1956: The *Highway Hi-fi* is a turntable for playing records while taking a spin.
DAVY, DAVY CROCKETT, KING OF THE WILD-
-WILD- -WILD- -WILD-
HIGHWAY HiFi
1965–'70s: *8-track* cassettes (and later compact cassette *tapes*) are the first truly portable format.
SHE'LL HAVE FUN, FUN, FUN 'TIL HER DADDY TAKES HER T-BIRD AWA
BEACH BOYS
1980s–'90s: *Compact disc* players arrive along with booming stereo systems.
COME ALOOOONG AAAAAND RIDE ON A FAAAAANTASTIC VOYAGE!
And beyond! *Satellite radio* and *Bluetooth* devices offer new ways to...
Crank it up!
LIFE IS A HIGHWAY I WANNA RIDE IT AL NIGHT LONG!
FM 2
SIRIUS
LIFE IS A HIGH-
AUDIO
APPS
HOME
OPTIONS
MUSIC

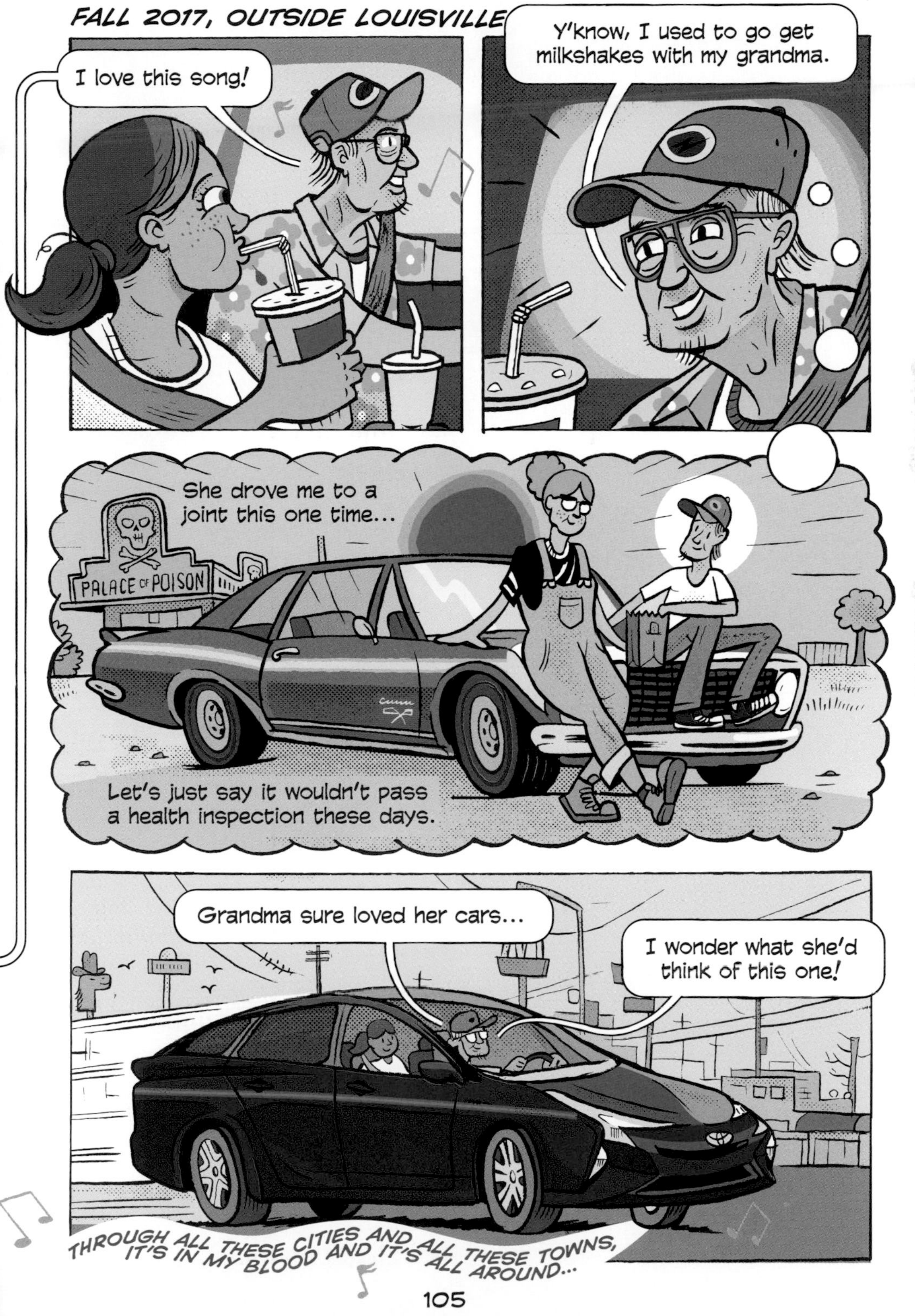
FALL 2017, OUTSIDE LOUISVILLE
I love this song!
Y'know, I used to go get milkshakes with my grandma.
She drove me to a joint this one time...
PALACE OF POISON
Let's just say it wouldn't pass a health inspection these days.
Grandma sure loved her cars...
I wonder what she'd think of this one!
THROUGH ALL THESE CITIES AND ALL THESE TOWNS, IT'S IN MY BLOOD AND IT'S ALL AROUND...

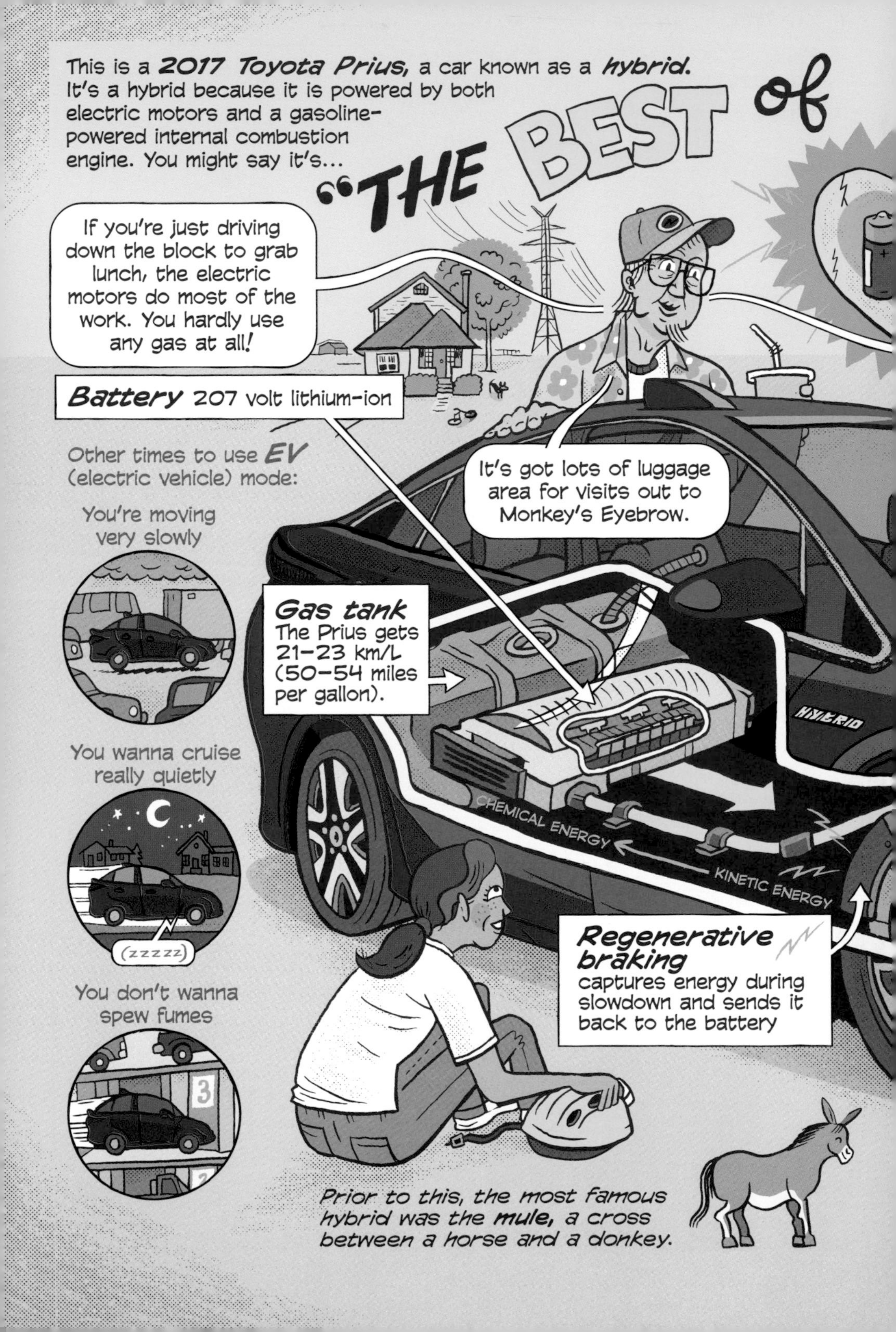
This is a 2017 Toyota Prius, a car known as a hybrid. It's a hybrid because it is powered by both electric motors and a gasoline-powered internal combustion engine. You might say it's...
"THE BEST of
If you're just driving down the block to grab lunch, the electric motors do most of the work. You hardly use any gas at all!
Battery 207 volt lithium-ion
Other times to use EV (electric vehicle) mode:
You're moving very slowly
You wanna cruise really quietly
(zzzzz)
You don't wanna spew fumes
3
It's got lots of luggage area for visits out to Monkey's Eyebrow.
Gas tank The Prius gets 21–23 km/L (50–54 miles per gallon).
HYBRID
CHEMICAL ENERGY
KINETIC ENERGY
Regenerative braking captures energy during slowdown and sends it back to the battery
Prior to this, the most famous hybrid was the mule, a cross between a horse and a donkey.

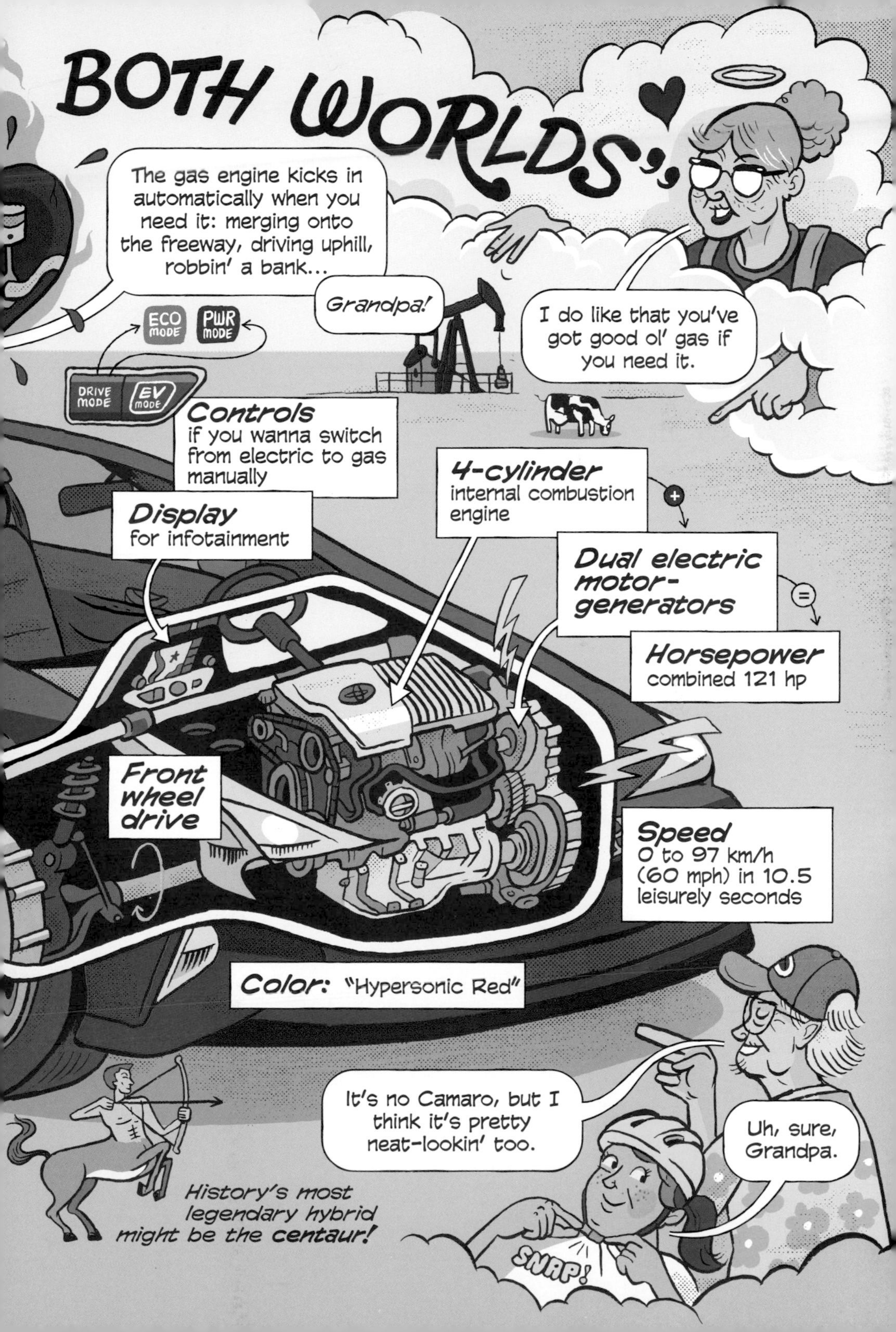
BOTH WORLDS,
The gas engine kicks in automatically when you need it: merging onto the freeway, driving uphill, robbin' a bank…
Grandpa!
I do like that you've got good ol' gas if you need it.
ECO MODE
PWR MODE
DRIVE MODE
EV MODE
Controls if you wanna switch from electric to gas manually
4-cylinder internal combustion engine
+
Display for infotainment
Dual electric motor-generators
=
Horsepower combined 121 hp
Front wheel drive
Speed 0 to 97 km/h (60 mph) in 10.5 leisurely seconds
Color: "Hypersonic Red"
It's no Camaro, but I think it's pretty neat-lookin' too.
Uh, sure, Grandpa.
History's most legendary hybrid might be the centaur!
SNAP!

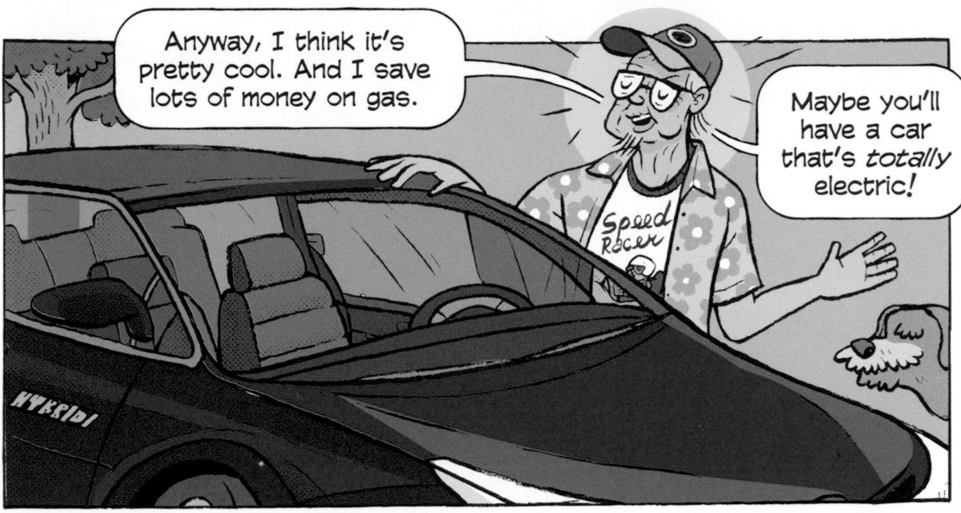
Anyway, I think it's pretty cool. And I save lots of money on gas.
Maybe you'll have a car that's *totally* electric!
Speed Racer
HYBRID

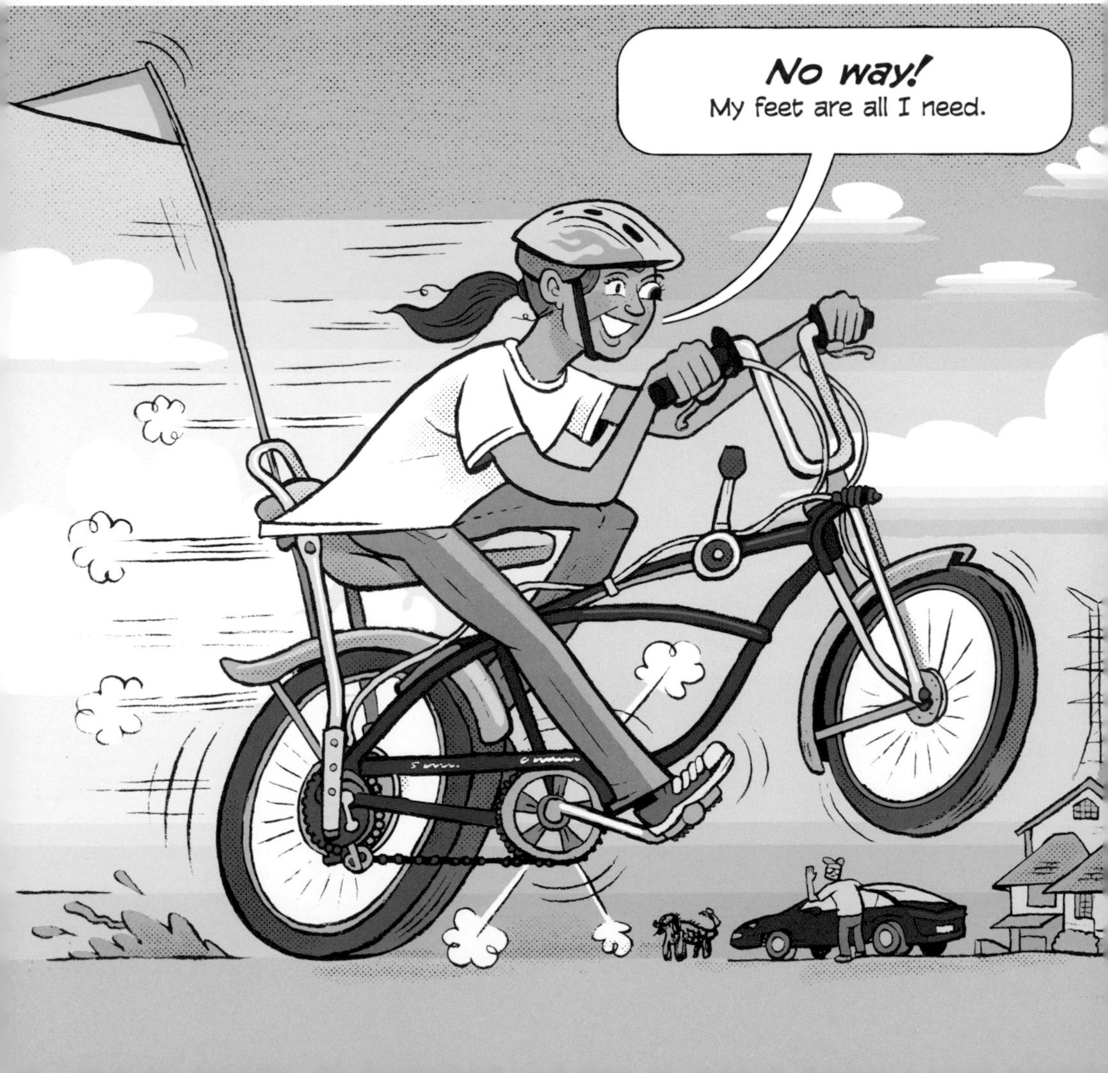
No way! My feet are all I need.

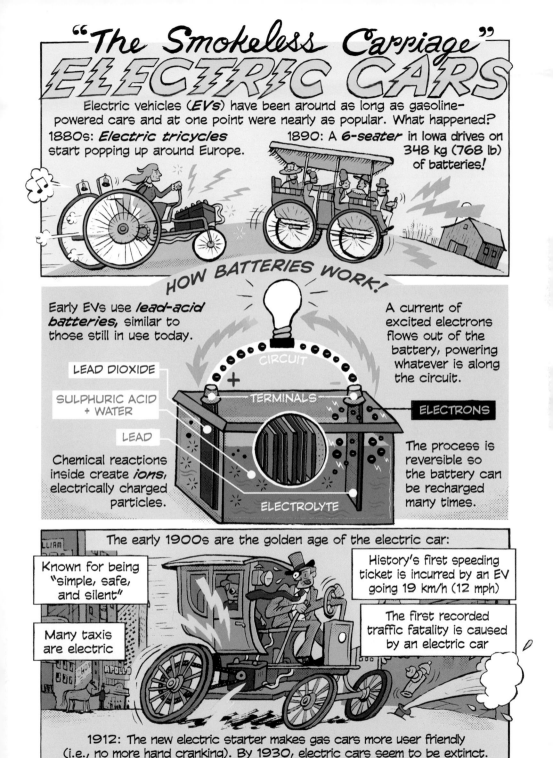

"The Smokeless Carriage"
ELECTRIC CARS

Electric vehicles (**EVs**) have been around as long as gasoline-powered cars and at one point were nearly as popular. What happened?

1880s: *Electric tricycles* start popping up around Europe.

1890: A *6-seater* in Iowa drives on 348 kg (768 lb) of batteries!

HOW BATTERIES WORK!

Early EVs use *lead-acid batteries*, similar to those still in use today.

LEAD DIOXIDE

SULPHURIC ACID + WATER

LEAD

Chemical reactions inside create *ions*, electrically charged particles.

CIRCUIT

TERMINALS

ELECTROLYTE

ELECTRONS

A current of excited electrons flows out of the battery, powering whatever is along the circuit.

The process is reversible so the battery can be recharged many times.

The early 1900s are the golden age of the electric car:

Known for being "simple, safe, and silent"

Many taxis are electric

History's first speeding ticket is incurred by an EV going 19 km/h (12 mph)

The first recorded traffic fatality is caused by an electric car

1912: The new electric starter makes gas cars more user friendly (i.e., no more hand cranking). By 1930, electric cars seem to be extinct.

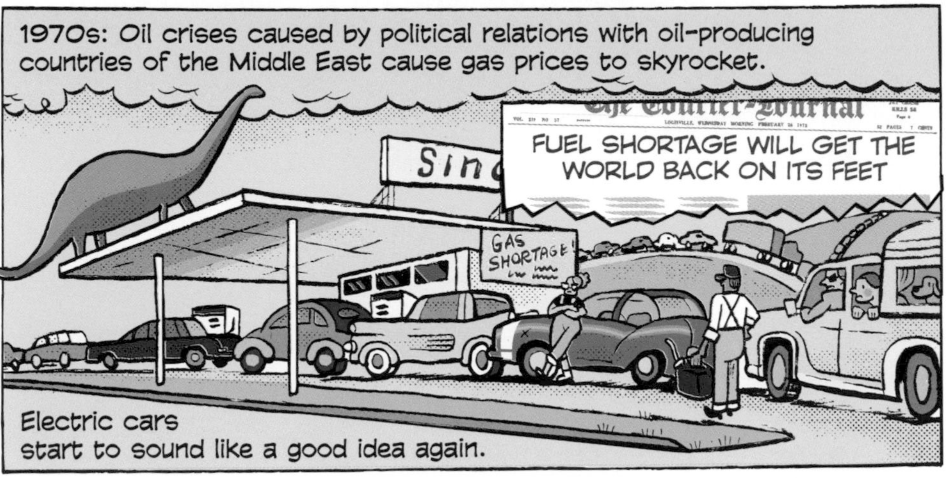
1970s: Oil crises caused by political relations with oil-producing countries of the Middle East cause gas prices to skyrocket.
FUEL SHORTAGE WILL GET THE WORLD BACK ON ITS FEET
GAS SHORTAGE!
Electric cars start to sound like a good idea again.

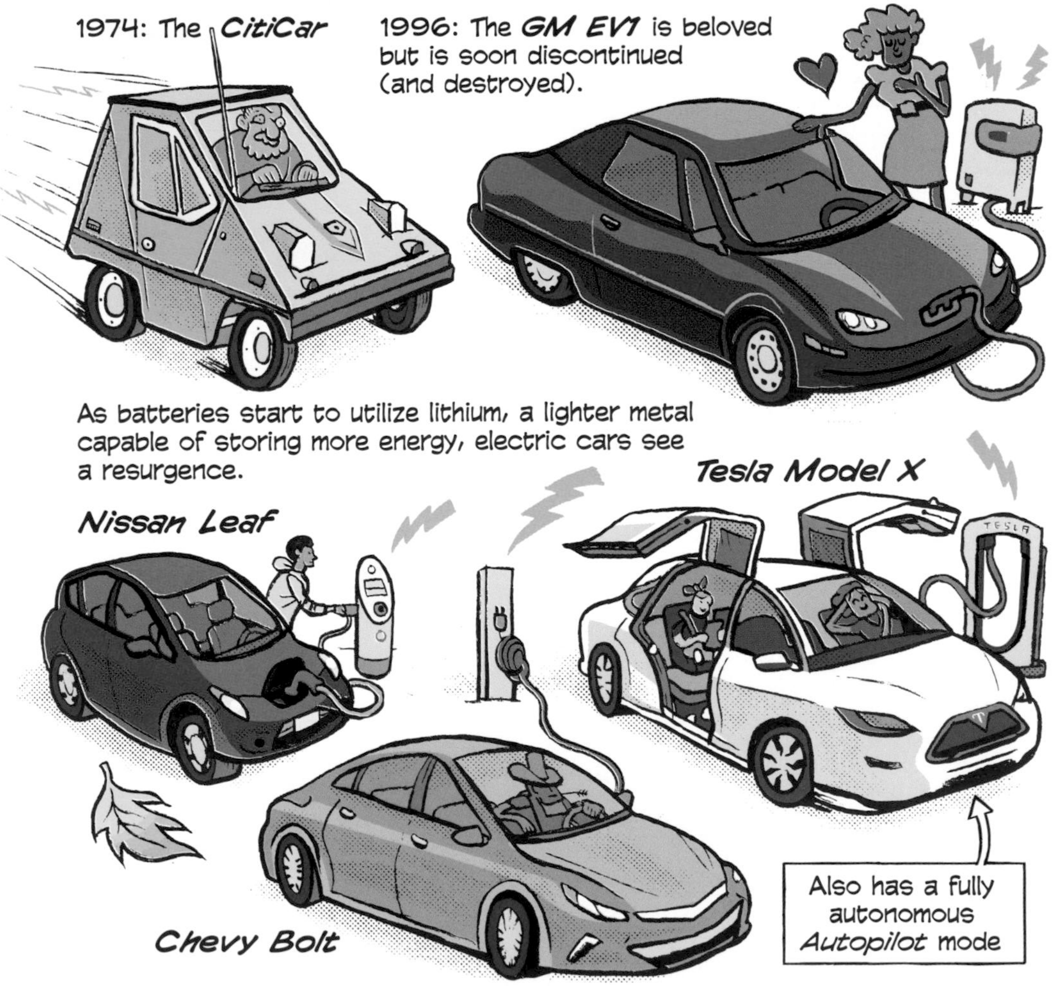
1974: The *CitiCar*
1996: The *GM EV1* is beloved but is soon discontinued (and destroyed).
As batteries start to utilize lithium, a lighter metal capable of storing more energy, electric cars see a resurgence.
Tesla Model X
Nissan Leaf
TESLA
Chevy Bolt
Also has a fully autonomous *Autopilot* mode

MARCH 2012, CALIFORNIA

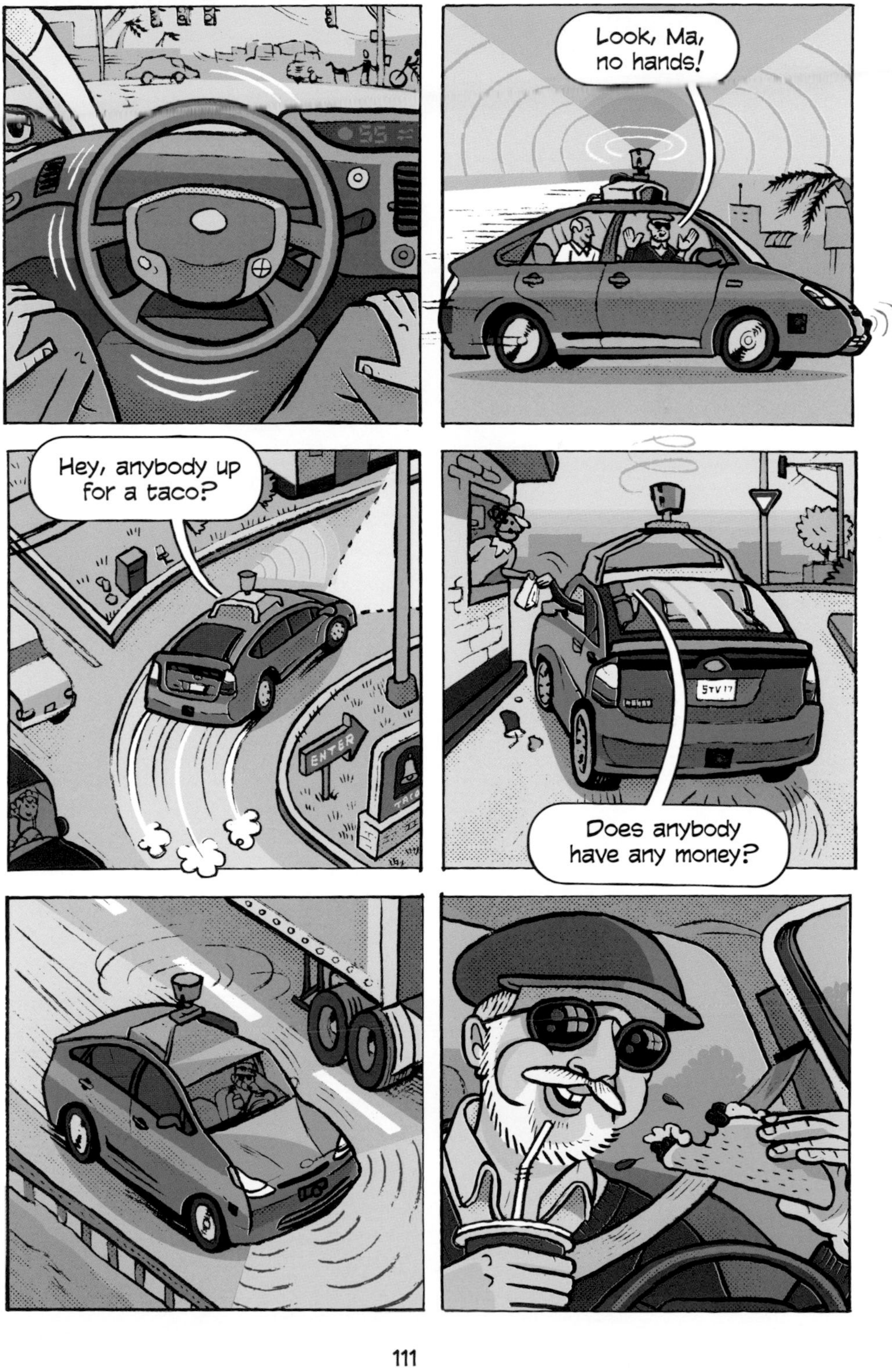
Look, Ma, no hands!
Hey, anybody up for a taco?
ENTER
Does anybody have any money?

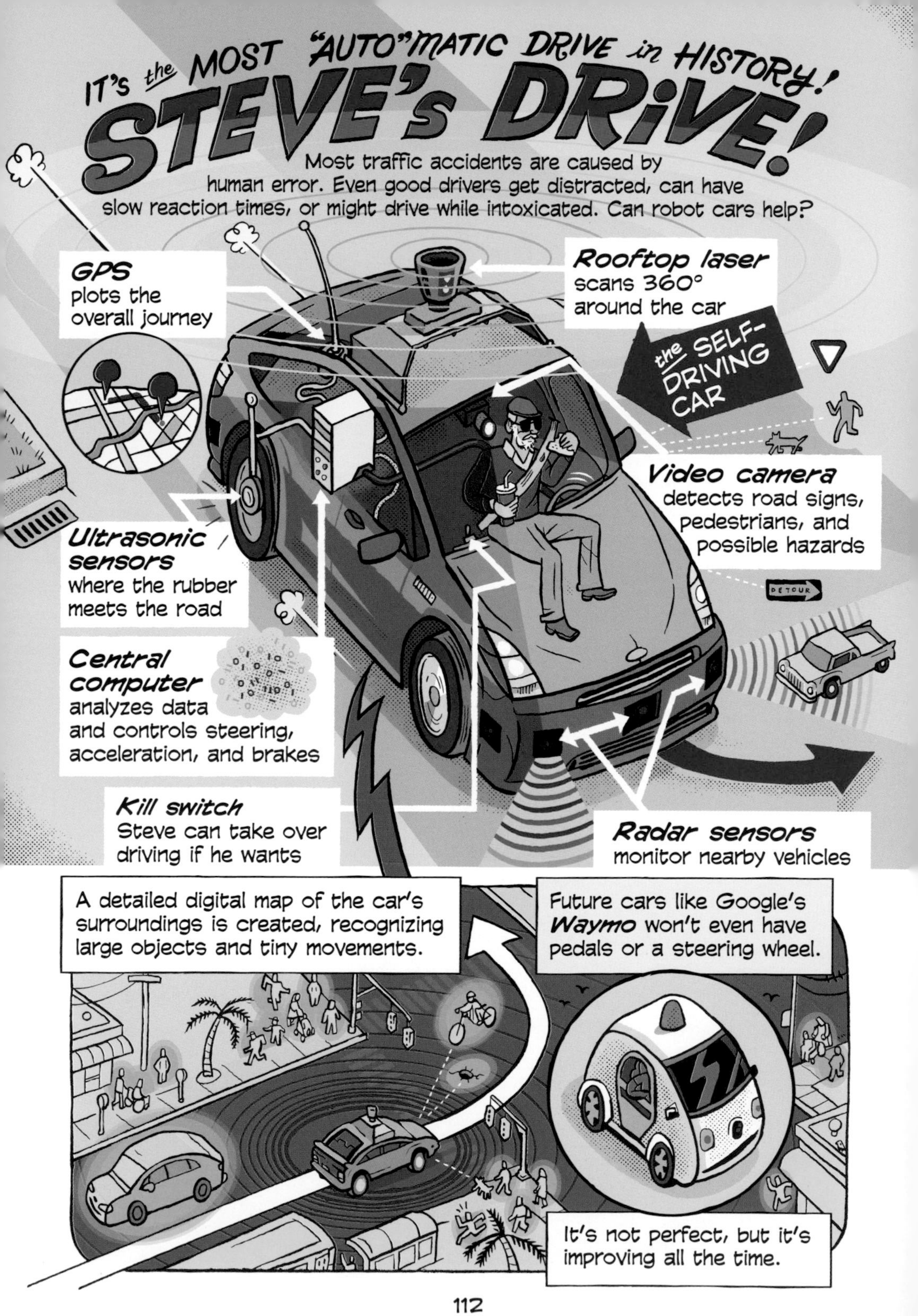

IT'S the MOST "AUTO"MATIC DRIVE in HISTORY!
STEVE'S DRIVE!
Most traffic accidents are caused by human error. Even good drivers get distracted, can have slow reaction times, or might drive while intoxicated. Can robot cars help?
GPS
plots the overall journey
Rooftop laser
scans 360°
around the car
the SELF-DRIVING CAR
Video camera
detects road signs, pedestrians, and possible hazards
DETOUR
Ultrasonic sensors
where the rubber meets the road
Central computer
analyzes data and controls steering, acceleration, and brakes
Kill switch
Steve can take over driving if he wants
Radar sensors
monitor nearby vehicles
A detailed digital map of the car's surroundings is created, recognizing large objects and tiny movements.
Future cars like Google's *Waymo* won't even have pedals or a steering wheel.
It's not perfect, but it's improving all the time.

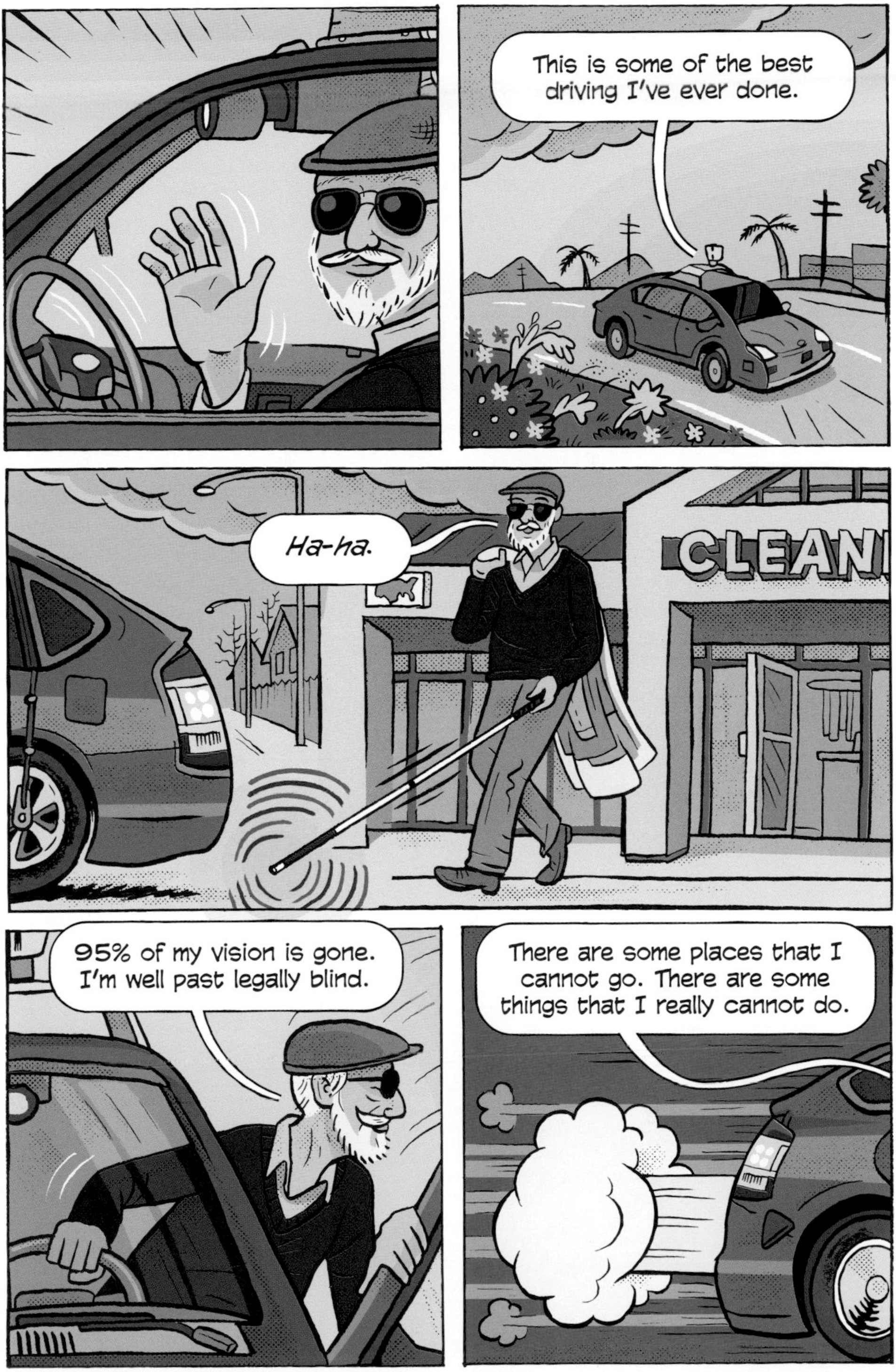
This is some of the best driving I've ever done.
Ha-ha.
CLEAN
95% of my vision is gone. I'm well past legally blind.
There are some places that I cannot go. There are some things that I really cannot do.

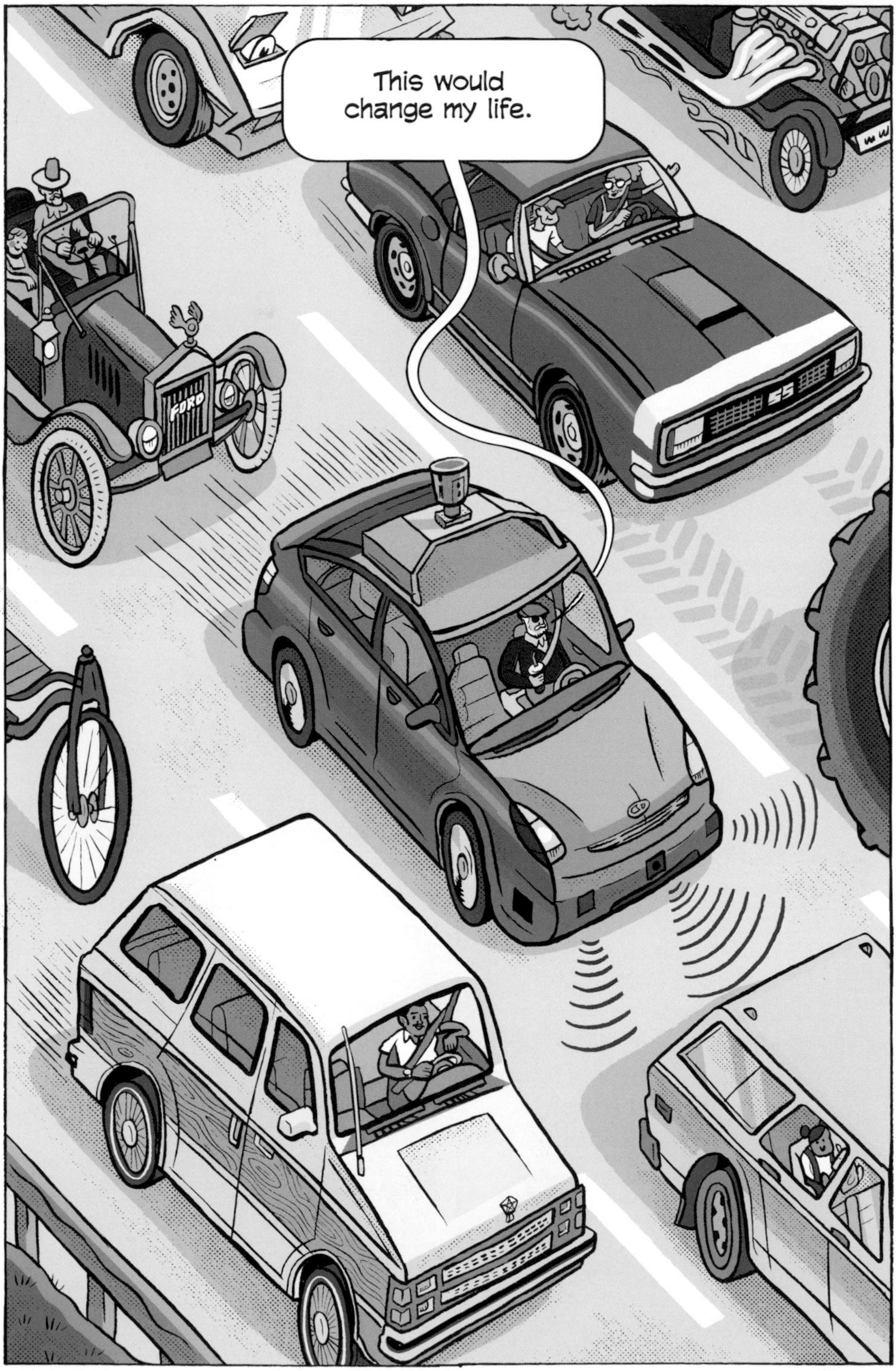
This would change my life.
FORD
SS

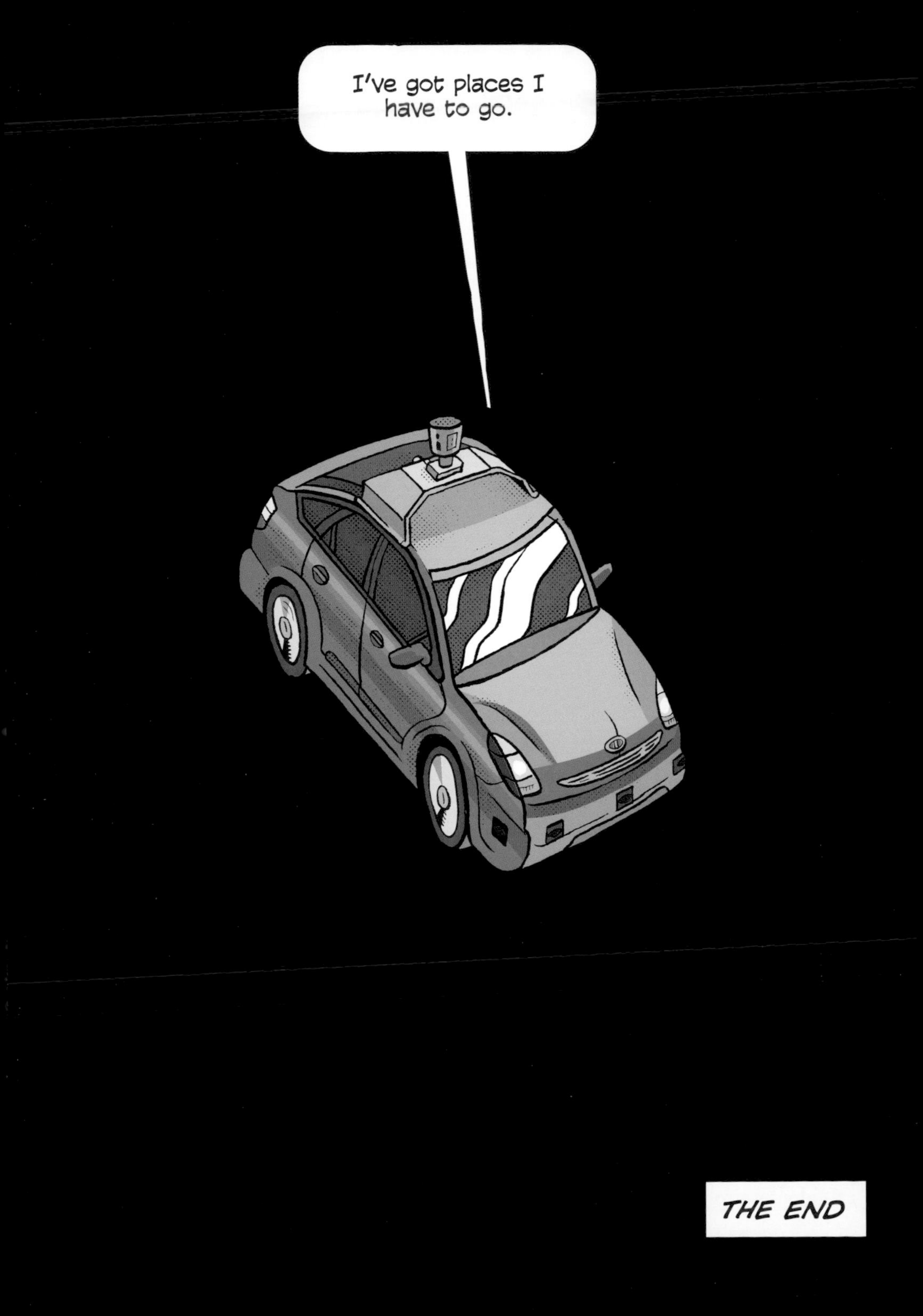
I've got places I have to go.
THE END

GLOSSARY

Aerodynamics The study of objects moving through air

Asphalt The sticky black petroleum-based substance often used for surfacing roads

Battery A storage container that converts chemical energy into electrical energy

Body The outer shell of a car

Camshaft The rotating shaft with egg-shaped protrusions that pushes open each spring-loaded intake and exhaust valve at exactly the right time

Carburetor A device that creates a mixture of fuel and air that varies from a fine spray at idle to a denser, faster flowing spray needed for full power; has been replaced by fuel injection for more precise control over the flow

Connecting rod Connects the piston to the crankshaft

Crankshaft The main shaft of the engine that is cranked by the pistons during combustion, turning the car's wheels

Cylinder The chamber in the engine where combustion occurs; most cars have between two and twelve

Distributor The device with an internal spinning rotor that sequentially delivers electrical charges to each cylinder in turn via the spark plugs

Electric vehicle (EV) A car powered by batteries and a motor rather than gasoline and a combustion engine

Fire triangle Symbol of the three things that create combustion:

Fossil fuel Energy sources, such as coal, petroleum, or gas, derived from remains of ancient organisms

Friction The resistance force between two surfaces rubbing together

Gasoline Petroleum refined into a volatile liquid and used as fuel for internal combustion engines

Horsepower A unit of power equal to 550 ft-lb per second (745.7 watts)

Hot rod A car modified for power, speed, or aesthetic appeal

Hybrid A car with both a gasoline engine and an electric motor(s), all of which can power it

Hydrocarbon A chemical compound of hydrogen and carbon, e.g., petroleum and natural gas

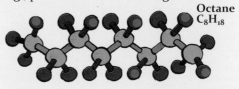

Octane C_8H_{18}

Ignition The process of starting the combustion of fuel in the cylinders of an internal combustion engine

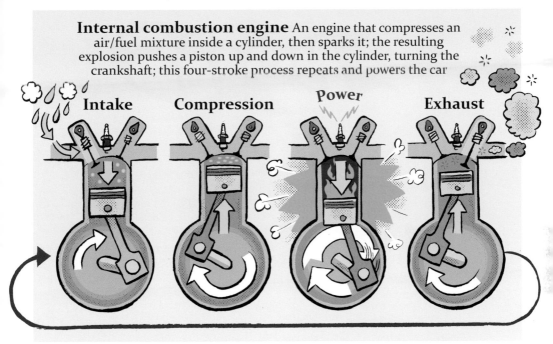

Internal combustion engine An engine that compresses an air/fuel mixture inside a cylinder, then sparks it; the resulting explosion pushes a piston up and down in the cylinder, turning the crankshaft; this four-stroke process repeats and powers the car

Intake　　**Compression**　　**Power**　　**Exhaust**

Lowrider A custom car lowered to drive nearly at road level

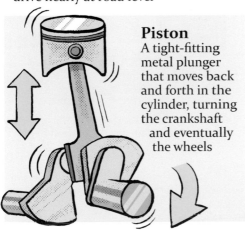

Piston
A tight-fitting metal plunger that moves back and forth in the cylinder, turning the crankshaft and eventually the wheels

Self-driving car A vehicle that uses sensors to navigate its environment and accelerates, steers, and brakes without the input of a human driver

Spark plug An electric device that ignites the air/fuel mixture, causing combustion

Starter The mechanism for starting an engine, typically activated by turning a key or pushing a button

Suspension The system of tires, springs, and shock absorbers that cushions the car from the road

Torque The measure of rotational force a car's engine is capable of producing

Transmission The system that transmits power from the car's engine to its wheels via a series of gears; can be automatic or manually operated

Valve The part of the engine that opens and closes, allowing air/fuel mixture into the cylinder and exhaust out

V8 A type of engine with 8 cylinders arranged in a V shape

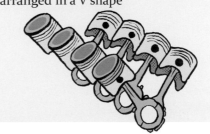

NOTES

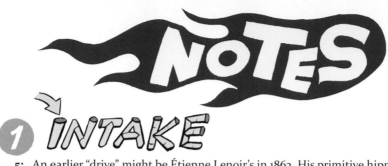

1 INTAKE

5: An earlier "drive" might be Étienne Lenoir's in 1863. His primitive hippomobile was slower than walking (and far less reliable).

8: Sometimes fire is visualized as a four-sided pyramid called the "fire tetrahedron," with the fourth side representing a chemical chain reaction. The fire triangle keeps the three ingredients (heat, fuel, and oxidizer) distinct from the surrounding chemical reaction.

11: The translation of the ancient inscription describing the early wheeled vehicle comes from Stuart Harris's paper "Bronocice Pot: Bags of Food in the Cart," 2013.

13: "Ferrari of Antiquity" comes from Alberto Rovetta, professor in robotics engineering at Polytechnic of Milan.

Most historians now believe Tutankhamun was not killed in a fiery chariot wreck, but from genetic frailty and malaria.

19: McKinley's reaction to the first presidential car ride was written about in the *Milwaukee Journal* in Jan. 1945: "After Steamer Jaunt, He Predicted Cars Wouldn't Replace Horses."

20: Carnot's book *Reflections on the Motive Power of Fire* explores how efficient an engine can be.

21: The joke about installing a Carnot engine in your car paraphrases David V. Schroeder's *An Introduction to Thermal Physics*, Addison-Wesley Publishing Co., San Francisco, CA, 1999.

HIGH-TEMPERATURE "FURNACE"
ENGINE
LOW-TEMPERATURE "REFRIGERATOR"
MECHANICAL WORK

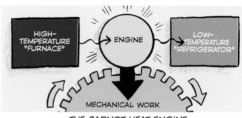

THE CARNOT HEAT ENGINE

22: Beau de Rochas had an earlier patent, but definitive accounts of Otto as the inventor of the modern four-stroke internal combustion engine come from Lynwood Bryant's articles "The Silent Otto" (1966) and "The Origin of the Four-Stroke Cycle" (1967), both in *Technology and Culture*.

26: Marcus may have been even more integral to the development of the car engine, but we'll never know. Many of his records and accomplishments were destroyed by Nazi revisionists.

2 COMPRESSION

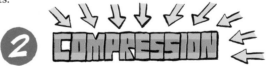

33–36: Details from this section pulled from Jackson's letters to his wife and from Ken Burns's documentary *Horatio's Drive: America's First Road Trip,* PBS, 2003.

42–43: Inspiration (and gadgets) for this section came from E. B. White's article "Farewell, My Lovely!" *The New Yorker*, May 16, 1936.

54–55: All engines are a bit different but this Chevy small-block 350 engine was chosen to dissect because of its longevity and popularity among hot-rodders and regular drivers alike.

56–57: Mighty Mouse was an animated superhero most famous on TV in the 1940s–'60s.

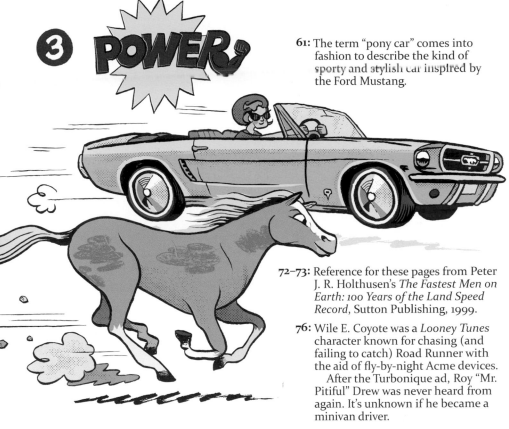

3 POWER

61: The term "pony car" comes into fashion to describe the kind of sporty and stylish car inspired by the Ford Mustang.

72–73: Reference for these pages from Peter J. R. Holthusen's *The Fastest Men on Earth: 100 Years of the Land Speed Record*, Sutton Publishing, 1999.

76: Wile E. Coyote was a *Looney Tunes* character known for chasing (and failing to catch) Road Runner with the aid of fly-by-night Acme devices.

After the Turbonique ad, Roy "Mr. Pitiful" Drew was never heard from again. It's unknown if he became a minivan driver.

79: The Voyager shares the title of "first minivan" with its twins the Dodge Caravan and Chrysler Town & Country.

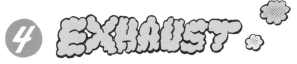

4 EXHAUST

95: There may be trucks longer or taller, but for sheer mass and hauling capacity the BelAZ 75710 dump truck is by far the most gigantic.

100: Dates for all the safey innovations are tricky to nail down. Often devices are invented years before they reach market and then only sporadically used. An entire book could be written just about the complicated history of the traffic light.

104–105: These stereos are playing songs that were popular for their times: Walter Donaldson's "You're Driving Me Crazy," Jackie Brenston's "Rocket 88" (often called the first rock 'n' roll record), "The Ballad of Davy Crocket," the Beach Boys' "Fun, Fun, Fun," Coolio's "Fantastic Voyage," and Tom Cochrane's "Life Is a Highway."

WALT DISNEY'S
DAVY CROCKETT,
PARKER • EBSEN
16 2/3 RPM
Side 1
HIGHWAY
Hi-Fi
CHRYSLER CORPORATION

110: For more about the tragic tale of the GM EV1 see the 2006 documentary *Who Killed the Electric Car?*

111–112: "Steve's Drive" is based on a video posted by Google to YouTube in 2012 entitled "Self-Driving Car Test: Steve Mahan."

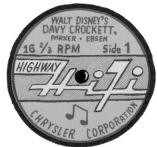

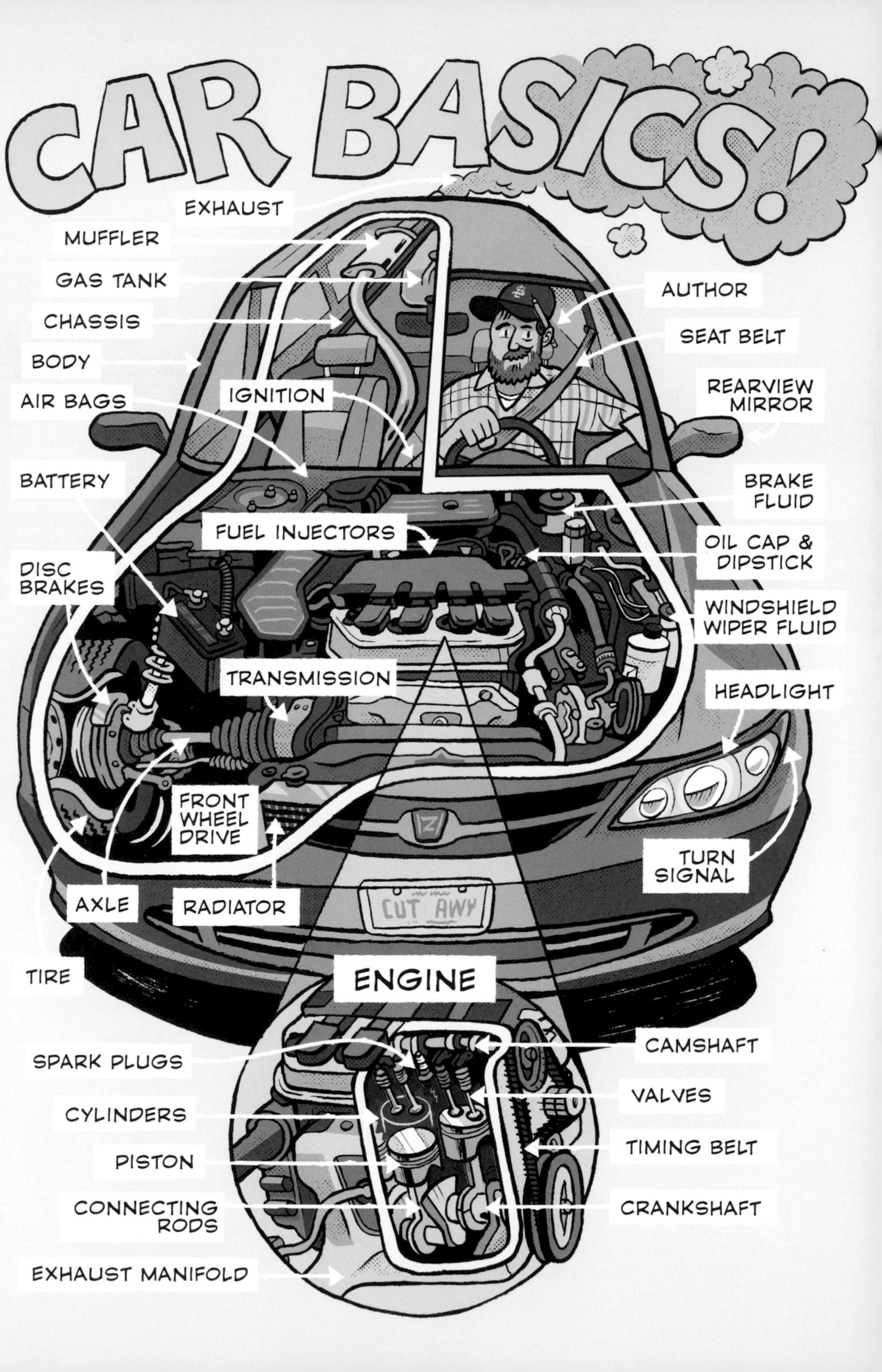
CAR BASICS!
EXHAUST
MUFFLER
GAS TANK
CHASSIS
BODY
AIR BAGS
IGNITION
AUTHOR
SEAT BELT
REARVIEW MIRROR
BATTERY
BRAKE FLUID
FUEL INJECTORS
OIL CAP & DIPSTICK
DISC BRAKES
WINDSHIELD WIPER FLUID
TRANSMISSION
HEADLIGHT
FRONT WHEEL DRIVE
TURN SIGNAL
AXLE
RADIATOR
CUT AWY
TIRE
ENGINE
SPARK PLUGS
CAMSHAFT
VALVES
CYLINDERS
TIMING BELT
PISTON
CONNECTING RODS
CRANKSHAFT
EXHAUST MANIFOLD

BIBLIOGRAPHY

Choate, Curt, et al. *Dodge Caravan, Plymouth Voyager & Chrysler Town & Country Repair Manual.* Haynes, 1994.

Chow, Lisa. "The Grand Challenge." Season 6, Episode 7. *StartUp Podcast.* Gimlet Media. October 27, 2017. Web.

Doeden, Matt. *Crazy Cars.* Lerner Publications, 2007.

Goldstone, Lawrence. *Drive!: Henry Ford, George Selden, and the Race to Invent the Auto Age.* Balantine Books, 2016.

Hennessy, Kathryn, and Beth Landis, eds. *Car: The Definitive Visual History of the Automobile.* DK Publishing, 2011.

Higgins, Melissa. *How the Wheel Changed History.* Essential Library of Inventors. Essential Library, 2016.

Ingrassia, Paul. *Engines of Change: A History of the American Dream in Fifteen Cars.* Simon & Schuster, 2013.

King, Frank O. *Walt and Skeezix,* Gasoline Alley comic strips from 1921 & 1922. Drawn & Quarterly, 2005.

Macy, Sue. *Motor Girls: How Women Took the Wheel and Drove Boldly into the Twentieth Century.* National Geographic, 2017.

Millar, Pete, and Carl Kohler, founders. *CARtoons Magazine.* Peterson Publishing, 1959–1991.

Mueller, Mike. *Chevy Small-Block V-8: 50 Years of High Performance.* Motorbooks, 2005.

Parissien, Steven. *The Life of the Automobile: The Complete History of the Motor Car.* Thomas Dunne Books, 2014.

Parks, Wally, ed. Hot Rod Magazine. Peterson Publishing, 1948–present.

Scarry, Richard. *Cars and Trucks and Things That Go.* Golden Books, 1974.

Acknowledgments! Thanks for technical assistance and general car know-how to Dr. Diandra Leslie-Pelecky, Steve Halachoulis, and Don and Doug Zettwoch. Thanks to the National Museum of Transportation and the Classic Car Club of St. Louis, as well as attendees of the NSRA Street Rod Nationals in Louisville, for letting me poke around and draw their cars. Thanks for research help to St. Louis Public and County Libraries. Special thanks to Leslie and Archie.

Spark Plug is also the name of Barney Google's beloved comic strip horse.

GET TO KNOW YOUR UNIVERSE!

SCIENCE COMICS

"An excellent addition to school and classroom libraries."
—*School Library Journal*

GET TO KNOW YOUR UNIVERSE!

SCIENCE COMICS
DINOSAURS
Fossils and Feathers

MK REED   JOE FLOOD

GET TO KNOW YOUR UNIVERSE!

SCIENCE COMICS
CORAL REEFS
Cities of the Ocean

MARIS WICKS

GET TO KNOW YOUR UNIVERSE!

SCIENCE COMICS
VOLCANOES
Fire and Life

JON CHAD

GET TO KNOW YOUR UNIVERSE!

SCIENCE COMICS
BATS
Learning to Fly

FALYNN KOCH

GET TO KNOW YOUR UNIVERSE!

SCIENCE COMICS
FLYING MACHINES
How the Wright Brothers Soared

ALISON WILGUS   MOLLY BROOKS

GET TO KNOW YOUR UNIVERSE!

SCIENCE COMICS
PLAGUES
The Microscopic Battlefield

FALYNN KOCH

GET TO KNOW YOUR UNIVERSE!

SCIENCE COMICS
DOGS
From Predator to Protector

ANDY HIRSCH

GET TO KNOW YOUR UNIVERSE!

SCIENCE COMICS
ROBOTS AND DRONES
Past, Present, and Future

MAIRGHREAD SCOTT   JACOB CHABOT

GET TO KNOW YOUR UNIVERSE!

SCIENCE COMICS
SHARKS
Nature's Perfect Hunter

JOE FLOOD

GET TO KNOW YOUR UNIVERSE!

SCIENCE COMICS
ROCKETS
Defying Gravity

ANNE DROZD   JERZY DROZD

GET TO KNOW YOUR UNIVERSE!

SCIENCE COMICS
TREES
Kings of the Forest

ANDY HIRSCH

GET TO KNOW YOUR UNIVERSE!

SCIENCE COMICS
SOLAR SYSTEM
Our Place in Space

ROSEMARY MOSCO   JON CHAD

GET TO KNOW YOUR UNIVERSE!

SCIENCE COMICS
THE BRAIN
The Ultimate Thinking Machine

TORY WOOLLCOTT   ALEX GRAUDINS

GET TO KNOW YOUR UNIVERSE!

SCIENCE COMICS
POLAR BEARS
Survival on the Ice

JASON VIOLA   ZACK GIALLONGO

GET TO KNOW YOUR UNIVERSE!

SCIENCE COMICS
WILD WEATHER
Storms, Meteorology, and Climate

MK REED   JONATHAN HILL

...And more books coming soon!